LIVING THE CATHOLIC

TRADITION

LIVING THE CATHOLIC

TRADITION

Philosophical & Theological Considerations

EDITED BY RENÉE KÖHLER-RYAN

FRANCISCAN UNIVERSITY PRESS

Franciscan University Press
1235 University Boulevard
Steubenville, OH 43952
740-283-3771
Distributed by:
The Catholic University of America Press
c/o HFS
P.O. Box 50370
Baltimore, MD 21211
800-537-5487
Cataloging-in-Publication Data available
from the Library of Congress
ISBN: 978-0-9995134-6-0
Cover Image: Stained glass window inside St. Mary's Cathedral in Sydney, Australia, courtesy of Wikimedia Commons
Printed in the United States of America.

CONTENTS

RENÉE KÖHLER-RYAN

INTRODUCTION

Traditions are intrinsic to human everyday life. They influence what we believe, say, and do, even when we take them for granted. They are central to families; to the ways we build our homes and cities; to how we grow and tend our food; to our work in laboratories; to how we greet each other formally and informally; and to our teaching and research in universities. Our political systems are steeped in traditions, and religious traditions are most essentially grounded in an overarching tradition. In Catholic thought, tradition is infused with a greater sense of faith seeking understanding, and understanding seeking faith. Only when we step back from all traditions can we attempt to assess their underlying meaning, so as better to understand and appreciate who we are and to recognize both our similarities and differences. The tools that we use to perform such a task are already embedded in what we have received from others before us. This book seeks to come to a greater appreciation of these points and to offer further avenues of reflection for scholars working within a particular tradition. Most contributions are from within the Catholic intellectual tradition, but this is not exclusively the case.

Arguably, traditions give us to ourselves in ways that we can only come to appreciate when we reflect upon them. To examine a tradition is to gain greater knowledge of self and of others. No tradition can truly know itself unless it has also encountered the traditions of others. As contemporary society becomes increasingly pluralist, it is all the more important to consider where we have come from and how we relate to one another through our traditions. Epistemologically, this has profound implications: what we are as humans can be further enlightened by thinking about how a variety of traditions influence and enrich each other. This then has ethical and political significance, as what we come to know about each other influences our thoughts and deeds. The variety of contributions to this volume illustrates how different approaches from within as well as outside disciplines that have their own traditions can help us to see what we might not otherwise acknowledge. This requires that those who converse about tradition trust one another as well as those from whom they have received these different modes of thinking and acting. Etymologically, tradition refers to what is handed over—from *tradere*.[1] This suggests a certain intimacy to the process. For to hand something to someone else brings both participants close to each other, as trust, receptivity, and generosity are all in play. Tradition relies on communities that together acknowledge what is good, so that there can be intergenerational giving and reception.

In 2013, participants at a conference at the University of Notre Dame in Sydney, Australia, responded to the question, *Tradition . . . today?* All involved came to appreciate the richness of the concept and meaning of tradition. At the same time, various threats to tradition became increasingly apparent. A tradition can be forgotten or lost or deliberately manipulated, particularly when those charged with handing on have not conveyed its inner meaning. Perhaps more interesting and somewhat troubling was the emergent idea that a tradition can change to such an extent that it only looks like its former self. Claims that one is being true to or working with a tradition need to be interrogated, and this constitutes the main work of the following contributions. Thus contributors explore what vivifies our sustained practices by finding what is meaningful and reflecting on the means by which we transmit perennial concerns. They thereby also allow us

1. *Oxford English Dictionary Online*, s.v. "tradition," accessed February 22, 2017, http://www.oed.com.ezproxy.sl.nsw.gov.au/view/Entry/204302?rskey=zHHpHv&result=1.

to reflect on the ways in which traditions can be undermined, either deliberately or by default.

In the lead-up to the conference, conveners sought to stimulate awareness and reflection in advance by publicizing images such as birthday candles, hot cross buns, and wreaths laid at a war memorial on Australia's ANZAC day. The final image in this series was the façade of St. Mary's cathedral in Sydney, captured at the moment that a light show superimposed its vibrant colors. The neo-Gothic church, so much a part of the relatively short history of the Catholic Church in Sydney, is at the same time in the tradition of medieval churches. These in turn derive from theological and philosophical reflections on what it means to belong to a particular tradition of faith. This representation of the confluence of a medieval worldview, relatively modern engineering (the cathedral was built in the nineteenth century), and contemporary digital technology provided an anchoring point for discussions of how traditions can interact and enrich one another. Simultaneously, the confluence of the medieval and the modern articulates the context within which the majority of contributors in this volume are writing. This is the milieu of the Catholic university, with its traditions of academic pursuit grounded in the middle ages and its context in the present day.

Such endeavors at the tertiary level can be traced most precisely to the earlier labors of philosophers and theologians dedicated to the quest for truth. The interrelationship of philosophy and theology is at the core of a Catholic university because of the medieval quest to find meaning in reality. Seeking ever more earnestly the intersections of faith and reason, medieval Catholic Europeans, usually clerics, devised systems of rigorous analysis and discussion as well as programs of study, and at the same time developed the hierarchically ordered graduations of bachelors, masters, and doctors. Today's secular universities owe much to these earlier thinkers, pushing the boundaries of inquiry while remaining focused on the importance of the human person, of community, and of seeking fulfillment both in this world and beyond. The academy as we know it has its roots in the pagan

Greek world; however, in its current form, it most closely resembles the university system that is the legacy of scholars questing for human and divine wisdom within a Christian tradition.

At its most secular, our academy might neglect some of the larger themes, concepts, and issues that were essential to the medieval university. Engaging with the idea of tradition has the benefit of refocusing attention while "broadening" our "horizon of Reason," as Pope Benedict XVI encouraged every university to do in his address at Regensburg University in 2006.[2] Taking up his challenge, academics can remember and even celebrate their roots. Traditions can be retrieved so long as they were always established in truth about the nature of reality and the nature of human beings. In his charter for Catholic Universities, Pope John Paul II reminded teachers and academics that all working within a Catholic university are ideally striving for the whole of truth,[3] situating their research within a common quest for the "a/ integration of knowledge; b/ a dialogue between faith and reason; c/ an ethical concern; and d/ a theological perspective."[4] Our readers will discern that all these dimensions are addressed within and between different contributions present herein. Thus *Living the Catholic Tradition: Philosophical and Theological Considerations* sits squarely and dynamically within the vocation of the Catholic university. It seeks, in the alignment of its three parts, to discuss what tradition is and the different ways in which it can be lived—morally, in community with each other, and in the arts.

Part I, "Philosophy, Theology, and the Problematic Nature of Tradition," proposes that tradition, considered in its complexity, yields

2. Benedict XVI, "Faith, Reason and the University: Memories and Reflections," Vatican website, September 12, 2006, http://w2.vatican.va/content/benedict-xvi/en/speeches/2006/september/documents/hf_ben-xvi_spe_20060912_university-regensburg.html.

3. John Paul II, *Ex Corde Ecclesiae*, Apostolic Constitution on Universities, Vatican website, August 15, 1990, http://w2.vatican.va/content/john-paul-ii/en/apost_constitutions/documents/hf_jp-ii_apc_15081990_ex-corde-ecclesiae.html, sec. 4.

4. John Paul II, *Ex Corde Ecclesiae*, sec. 15.

fundamental principles for reflection. Matthew Levering begins by asking whether Catholic tradition is "invented" or "received." Specifically addressing the fraught nature of Terrence Tilley's understanding of tradition, Levering demonstrates that this contemporary theologian ultimately dissents from the foundations of Tradition that one can find in the New Testament and hence undermines our capacity to appreciate how the concept of tradition interacts with Tradition. Gerard Gleeson's "The Incarnation: Debate and Development in Catholic Tradition" follows and reminds us of the way that theological development of Catholic doctrine—in this case the doctrine of Christ's personhood—continues to be a source of inspired inquiry. His chapter develops John Cardinal Henry Newman's approach to doctrine, arguing that by building on the doctrine of the Council of Chalcedon, we can think anew the mystery of the Incarnation. Speaking of Christ as one person with two natures thus enables us to know the one *theandric* nature of the Incarnate Word: Christ is known to be human in a divine way, and divine in a human way. Gleeson claims that this theology is legitimate, valuable, and a promising development of our tradition. Finally, Renee Kohler-Ryan ends this section by considering the problem of evaluating what constitutes a traditional architectural style in the Catholic tradition. In "Keeping Truth in Style: Tradition and Scandals in Roman Catholic Ecclesiastical Architecture," she argues that while it might be tempting to claim that the Roman Catholic Church has discovered all the truest ways architecturally to express its relationship to God, the organic nature of tradition suggests that present styles of church building have not exhausted the possibility for articulating this affiliation. Using the work of St. Augustine, T. S. Eliot, and Benedict XVI, she argues that new styles can never fully capture discoveries about our relationship to God as the fullness of Truth. And so she asks: What might be the next glorious architectural scandal on the horizon of tradition and truth?

Part II is titled "Living the Catholic Tradition: Morality." Therein, Most Reverend Anthony Fisher first observes that contemporary thought has come some way in recovering a tradition that is hospitable to genuinely Catholic moral thought, one in which narrow and partisan approaches to morality are challenged by an appreciation of the demand to take the whole human person into account. New approaches to Scripture, the Church Fathers, the Scholastics, and the Magisterium provide resources for the contemporary Catholic theologian. At the same time, a tradition of reflection that gives precedence to practical reason is being heard again, and various thinkers are recovering virtue, community, and beauty in ethics. This enables the moral theologian more clearly to discern the path toward a specifically Catholic contribution to ethics as the tradition particular to Catholic ethics encourages us to explore an increasing array of avenues of contemporary thought. E. Christian Brugger, in his "Reason's 'Wax Nose': Moral Self-Determination and the Epistemic Death of Natural Law," brings together two claims of one Catholic thinker to ask how effectively language about natural law can speak to a pluralistic secular age. On the one hand, in his prepapal writings, Joseph Ratzinger expressed the view that the language of natural law could make no difference in a secular society where there is no common agreement about the terms of ethical knowledge. On the other hand, as Benedict XVI, he stated that natural law is "the only valid bulwark against the arbitrary power or the deception of ideological manipulation."[5] It seems, then, that discussions of natural law are both necessary and insufficient. They could halt contemporary society from becoming increasingly disconnected from reality. At the same time, they risk not being heard or understood. Brugger leaves the reader to contemplate how we might overcome this stalemate. His contribution is, then, a challenge to contemporary men and women seeking to live the good life in light of the tradition in which they believe.

Part III, "Living the Catholic Tradition: Politics, Vocation, and Ed-

5. Benedict XVI, "Address of His Holiness Benedict XVI to the Participants in the International Congress on Natural Moral Law," February 12, 2007, Vatican website, http://www.vatican.va/holy_father/benedict_xvi/speeches/2007/february/documents/hf_ben-xvi_spe_20070212_pul_en.html.

ucation," brings us directly into the realm of public life, asking questions about the relationships that politics, vocation, and education all have with traditions. John Finnis begins with a chapter discussing four theses and their relations to the law and justice under the labels of Creation, Freedom, Justice (and Humanity), and Faith (as intelligent and rational acceptance of divine revelation). Finnis identifies the inception points of these concepts, showing that in each instance, a concept we now take for granted emerged as a result of a rupture from the past and from the whole surrounding matrix of civilizations and cultures. Each of these new conceptual insights developed and deepened in a way that enabled a transformation in society that subsequently led to the creation of universities. At the same time, this process provided the foundations of the disciplines of philosophy and of law, which are central elements of the political context. Mark Kingwell's "Fugitive Democracy: A Gift in Time" extends the consideration of the political by exploring the relationship of democracy to time. Kingwell argues that at the heart of democracy we find a gift economy, which depends on constant renewal through *kairotic* ruptures. Democracy, in his view, can only live up to its promise when it extends beyond politics, operating fundamentally as a gift handed on through ordinary time—but at the same time one that goes beyond. *Kairos* is an ancient pagan concept that refers to a transcendent occurrence. Kingwell transports it into the context of democracy and thereby highlights what he thinks of as "radical ruptures in the fabric of social life," which are essential to realizing the trusteeship upon which democracy depends. Unrepeatable moments in political life constitute these ruptures and at the same time sustain the promise of democracy. Finally, Mary Prudence Allen, RSM, contributes a chapter that discusses personal identity by asking, "Does the Religious Vow of Obedience Impede or Assist Our Development?" Sister Allen relies on Karol Wojtyła's emphasis, in *The Acting Person*, on the integration of authentic ways of participating in intersubjective communities of persons. Taking this discussion as her foundation, she traces the principles and ways of living out obedience within the Christian tradition. Allen draws upon St. Augustine, St. Benedict, Venerable Catherine McAuley, and various Magisterial documents prior to the Second Vatican Council before moving to explore new articulations of the vow of obedience in the Second Vatican Council and postconciliar documents. Allen ends with a response to contemporary critiques of the vow of obedience from the perspective of philosophical anthropology. Namely, she argues that the tradition of obedience in the Church, which is configured differently in each of the three primordial vocations in the Church—of religious consecration, sacramental marriage of laymen and laywomen, and priestly ordination—fundamentally depends on mutual submission and service. Understanding this brings us to a greater appreciation of the tradition of Revelation, and at the same time of ourselves. *Living the Tradition: Philosophical and Theological Considerations* thereby ends with some of the most concrete considerations of what it means to live within the Catholic tradition.

A volume such as this owes many debts of gratitude. The Institute for Ethics and Society of the University of Notre Dame Australia, under the direction of Professors Hayden Ramsay and Sandra Lynch, organized the conference that gave rise to most of the contributions to this volume, and they were aided by an administrative staff that included Trish Egan, Elle Glynn, Daniel Griffiths, and GayL Purchase. After the conference, Matthew Beard took over the task of collecting papers for editing. The ultimate task of editing then came to me, with the aid of François Fontaneau. Finally, thanks are owed to Franciscan University Press, particularly to Stephen Lewis and Sarah Wear, for their enthusiasm about this fine collection of essays, and for their patience throughout the review process and final processes of publication. The manuscript benefited from the comments, commendations, and incorporated recommendations of two external reviewers, Professors Robert Fastiggi and Anthony C. Sciglitano. Finally, Ashleigh McKown stands in the great tradition of gracious and meticulous copy editors; her work is greatly appreciated.

PART I

PHILOSOPHY, THEOLOGY, AND THE PROBLEMATIC NATURE OF TRADITION

MATTHEW LEVERING

1 • CATHOLIC TRADITION

Invented or Received?

During its discussion of Tradition, having affirmed that Jesus Christ summed up divine revelation in himself, *Dei Verbum* observes that "God graciously arranged that the things he had once revealed for the salvation of all peoples should remain in their entirety, throughout the ages, and be transmitted to all generations."[1] According to *Dei Verbum*, Jesus Christ gave his Apostles the mission of communicating the Gospel to all humans. The Apostles did so in two ways, through oral teaching and through sacred writings, both of which were guided by the Holy Spirit. They also appointed successors (bishops) who share even today in the task of handing on the Gospel in its fullness.[2]

This chapter originally appeared in my *Engaging the Doctrine of Revelation: The Mediation of the Gospel through Church and Scripture* (Grand Rapids, MI: Baker Academic, 2014). Used by permission of Baker Academic, a division of Baker Publishing Group.

1. See *Dei Verbum*, §7, in *Vatican Council II*, vol. 1, *The Conciliar and Post Conciliar Documents*, ed. Austin Flannery, OP (Northport, NY: Costello, 1996), 753.

2. Apostolic succession allows for development of doctrine in specifying the role and duties of bishops (and of the bishop of Rome), without thereby supposing that a merely functional, rather than sacramental, succession existed in the earliest Church. For a proposal regarding the stages of this doctrinal development and the reasons for it, see John Henry Newman, *An Essay on the Development of Christian Doctrine* (Notre Dame, IN: University of Notre Dame Press, 1989), 148–65. For a more recent historical reconstruction, see, e.g., John M. Rist, "The Origin and Early Development of Episcopacy at Rome," in *What Is Truth? From the Academy to the Vatican* (Cambridge: Cambridge University Press, 2008), 201–32.

On this basis, *Dei Verbum* explains the nature of Tradition as follows: "Tradition transmits in its entirety the word of God which has been entrusted to the apostles by Christ the Lord and the Holy Spirit. It transmits it to the successors of the apostles so that, enlightened by the Spirit of truth, they may faithfully preserve, expound and spread it abroad by their preaching."[3]

Tradition, then, is the Church's mode of transmitting "the word of God," which Christ and the Holy Spirit "entrusted to the apostles."[4] Tradition is the handing on the salvific realities of the Gospel, and as such, Tradition can be found in the Church's "doctrine, life, and worship."[5] Tradition is the Church's faithful communication of the doctrines and practices of Christian faith across the generations. Tradition is closely connected to Scripture, because the Church hands on

3. *Dei Verbum*, §9, 755. For further discussion of *Dei Verbum*'s view of Tradition, which itself constitutes a development of earlier Catholic teaching on Tradition, see Avery Dulles, SJ, "Revelation, Scripture, and Tradition," in *Your Word Is Truth: A Project of Evangelicals and Catholics Together*, ed. Charles Colson and Richard John Neuhaus (Grand Rapids, MI: Eerdmans, 2002), 35–58, at 50–53; Benedict Thomas Viviano, OP, "The Normativity of Scripture and Tradition in Recent Catholic Theology," in *Scripture's Doctrine and Theology's Bible: How the New Testament Shapes Christian Dogmatics*, ed. Markus Bockmuehl and Alan J. Torrance (Grand Rapids, MI: Baker Academic, 2008), 125–40. See also Avery Dulles, SJ, "Tradition: Authentic and Unauthentic," *Communio* 28 (2001): 377–85.

4. In his chapter "Tradition and the Tacit," Andrew Louth emphasizes "an inarticulate living of the mystery, the tacit dimension, which is the heart of tradition, and from which theology must spring if it is to be faithful to the truth it is seeking to express." *Discerning the Mystery: An Essay on the Nature of Theology* (Oxford: Oxford University Press, 1983), 95.

5. *Dei Verbum*, §8, 754. Pelikan offers a helpful distinction between tradition as idol and as icon: "Tradition becomes an idol, accordingly, when it makes the preservation and the repetition of the past an end in itself; it claims to have the transcendent reality and truth captive and encapsulated in that past, and it requires an idolatrous submission to the authority of tradition, since truth would not dare to appear outside it. . . . Tradition qualifies as an icon . . . when it does not present itself as coextensive with the truth it teaches, but does present itself as the way that we who are its heirs must follow if we are to go beyond it—to a universal truth that is available only in a particular embodiment" (Pelikan, *The Vindication of Tradition* [New Haven, CT: Yale University Press, 1984], 55–56). Tradition mediates rather than encapsulates divine revelation.

the sacred writings as part of the faithful communication of divine revelation as summed up in and taught by Jesus Christ.

This view of Tradition, however, has been strongly challenged on various fronts. While considering themselves to be the representatives of the Church's true Tradition, the sixteenth-century Reformers sought to rid the Church of a number of doctrines and practices that, in their view, were foreign to the Gospel and were instead human inventions recognizable by their lack of accord with Scripture, such as papal supremacy, eucharistic sacrifice, merit, purgatory, various Marian doctrines, and so forth.[6] Along these lines, the eminent

6. See Jaroslav Pelikan, *The Christian Tradition: A History of the Development of Doctrine*, vol. 4, *Reformation of Church and Dogma (1300–1700)* (Chicago: University of Chicago Press, 1984), 127–244. As Pelikan puts it in *Vindication of Tradition*, "The claim that the papacy had been divinely instituted and hence possessed supernatural authority was untenable, Luther and his colleagues charged, in the light of history, which showed that the institutions, the practices, and even the doctrines of the church had changed over centuries. 'As it was in the beginning, is now, and ever shall be, world without end' applied to God and to the word of God, but not to the ever-mutable tradition of the church. Trained as many of them were in the critical methodology and 'sacred philology' of Renaissance humanism, the Protestant Reformers helped to lay the foundations for historical research into the genesis and the evolution of cherished traditions that had come down from the Middle Ages and from the church fathers. By this research they exploded the assumption of a 'consensus of the centuries,' upon which the authority of tradition rested. What the Reformation of the sixteenth century had done in its historical critique of the papacy or the sacraments or the legends of the saints, the Enlightenment of the eighteenth century did to many other sacred traditions, including some traditions that the mainstream of the Protestant Reformation had declared out of bounds for such destructive criticism" (44–45). For emphasis on the Reformers' appreciation of their debt to tradition, see H. Ashley Hall, "The Development of Doctrine: A Lutheran Examination," *Pro Ecclesia* 16 (2007): 256–77. Colin Gunton argues that John Calvin was a "traditionalist" on the grounds that "he believed that the church had left the main road and that the Reformation was calling it back to its true course." *A Brief Theology of Revelation* (London: T&T Clark, 1995), 83. Timothy George argues that the Reformers greatly valued Tradition but not at the expense of Scripture: "Evangelicals can affirm the coinherence of sacred Scripture and sacred Tradition, but not their coequality." "An Evangelical Reflection on Scripture and Tradition," in *Your Word Is Truth*, 9–34, at 34. See also the erudite defense of *sola scriptura* offered by John Woodbridge in his "The Role of 'Tradition' in the Life and Thought of Twentieth-Century Evangelicals," in *Your Word Is Truth*, 103–46.

nineteenth-century Reformed theologian Herman Bavinck argues that "Scripture is the only adequate means of guarding against the corruption of the spoken word and of making it the possession of all human beings. . . . The brevity of life, the unreliability of memory, the craftiness of the human heart, and a host of other dangers that threaten the purity of transmission all make the inscripturation of the spoken word absolutely necessary if it is to be preserved and propagated."[7] He holds that only Scripture—and certainly not the Church's handing on of the Gospel—is given infallibility by Christ and his Spirit. For Bavinck, therefore, "It is untenable to say that today we continue to receive Christian truth apart from Scripture. In the first century something like that was possible, but the streams of tradition and Scripture have long since converged, and the former has long been incorporated into the latter."[8]

7. Herman Bavinck, *Reformed Dogmatics*, vol. 1, *Prolegomena*, ed. John Bolt, trans. John Vriend (Grand Rapids, MI: Baker Academic, 2003), 471. From a different theological perspective but with the same historical judgment, James Barr comments that "Protestantism was right to observe that Catholic traditions as they grew had failed to provide adequate safeguards against the possibility that the interpretative tradition might come to dominate the scripture and would thus distort its own meaning." *Holy Scripture: Canon, Authority, Criticism* (Oxford: Oxford University Press, 1983), 29; cf. 31. Barr, however, goes on to add that "the traditional 'Catholic' and 'Protestant' roles come to be reversed: the facts of scripture are once again obscured through the imposition of a tradition, but this time it is not a medieval Catholic tradition, it is a Protestant tradition, built upon the insights of the seventeenth century and anxious to maintain these insights *against* the evidence of the text of scripture or at least against the fact that quite different interpretations of the text are possible. . . . Biblical authority on Protestant terms (on Catholic or Orthodox terms it may be otherwise) exists only where one is free, on the ground of scripture, to question, to adjust, and if necessary to abandon the prevailing doctrinal traditions" (31; cf. 36–37, on the Reformation and historical criticism).

8. Bavinck, *Reformed Dogmatics*, 472. Bavinck argues further, "The church cannot perform this ministry of the word. It is nowhere promised infallibility. Always in Scripture the church is referred to the objective word, 'to the teaching and to the testimony' [cf. Isa 8:20]. Actually even Rome does not deny this. The church, i.e., the gathering of believers, is not infallible in the understanding of Rome, neither is the gathering of bishops, but only the pope. The declaration of papal infallibility is proof of the Reformation's thesis of the unreliability of tradition, the fallibility of

More recently, Kevin Vanhoozer has posed the same problem from a Reformed perspective. Vanhoozer grants that the Holy Spirit has been at work in the Church, and not solely in inspired Scripture. But he too warns against exaggerating the place, let alone the supposed infallibility, of the Church's mediation or "performance" of the Gospel.[9] In his view, the work of the Holy Spirit, as the work of the Lord of the covenant, risks being conflated with the work of the people of God if one supposes that the Church's doctrinal performance of the Gospel is always on key. The Spirit that works in the Church does so to point to Christ's glory, not to the Church's. When it comes to Jesus Christ, Vanhoozer suggests, our knowledge derives from Scripture. Guided by the Spirit, the Church strives to "perform" or actualize this knowledge. Vanhoozer therefore concludes, "The real

---

the church, and even of the necessity of Scripture. For this declaration of infallibility implies that the truth of the revealed word is not or can not be preserved by the church as the gathering of believers, inasmuch as the church is still liable to error. The truth of the revealed word can be explained only in the light of the special assistance of the Holy Spirit of which, says Rome, the pope is the beneficiary. Rome and the Reformation agree, accordingly, that the revealed word can be preserved in its purity only by the institution of the apostolate, i.e., by inspiration. And the controversy between them pertains only to whether that apostolate has ceased or is continued in the person of the pope" (472). For important clarifications and corrections from a Catholic perspective, see Avery Dulles, SJ, *Magisterium: Teacher and Guardian of the Faith* (Ave Maria, FL: Sapientia Press, 2007), 64–72. See also the position of the Orthodox theologian Stylianos Harkianakis, who (like Bavinck) rejects papal infallibility but who (like Dulles) affirms the infallibility of the Church: *The Infallibility of the Church in Orthodox Theology* (Redfern: St. Andrew's Orthodox Press, 2008). For study of influential Catholic theologians who debated papal infallibility in the two centuries prior to the definition (with an eye to Vatican II's *Lumen Gentium*), see Richard F. Costigan, SJ, *The Consensus of the Church and Papal Infallibility: A Study in the Background of Vatican I* (Washington, DC: Catholic University of America Press, 2005).

9. As Carl E. Braaten puts it from a Lutheran perspective, "The church is *simul iustus et peccator* until the rule of glory (*regnum gloriae*) because the eschatological righteousness it appropriates in faith reveals the sinful imperfections of its concrete life as a church. The eschatological power of the gospel relativizes all the structures of the church and of its tradition. Nothing in and of the church can be exempt from the criticism that emanates from the eschatological word of God in the Christ-happening." *Mother Church: Ecclesiology and Ecumenism* (Minneapolis: Fortress Press, 1998), 55.

theological issue at stake in the debate over the relative authority of Scripture and tradition (not that one has to take sides, only prioritize) is actually *Christology*. Are there postcanonical, Spirit-inspired or -illumined insights into the way of Jesus Christ that do not have the canonical testimony to Christ as their ultimate source and norm?"[10] To this question, I would answer no, so long as what counts as canonical testimony can be illuminated by typological reasoning and by the postcanonical Church (e.g., via liturgical practice).[11]

Catholic theology of Tradition has also been challenged in recent years by concerns that, having first emerged within classical Protestant liberalism, now dominate much of the Catholic theological academy.[12] Many contemporary Catholic theologians reject the Church's view of Tradition (and of Scripture, for that matter). These Catholic theologians do not embrace biblical authority in the way that the Reformers did, but instead tend to see *both* Scripture and Tradition principally as human constructions.[13] The result is that they can no

10. Kevin J. Vanhoozer, *The Drama of Doctrine: A Canonical-Linguistic Approach to Christian Theology* (Louisville, KY: Westminster John Knox Press, 2005), 189.

11. See Yves M.-J. Congar, OP, *Tradition and Traditions: An Historical and Theological Essay*, trans. Michael Naseby and Thomas Rainborough (New York: Macmillan, 1967), esp. 376–424. Commending Irenaeus's view of the relationship of Scripture and Tradition, Congar observes, "We are not talking here, in Tradition, of *particular truths* not contained in the scriptural deposit or at least not in that which Scripture bears witness to. St. Irenaeus even says that there could be no truths which the apostles did not pass on in a public manner. No; we are talking here of the meaning of the whole. If we can find in 'Tradition' particular truths which were not expressed in Scripture, this will doubtless be due to Tradition's own proper genius, by means of the 'analogy of faith', in other words, thanks to the light that can be thrown on some particular question by the interrelation of various truths with one another, with their centre and with the end term of the whole investigation. This is peculiarly the case with the two Marian doctrines defined in the modern period, the Immaculate Conception and bodily Assumption of the Mother of God" (*Tradition and Traditions*, 391). See also Hans Boersma's "On Baking Pumpkin Pie: Kevin Vanhoozer and Yves Congar on Tradition," *Calvin Theological Journal* 42 (2007): 237–55. For further discussion, see my *Mary's Bodily Assumption* (Notre Dame, IN: University of Notre Dame Press, 2015).

12. For comment see Braaten, *Mother Church*, 72.

13. Nicholas Lash observes that "if human experience is a constitutive element

longer hear the Gospel as a divinely authoritative word with doctrinal content that transcends the vicissitudes of history even while being embedded in particular times and places.[14] In the debates between

---

in revelation, then we are tempted to ask the question: Are we to conceive of revelation as a matter of man's understanding of himself and of his future, or as coming to him from 'outside'? To put the question in this way, as a matter of mutually exclusive alternatives, is to confuse the issue. . . . Nevertheless, it is not easy to take with sufficient seriousness the function of human experience and self-understanding in the process of revelation, while at the same time safeguarding the God-given nature of that revelation." *Change in Focus: A Study of Doctrinal Change and Continuity* (London: Sheed and Ward, 1973), 13. Even if the two ways of conceiving revelation are not "mutually exclusive alternatives," the latter conception must for the Christian retain a strong priority at every stage.

14. As biblical scholar Dale C. Allison Jr. (a convert to Orthodoxy) puts this skepticism, "Matthew amended Mark to advance a higher Christology, and ideological tinkering must have gone on from the start. The questions all this raises are obvious." *The Historical Christ and the Theological Jesus* (Grand Rapids, MI: Eerdmans, 2009), 86. By contrast, consider Karl Barth's famous challenge to liberal Protestantism in the opening words of the preface to the first edition (reprinted in the 6th ed.) of his *The Epistle to the Romans*, trans. Edwyn C. Hoskyns (Oxford: Oxford University Press, 1933), 1: "Paul, as a child of his age, addressed his contemporaries. It is, however, far more important that, as Prophet and Apostle of the Kingdom of God, he veritably speaks to all men of every age. The differences between then and now, there and here, no doubt require careful investigation and consideration. But the purpose of such investigation can only be to demonstrate that these differences are, in fact, purely trivial. . . . my whole energy of interpreting has been expended in an endeavour to see through and beyond history into the spirit of the Bible, which is the Eternal Spirit. What was once of grave importance, is so still." For an effort to respond to liberal Judaism, while granting the truth of its critique of Scripture's historicity, see James L. Kugel, *How to Read the Bible: A Guide to Scripture, Then and Now* (New York: Free Press, 2007). His criticism of the canonical approach of Brevard Childs and others provides a window into his own solution, which I find intriguing but inadequate: "Faced with the theological problems posed by modern biblical scholarship, canonical critics correctly insist that a text's original meaning is not necessarily its only meaning, indeed, that the original constituents of the Bible necessarily took on new meaning as soon as they began to be supplemented and edited and ultimately placed in a larger environment of texts, the biblical canon. But this apparently historical argument takes no account of what those texts actually meant at the time of their canonization. That is, canonical criticism draws the line at the canonical *text*. It does not seem to realize that the earliest 'community of believers' canonized not only the text but their own peculiar way of reading and interpreting it. There was nothing optional about the latter: it *was* what the text meant" (679).

some Catholic theologians and the Church's Magisterium, a central issue has therefore been the doctrinal content and authority of Tradition, understood as the Church's ability to faithfully hand on the truth about Jesus Christ.

For this reason, the present essay focuses not on classic works of the past century such as Yves Congar's *Tradition and Traditions* but on a more recent, and representative, contribution: Terrence Tilley's *Inventing Catholic Tradition*.[15] Tilley sets forth a theology of "Catholic tradition" rooted in what he takes to be the necessity—in light of historical studies that in his view demonstrate frequent doctrinal invention and rupture—of the "abandonment of development as a credible theory of doctrinal change."[16] He envisions Catholic tradition as a continual

15. For a discussion of Tilley's book that makes clear how widely his views are shared, see the responses by Ann Riggs, Elizabeth A. Johnson, William L. Portier, and Roberto Goizueta, "Terrence W. Tilley's *Inventing Catholic Tradition*: Four Perspectives," *Horizons* 28 (2001): 105–19. Goizueta notes, "Tilley has given us what should rank as one of the most important scholarly treatments of this key theological concept since the publication of Yves Congar's magisterial *Tradition and Traditions*" (114), and he goes on to say, "Contemporary battles between conservatives and liberals are often, I would suggest, battles between two equally *modern* interpretations of tradition. Both sides presuppose an objectified, abstract, conceptual notion of tradition; one reifies tradition by constructing idols of the *tradita* while the other, mistakenly identifying the reification with the reality, rejects the *tradita* altogether" (114). Goizueta does not give an example of scholars who construct "idols of the *tradita*," and it seems to me that he is constructing a straw man here, since it is in fact "Congar's magisterial *Tradition and Traditions*" that now represents the "conservative" view. Of the four contributors to this symposium, Portier raises by far the most concerns; in particular, he rightly urges that Tilley interact with the theologians and philosophers of the *nouvelle théologie*. He concludes by emphasizing his "deep appreciation and admiration for Tilley's project as a whole and for his practice-oriented approach to tradition in this book. The intellectualist mainstream of Catholic theology in the United States badly needs a shot of Tilley, with his corrective emphasis on act over text, practice over belief" (111). My concern is that Tilley's oppositional framework of "practice over belief" deracinates the latter and thereby undermines the former.

16. Terrence W. Tilley, *Inventing Catholic Tradition* (Maryknoll, NY: Orbis, 2000), 82. As Maurice Wiles puts it sardonically in response to Owen Chadwick's work on doctrinal development, "I find little cause for surprise that his historical researches should not have given rise to much modern theological discussion of the question of doctrinal

reinvention of the practice of Catholic faith, without enduring doctrinal truth. After surveying the argument of his book, I compare his position with some of the ways in which Scripture presents παράδοσις ("tradition"). I argue that the difference between Tradition and tradition—the latter being merely human and conveying no enduring doctrinal truth—is inscribed in Scripture itself.[17] The New Testament's

---

development. The historical story is full of fascination. One reads and one admires; one admires not only the narrator of the story but also the characters within it; one admires the characters within it; one admires the broad sweep of their intellectual convictions and the detailed subtlety of their individual reasonings. But it is like reading a debate about the movements of the planets before the invention of the telescope. The general problems with which they were concerned are real problems; but the particular problems to which they addressed themselves so vigorously are not ours; and, more emphatically still, the way in which they approached them cannot be ours. . . . The study of doctrinal development is a study of importance; but the debates of the eighteenth and nineteenth centuries must not be expected to throw any great light on the road we have to tread in pursuit of it at the present time. The most obvious of all divisions concerning the nature of doctrinal development in the life of the Church lies between those who consider all such development as has received the accredited sanction of the Church to be wholly true and those who believe it to include an element of error." Wiles, *The Making of Christian Doctrine: A Study in the Principles of Early Doctrinal Development* (Cambridge: Cambridge University Press, 1967), 1–2; cf. 11. Wiles is right about this point of division, but he is wrong that the nineteenth-century debates are now theologically irrelevant, even for Protestants. For Wiles, the rejection of the absolute inerrancy of Scripture entails the rejection of an infallible Church (and thus of infallible dogma), but in making this argument he overlooks that one can hold to scriptural inerrancy without supposing that this inerrancy applies in every way (e.g., to scientific and historical matters) and without denying a certain kind of real theological diversity in Scripture. For a better way forward, see Richard Schenk, OP, "*Officium Signa Temporum Perscrutandi*: New Encounters of Gospel and Culture in the Context of the New Evangelization," in *Called to Holiness and Communion: Vatican II on the Church*, ed. Steven Boguslawski, OP, and Robert Fastiggi (Scranton, PA: University of Scranton Press, 2009), 69–105.

17. See also the helpful discussion in Congar, *Tradition and Traditions*, 7–22. Regarding Paul's view of "tradition," e.g., Congar observes that "Paul makes of the acts of transmission (παραδιδόναι) and reception (παραλαμβάνειν), or of conservation and holding (κατέχειν, κρατεῖν), the very structure or law of the régime of faith by which the communities were built up. The *content* of this 'tradition' is seen to be composed of two groups of objects. On the one hand, there is the basic message of the faith, which must be received as a word *from God*. It is essentially centered on the death and resurrection of Christ. . . . Besides the central message of the faith, Paul

various negative references to παράδοσις caution believers against conceptions of "tradition" similar to Tilley's, whereas the New Testament's positive references to "tradition" resonate broadly with *Dei Verbum*'s position on Tradition. As Edith Humphrey points out, for the New Testament, "the idea of tradition includes an act of giving (*didōmi*) over (*para*), a gift that is given over (*paradosis*), and an implied reception of that gift."[18] If that gift is in fact at bottom a human invention, it is not the παράδοσις upon which the New Testament insists.

Tradition as Faithful Reinventing: Terrence Tilley's *Inventing Catholic Tradition*

In *Inventing Catholic Tradition*, Terrence Tilley argues for three major points that significantly affect how Catholics think about Tradition, and that make appropriate the lower-case "t" that Tilley uses for "tradition" throughout the book. These three points are the relativization of propositional truth, the view that Catholic tradition has no definite content or starting point, and the view that Catholic tradition evolves in a non-teleological fashion.[19] All three points are mistaken, in my

'transmits' to the communities rules concerning their internal discipline or Christian behaviour ('parainesis'). . . . When dealing with St Paul, we should not separate too sharply the 'tradition' of the paschal faith from the 'tradition' of apostolic rules of conduct. Both 'build up' the community. Together they integrate the true religious relationship which the faithful must have with God in Christ" (9–10). Congar goes on to argue that the practices are less binding than the doctrines: "However, the two categories of 'tradition' are not entirely of equal standing: the events and doctrines *de Christo*, the objects of the kerygma, have an absolute and immutable character—they are 'fundamental' (1 Cor 3.10; Gal 1.6*ff.*)—which is not possessed by those rules of conduct laid down by the apostles under the guidance of the Holy Spirit, and which we can see would be open to modification, or at least growth, according to the needs of the historical life of the Church" (11). While agreeing with Congar regarding Paul's communication of "doctrines" that "have an absolute and immutable character," I would add that certain practices or "rules of conduct" laid down by Paul also have that character, although this requires careful working out in particular instances.

18. Edith M. Humphrey, *Scripture and Tradition: What the Bible Really Says* (Grand Rapids, MI: Baker Academic, 2013), 26.

19. For related perspectives on Catholic tradition, see also such works as Edward Schillebeeckx, OP, *Church: The Human Story of God*, trans. John Bowden (New

York: Crossroad, 1993); Claude Geffré, *The Risk of Interpretation: On Being Faithful to the Christian Tradition in a Non-Christian Age*, trans. D. Smith (New York: Paulist Press, 1987); Lieven Boeve, *Interrupting Tradition: An Essay on Christian Faith in a Postmodern Context* (Louvain: Peeters, 2003). See also George Tyrrell's 1898 essay "Sabatier on the Vitality of Dogmas," in his *The Faith of the Millions: A Selection of Past Essays* (London: Longmans, Green, 1904), 115–35, in comparison with the essays of Tyrrell's later period that we find in his *Through Scylla and Charybdis or The Old Theology and the New* (London: Longmans, Green, 1907), esp. "Semper Eadem II," " 'Theologism'—A Reply," "Revelation," "Mysteries," and "The Rights and Limits of Theology." On Tyrrell, see, e.g., Oliver P. Rafferty, "Tyrrell's History and Theology: A Preliminary Survey," in *George Tyrrell and Catholic Modernism*, ed. Oliver P. Rafferty (Dublin: Four Courts Press, 2010), 21–37, esp. 33. Special mention should be made here of John E. Thiel's *Senses of Tradition: Continuity and Development in Catholic Faith* (Oxford: Oxford University Press, 2000), published in the same year as Tilley's book. Like Tilley, Thiel is indebted to the epistemological pragmatism of Wilfrid Sellars, who argues that (in Thiel's words) "what is called knowledge takes shape in an integrated network of revisable claims" and that "this meaningful whole is enmeshed in time and culture, ever aligning its interrelated claims for meaning to the circumstances in which knowledge—and faith—is practiced" (28–29). Thiel first engages what he calls the "literal sense of tradition"—namely, its communication of universally true expressions of the gospel in faith and practice—as Thiel points out, however, the seeming stability and universality of this literal sense is tied to the "continuing interpretation of divine revelation made and remade in every successive moment by the Christian community" (55). From this hermeneutical perspective, Thiel argues that there is room for further "senses" of tradition that allow for breaks and ruptures. Specifically, he proposes three further "senses" of tradition: "development-in-continuity" (represented in different ways by Johann Sebastian Drey, Johann Adam Möhler, John Henry Newman, and various reception theories); "dramatic development" (represented by John T. Noonan's *A Church That Can and Cannot Change*, by some teachings of Vatican II, and by the lack of widespread contemporary reception of the Church's teachings on birth control and the ordination of women); and "incipient development" (represented by some cultural and theological changes instigated by feminist anthropology). In this way, Thiel joins development-as-continuity with development-as-rupture, now under the one rubric of "tradition." Thiel's opponent here is the view of "the universality of the Church's common faith as an originary given, trickling down from the Great Church through the local churches into the life of every believer and informing the ever smaller times and places of ecclesial experience with an infallibility as grand as it is fixed" (150). He conceives of his position as balancing the principles of renewal and reception (through novelties and ruptures) with the principles of continuity and universality: prior to the eschaton, we can have only historically partial views of the configuration of the Catholic tradition, rather than an "epic" or God's-eye view (cf. 14–15, view. My first task is therefore to survey Tilley's argument in some detail.

Of the three points, the first is particularly crucial because it shapes the second and third in a determinative way. To understand Tilley's critique of propositional truth, we should start with his broader account of truth. He thinks that it can no longer be held that truth arises from the adequation of the mind to being. Like Immanuel Kant, Ludwig Wittgenstein, and many others, Tilley considers that there are no "concepts of reality independent of our concepts," with the result that we cannot get below or behind our conceptual and narratival mental structure to know reality (being) in a deeper or more direct fashion.[20] Although he recognizes that there are philosophical realists who have disputed this Kantian claim by appealing to the manifestation of being and the act of judgment, Tilley does not advance arguments against contemporary or classical philosophical realists. Instead, he states that "at the beginning of the twenty-first century, foundational realism has been shown to be untenable, at least in any form strong enough to support a metaphysical system necessary to guaranteed epistemic claims."[21] In the past, there were

156–60, 193–95, 210–11). To my mind, Thiel's account of tradition, while much more theologically nuanced than Tilley's, reduces in the end to Tilley's. For both, tradition is a site of contradictory breaks and ruptures, and for both it is naïve to understand propositional teachings (of Scripture, of the Church) as articulating universal truth owing to their adequation, in the act of judgment, to reality. The result is an amorphous, fundamentally anti-dogmatic view of the content of revelation, whose real content will only be known at the eschaton. For a response to Thiel on *Humanae Vitae* and "dramatic development," see Janet E. Smith, "The *Sensus Fidelium* and *Humanae Vitae*," in *Called to Holiness and Communion*, 291–319.

20. Tilley, *Inventing Catholic Tradition*, 168. For further discussion, see Tilley's *The Wisdom of Religious Commitment* (Washington, DC: Georgetown University Press, 1995). and his *Talking of God: An Introduction to Philosophical Analysis of Religious Language* (Mahwah, NJ: Paulist Press, 1978). See also Tilley's "Toward a Practice-based Theory of Tradition," in *Tradition and Tradition Theories: An International Discussion*, ed. Torsten Larbig and Siegfried Wiedenhofer (Berlin: LIT Verlag, 2006), 247–80, which provides an essay-length version of his *Inventing Catholic Tradition*.

21. Tilley, *Inventing Catholic Tradition*, 168. Numerous scholars disagree with Tilley

philosophical realists who considered that our knowing apprehends being, but in the twenty-first century, this is apparently no longer an option that can be taken seriously.

If so, then are all knowledge claims merely mental constructs, so that no claim can be considered truer than any other claim? Indebted to Wilfrid Sellars, Tilley argues that one can be "radically constructivist" without thereby being "anti-realist."[22] For Tilley, humans construct our languages, from which follow linguistic acts in which we strive to advance particular claims. Our linguistic acts depend upon our constructed languages; the view that our conceptual judgments directly access reality or being is therefore misguided. In describing the position of anti-realists, Tilley observes that their position arises from a rejection of realist and foundationalist theories. "Philosophers from Plato to the present have construed a foundational-realist theory of truth, in which our knowledge is grounded in the 'fact' that our true claims mirror the world-as-it-is-in-itself (realism) and the 'fact' that the-way-the-world-is-in-itself is just what makes our claims true (foundationalism)."[23]

Having accepted that we cannot know reality in itself (being), Tilley is necessarily a "constructivist," but he argues that there is room for a constructivist position that, even in rejecting foundationalism, still leaves room for a form of "realism." Namely, we might not be able to measure our truth-claims by their adequation to the real, but we can at least admit that when our truth-claims are borne out by empirical evidence, then this may well be the result of their being true. The real cannot ground our truth-claims, because our truth-claims

here, as do I. For arguments in favor of realism, see, e.g., Francesca Aran Murphy, *God Is Not a Story: Realism Revisited* (Oxford: Oxford University Press, 2007); Denys Turner, *Faith, Reason and the Existence of God* (Cambridge: Cambridge University Press, 2004); Ian Markham, *Truth and the Reality of God: An Essay in Natural Theology* (Edinburgh: T&T Clark, 1998). For an influential position with affinities (despite a different conceptual vocabulary) to that of Tilley, see David Tracy's *Blessed Rage for Order: The New Pluralism in Theology* (New York: Seabury Press, 1975); cf. Thiel, *Senses of Tradition*, 198–203.

22. Tilley, *Inventing Catholic Tradition*, 156.

23. Tilley, *Inventing Catholic Tradition*, 158.

arise from our language rather than from direct contact (via the act of judgment) with what is, but when our truth-claims are borne out empirically, this result may be taken as "an *effect* of our getting our claims right."[24] Again, this empirical evidence cannot be taken to ground our truth-claims, because we obtain empirical evidence precisely through "our constructed concepts and practical investigations."[25] But when empirical or practical evidence shows us that a particular truth-claim is generally reliable, this result can confirm us in the view that our truth-claim (a mental construct) reflects reality. We can obtain this form of realism without having to accede to the foundationalist claim that we can have access to being in such a way that reality, as such, is what measures the truthfulness of our conceptual truth-claims. For Tilley, therefore, practice has priority both in how we articulate truth-claims and in how we judge the truthfulness of truth-claims.[26]

It follows that truth-claims about the triune God or Christ Jesus have their meaning within the Church's practice-generated languages. The truthfulness of such truth-claims can be judged, or appraised (to use Tilley's term), solely in terms of the empirical and practical results that will be perceptible in local congregations of Christians.[27]

24. Tilley, *Inventing Catholic Tradition*, 160.

25. Tilley, *Inventing Catholic Tradition*, 162.

26. Here I think of Gordon Kaufman's argument for provisionality of biblical and creedal conceptions of God on the grounds that "the only God we should worship today—the only God we can afford to worship—is the God who will further our humanization, the God who will help to make possible the creation of a universal and humane community" as it is understood today. *God, Mystery, Diversity: Christian Theology in a Pluralistic World* (Minneapolis: Fortress Press, 1996), 29. See also John Hick, *The Metaphor of God Incarnate* (London: SCM Press, 1993), 161. For better approaches to the relationship between doctrine and practice, see Colin Gunton's *A Brief Theology of Revelation* (London: Edinburgh, 1995), 93–95; Terrence Merrigan, "The Image of the Word: Faith and Imagination in John Henry Newman and John Hick," in *Newman and the Word*, ed. Terrence Merrigan and Ian T. Ker (Louvain: Peeters, 2000), 5–47, esp. 27–47.

27. For background, see Edward Schillebeeckx, OP, *God the Future of Man*, trans. N. D. Smith (New York: Sheed and Ward, 1968), esp. chap. 6; see also Thiel's account of the contextuality, ambiguity, and obscurity that characterize the act of faith and his related account of the *sensus fidei* and *consensus fidelium*, in Thiel, *Senses of Tradition*,

These appraisals are changeable, and thus so are the truth-claims of any religious tradition, including the Catholic one. Tilley gives five "rules of thumb" or "adaptable standards" for the practice of appraising "religious claims."[28] Religious claims must uncover something about "the world in which we live"; they must fit with other recognized facts; they must enable authenticity rather than self-deception; they must enable fidelity to others and to the tradition (a fidelity that does not require repetition and that often requires rupture); and they must "help create lives of truthfulness."[29] In short, although we cannot know God the Trinity or Jesus Christ in any direct way, we can make truth-claims about such things and measure the truth of these claims by the results that they produce in us. The Catholic tradition's

---

chap. 5. Along the same lines as Tilley, Thiel concludes, "Like all discernments, comprehensive discernments of the *sensus fidei* that unify all four senses of tradition have a host of incarnational and pneumatological criteria that measure their authenticity. And yet, like all discernments, comprehensive discernments follow no rules that specify their practice. Like all discernments, they prove themselves by practice, by an enacted faithfulness that gains authority by showing how the power of renewal bolsters the tradition's constancy and how the tradition's constancy extends as far as and into discernments of striking renewal. Although this authority remains ambiguous as tradition continues to unfold—and although this ambiguity can be disconcerting to some in the community of the faithful who are inclined to think of the Spirit's infallible truth dwelling only in those times, places, persons, and events in which faithfulness already has been enacted—its ambiguity is rightly named the mystery of the Spirit's presence, the source and the means of all authority that truthful discernments in search of tradition might possess" (*Senses of Tradition*, 185–86).

28. Tilley, *Inventing Catholic Tradition*, 164.

29. Tilley, *Inventing Catholic Tradition*, 164, 166. Cf. here a list offered by Thomas H. Groome, which, despite serving a different purpose, bears notable similarities with Tilley's list: "When it comes to interpreting Christian Story, it would surely help to have guidelines for making reliable interpretations and drawing out what is most life-giving. I will suggest five. In summary, Christian communities and persons should approach their scriptures and traditions: (1) as a great unfolding Story of the vital partnership between God and humankind; (2) bringing life to interpret Christian Story and Christian Story to interpret life; (3) expecting to encounter old and new spiritual wisdom; (4) being alert for distortions and forgotten legacies; and (5) always choosing *for life for all*." *What Makes Us Catholic: Eight Gifts for Life* (New York: HarperCollins, 2002), 19.

task will be to seek increasingly to make truth-claims that "free a person and community to live in truthful ways."[30]

The Catholic tradition therefore should embrace the reality of ever-changing appraisals of its truth-claims, as one would expect in light of the ever-changing practices and contexts in which Christians live. Tilley observes, "What makes living religious traditions different from delusive or silly systems is that religious traditions' claims are subject to ongoing appraisal and modification."[31] We cannot an-

30. Tilley, *Inventing Catholic Tradition*, 166; see also Tyrrell, *Through Scylla and Charybdis*, 175 and elsewhere. It is unclear how Tilley knows what counts as suitable "results," human "authenticity," "truthful ways," and so forth. Abstracted from the instruction of the Word in his Spirit-filled Church, how can we know when we have found Christian authenticity? For discussion, see Guy Mansini, OSB's helpful "Experience and Discourse, Revelation and Dogma in Catholic Modernism," forthcoming in *Nova et Vetera*. See also the concerns expressed in Hans Urs von Balthasar, *The Moment of Christian Witness*, trans. Richard Beckley (San Francisco: Ignatius Press, 1994).

31. Tilley, *Inventing Catholic Tradition*, 169. Applying this to the Catholic Church, Rosemary Radford Ruether and Eugene C. Bianchi argue that "Catholics must shake off the intellectual lethargy that, for too long, has allowed them to acquiesce in the view that the present church structure is divinely mandated for all time. They must begin to ask the hard questions about the relationship between historical realities and theological and ethical norms." "Introduction," in *A Democratic Catholic Church: The Reconstruction of Roman Catholicism*, ed. Eugene C. Bianchi and Rosemary Radford Ruether (New York: Crossroad, 1993), 7–13, at 7. Bianchi and Ruether seek to identify the Church's "basic message and ministry to society" and to ask "what kind of social ordering of human relationships best approximates, even if always imperfectly, redemptive relationality" (13). The Church, on this view, needs to be refounded in a radical way in order to mediate redemption. See also Edward Schillebeeckx, OP's effort to reconceive Catholic ecclesiology on the basis of what he discovers to be "the heart of the gospel message." *Church: The Human Story of God*, trans. John Bowden (New York: Crossroad, 1993), xiii. Schillebeeckx argues that the Church is indefectible only insofar as it continually reinvents itself so as to overcome its own errors, and Schillebeeckx thinks that he is able to identify these errors. In addition to pressing for a democratic restructuring of the Catholic Church, Schillebeeckx proposes that Christian communities must no longer be divided by doctrinal differences: "All local and confessional churches are 'church' to the degree that they can affirm, encourage and further *communio*, communication, with other local churches" (197). See also the conclusion to Daniel Speed Thompson's *The Language of Dissent: Edward Schillebeeckx on the Crisis of Authority in the Catholic Church* (Notre Dame, IN: University of Notre Dame Press,

ticipate in advance the new practices and contexts that will cause our truth-claims to shift. But we can be assured that insofar as the claims generated by our practices/languages result in human authenticity, then we have spoken truly for that moment at least, and have spoken in a manner that reveals our sacramental ability to manifest "God's grandeur" in our lives.[32] We may need to speak in an entirely different way in the future, and that too would manifest God's grandeur insofar as it fosters human authenticity. We cannot directly know about God (or Christ Jesus, or salvation, or other realities), but we can measure our truth-claims by the communities that they foster. We can know something about ourselves, and if what we discover about ourselves reveals authenticity, then we can judge from these results that our truth-claims about divine realities must be true at least for the moment, given the imperatives of our current practices and contexts.

Everything, then, boils down to the authenticity of believers in

---

2003), 147–62, as well as Paul Lakeland's identification of the Church's "essentials" in his *The Liberation of the Laity: In Search of an Accountable Church* (New York: Continuum, 2003), 260–62. A better view was articulated by Karl Barth in 1936: "It was and is needful that someone somewhere should make a stand against the excessive claims of all church movements, and assert that the union of the churches is a thing which cannot be manufactured, but must be found and confessed, in subordination to that already accomplished oneness of the Church which is in Jesus Christ. . . . Let us not deceive ourselves. The union of the churches into the oneness of the Church would mean more than mutual tolerance, respect, and cooperation; more than readiness to hear and to understand each other; more than an emotional sense of oneness in the possession of some ineffable common link; more than that we, being one in faith, hope, and charity, could worship together in one accord. Above all it would mean, as the decisive test of unity, that we should join in making confession of our faith and thus should unitedly proclaim it to the world, and so fulfill that commandment of Jesus on which the Church is based. The message and witness, given by the Church's teaching, order, and life, must utter one voice, however manifold in the diversity of languages, gifts, places, and persons. A union of the churches in the sense of that task which is so seriously laid upon the Church would mean a union of the confessions into one unanimous confession. If we remain on the level where confessions are divided, we remain where the multiplicity of the churches is inevitable." *The Church and the Churches* (Grand Rapids, MI: Eerdmans, 2005), 39–41.

32. Tilley, *Inventing Catholic Tradition*, 170.

our local contexts and circumstances. Our truth-claims about God the Trinity, Jesus Christ, salvation, and so forth arise out of our practices/languages, and the truthfulness of these claims is appraised in terms of whether they foster authentic practices here and now. What "Catholic tradition" means, then, is the ongoing set of appraisals and revised truth-claims in light of ever new practices and contexts, truth-claims that may be about God but, because our practices and languages constitute our knowledge, can be appraised for truthfulness only in terms of us. Because we are ever changing, the appraisals and truth-claims of "Catholic tradition" are ever changing.[33]

Tilley accepts that "in one sense, our basic grammar is already defined in the *regula fidei*, the Creed."[34] But he makes clear that creedal statements are elastic insofar as "terminology can remain constant while the significance of terms changes, sometimes radically."[35] Given that the Church clearly defined the seven sacraments only in the medieval period, sacramental theology appears to be particularly prone to such change. All theological claims, however, can be shown to conceal (whether more or less openly) a history of invention and rupture. Examples that Tilley gives include the inculturation of the concept of original sin and redemption, the variety of Christologies, and the subtleties of Trinitarian theology. This is no less true in the Bible than in the history of the Church: "Believers' faith presumes that the Bible is

33. For an exemplification of this viewpoint from the perspective of "critical theology," see Elisabeth Schüssler Fiorenza, "A Discipleship of Equals: Ekklesial Democracy and Patriarchy in Biblical Perspective," in *Democratic Catholic Church*, 17–33. For background, see Edward Schillebeeckx, OP, "The New Critical Theory and Theological Hermeneutics," in *The Understanding of Faith: Interpretation and Criticism*, trans. N. D. Smith (New York: Sheed and Ward, 1974), 124–55; see also, on the status of dogma within theologies founded upon and ordered to praxis, Matthew L. Lamb, "Political Theory and Enlightenment: Toward a Reconstruction of Dogma as Socially Critical," in *Solidarity with Victims: Toward a Theology of Social Transformation* (New York: Crossroad, 1982), 100–115; William L. Portier, "Edward Schillebeeckx as Critical Theorist: The Impact of Neo-Marxist Social Thought on His Recent Theology," *The Thomist* 48 (1984): 341–67.

34. Tilley, *Inventing Catholic Tradition*, 12.

35. Tilley, *Inventing Catholic Tradition*, 11.

in some sense *given* by God to humanity. Historical research seems to show that the Bible is *made* by human processes. Not only are books in the Bible composites of earlier traditions, but also evident inconsistencies can be found within and between its books."[36] Such inconsistencies profoundly mark Christian communities over time, and in fact such inconsistencies are present in all communities that possess traditions. As Tilley says, "A verbal token, translated from language to

36. Tilley, *Inventing Catholic Tradition*, 13–14. For the risks involved here, see John Betz, "Glory(ing) in the Humility of the Word: The Kenotic Form of Revelation in J. G. Hamann," *Letter & Spirit* 6 (2010): 141–79, at 173. From a perspective that accords with Tilley's, see John J. Collins's *The Bible after Babel: Historical Criticism in a Postmodern Age* (Grand Rapids, MI: Eerdmans, 2005), and *Encounters with Biblical Theology* (Minneapolis Fortress Press, 2005). In his introduction to the latter volume, Collins responds to concerns raised by Jon D. Levenson. Collins argues that "not all traditions are alike. While historical criticism is itself a tradition, it is a tradition of a very different order from religious orthodoxy, as it does not require the a priori acceptance of any particular conclusions. It is neither committed nor opposed in principle to any particular reconstruction of the history of Israel, or to the unity or divine origin of the Bible. Any position can be defended, so long as evidence is adduced and arguments are made. A confessional approach, such as that advocated by Levenson and many others, wants to privilege certain positions and exempt them from the requirement of supporting arguments, thus in effect taking biblical theology out of the public discussion" (*Encounters with Biblical Theology*, 3). But the question is whether historical reconstructions could ever demonstrate the "unity" of a set of widely diverse ancient Near Eastern texts. It is the faith community that perceived the unity of these texts as one Bible. Historical-critical commitment to bracketing the faith community results in the privileging of a certain position regarding "the unity or divine origin of the Bible." Collins goes on to grant that "faith in supernatural beings or events can never be confirmed by historical or literary research" (4). Surely this is a significant, though obvious, admission regarding the study of texts that consistently bear reference to God, but Collins does not seem to notice the significance, other than to emphasize that the "God" who figures in the texts is simply a human construction. Collins adds that some things can be confirmed by historical research, such as "the gap between the biblical 'history of salvation' and the history reconstructed by modern scholarship. . . . Appeals to faith are of little help here, as it is difficult to see the virtue in continuing to affirm on a theological level what has been shown to be erroneous on the historical" (4). If on the theological level we affirm the living God's election and formation of the people Israel, however, it would seem that we could allow that some events did not happen without thereby negating the active and unique presence of the living God in the historical formation of Israel.

language and historical context to historical context, connected with different concepts to get its significance, and embodied in different cultures and practices, cannot simply 'mean the same thing.'"[37]

These reflections have already involved us in the second central point that Tilley's book makes. In Tilley's view, the Catholic tradition has no definite content and no definite starting point, and the Catholic tradition evolves in a non-teleological fashion. Again, this should be seen in light of his critique of propositional knowledge, as opposed to practical knowledge measured by the authenticity of believers. With regard to attempts to locate an essential doctrinal core that has been handed down in the Catholic tradition across the centuries, he observes that "even if there were clear verbal continuity in formulating 'essential' concepts and propositions of the tradition, there is great difficulty in determining the meanings of those concepts."[38] Along these lines, he suggests that the notion of a "deposit of faith" is profoundly misleading.[39] He explains, "The contexts in which that 'core' is expressed radically affect the expression; and if there is a 'deposit of faith' or other 'core' of a tradition, there can be no direct

37. Tilley, *Inventing Catholic Tradition*, 34. See also his remark that "historical investigations have shown that there have been marked shifts in the content of practices and beliefs we accept as 'given' on the basis of tradition. Appeals to warrant contemporary beliefs on the grounds that they are traditional are always subject to overturning by historical research—and that frequently happens" (27–28).

38. Tilley, *Inventing Catholic Tradition*, 35.

39. Joseph Ratzinger agrees that simply to affirm that revelation was closed at the death of the last Apostle is "far too simplistic," but he suggests that a middle ground is possible: "revelation is indeed closed in terms of its material principle, but it is present, and remains present, in terms of its reality. Putting it another way: We are faced with a concept according to which revelation does indeed have its ἐφάπαξ, insofar as it took place in historical facts, but also has its constant 'today,' insofar as what once happened remains forever living and effective in the faith of the Church, and Christian faith never refers merely to what is past; rather, it refers equally to what is present and what is to come." "The Question of the Concept of Tradition: A Provisional Response," in *God's Word: Scripture—Tradition—Office*, ed. Peter Hünermann and Thomas Söding, trans. Henry Taylor (San Francisco: Ignatius Press, 2008), 41–89, at 86–87.

access to that 'core.' All communicable expressions are necessarily contextualized expressions."[40]

40. Tilley, *Inventing Catholic Tradition*, 35. The problems with "contextual" theologies are well articulated in Vladan Perišić, "Can Orthodox Theology Be Contextual?," *St. Vladimir's Theological Quarterly* 56 (2012): 399–413. For an approach that while theologically much richer has certain affinities with Tilley's, see David Brown, *Tradition and Imagination: Revelation and Change* (New York: Oxford University Press, 1999). Like Tilley, Brown rejects "the 'deposit' view of revelation which has so dominated most of the history of Christianity" (107). He argues that historical criticism requires that theologians let go of claims about Jesus that differentiate him from his times: "As I understand matters, modern biblical scholarship has forced upon us a very different understanding of the nature of the incarnation from that which prevailed through most of Christianity's history. Gone is the incarnate Lord who remained transcendent to the ambiguities of history and in his place has come someone so thoroughly shaped by the social setting in which he found himself that in retrospect we must declare some at least of his beliefs false. It is not just a matter of easily containable error such as the three-decker universe or the authorship of the Pentateuch and Psalms but also some beliefs which helped profoundly to shape the very substance of his message. Probably he thought that the end of the world as we now know it was imminent, and as a corollary he may well have died disappointed or in despair. Perhaps also he presumed continuing obedience to Jewish law. Most significantly of all, the human Jesus had no consciousness of his own divinity. Such admissions are often thought to carry with them the automatic demise of orthodox Christian belief. But . . . it will be my contention that, so far from this being so, such discoveries can instead be very effectively employed towards the actual strengthening of incarnational doctrine. The incarnation has now become a total identification with our humanity and its limitations. Though such extensive accommodation to the human condition inevitably generates major problems concerning the adequate translation of some aspects of Jesus' teaching from his world to our own, the benefits in my view far outweigh the losses. We now have a fellow-human being with whom we can unqualifiedly identify, with all that implies for our understanding of 'salvation'" (108–9; cf. Brown's chap. 6). But the question is whether historical-critical scholarship really does compel this view of Jesus's consciousness. How can historical-critical scholarship obtain this privileged access, contradicting at least a significant strand of the Gospels' witness, into what Jesus knew or thought he knew? Brown seems to me here to build his "incarnational doctrine"—which amounts to the view that a credible incarnation would require that Jesus, at least prior to his exaltation, "knew" only what other Jews of his day thought they knew—on the foundation of alleged historical-critical certainties about Jesus's consciousness, surely a domain that radically eludes historical-critical certitude. In his doctrine of tradition, Brown is right to see (with historical-critical scholars) "how deeply a developing tradition has helped shape the thinking of the biblical writers" (112), but I do not see why

If traditions are ever changing, so that their propositional content is never stable, are traditions worth having? Tilley thinks that they are not only unavoidable, but also worth having so long as they recognize themselves to be ever-changing constructions whose truthfulness is measured by whether they foster authentic practices. Failure to recognize their instability does not result in more stability. Tilley argues that instead it leads to efforts by authorities to impose their will by innovating under the guise of preserving a tradition. Such imposition, for Tilley, is an illegitimate form of "inventing" tradition. While changing a tradition is good and necessary, a bad "invention" is a change that is *deliberately* invented and imposed (as if it were no change at all) by sheer power. Tilley holds that the main engine of such deliberate, cloaked "invention" in Catholic history has been the Roman Magisterium, especially in the past half century.[41]

---

this should lead to conflating Scripture and the Church's ongoing tradition. Having argued that the difference between the Gospels and tradition are "differences of degree rather than kind" (112), Brown finds himself having to account for later doctrinal development at best in terms of "pressure . . . from various New Testament trajectories" (286) without being able to defend the normative status of the apostolic witness to Jesus Christ (see 111, 300). We can certainly grant both that there is inconsistency and diversity in Scripture, and that conceptual/imaginative reflection over time resulted in new ways of understanding events and narratives (doctrinal development or "evolving tradition"; see p. 300), but this need not entail the denial of the existence of an intelligible "deposit" of revelation and thus also of a closed, uniquely inspired biblical canon. For further discussion of Brown's work, see William J. Abraham, "Scripture, Tradition, and Revelation: An Appreciative Critique of David Brown," in *Theology, Aesthetics, and Culture: Responses to the Work of David Brown*, ed. Robert MacSwain and Taylor Worley (Oxford: Oxford University Press, 2012), 13–28.

41. See Tilley, *Inventing Catholic Tradition*, 36–43, drawing upon various essays in Eric Hobsbawn and Terence Ranger, eds., *The Invention of Tradition* (Cambridge: Cambridge University Press, 1983). Tilley's examples of such cloaked "inventions" range from the divergence of *Dignitatis Humanae* from nineteenth-century papal teachings about religious freedom, to the shifting of the altar in the celebration of the Eucharist (which, he argues, changed the Eucharist by obliterating its sacrificial symbolism), to the Congregation for the Doctrine of the Faith's rejection of inclusive-language translation (a rejection that Tilley finds particularly appalling, given that the Septuagint had also employed a relatively free translation style). Given Tilley's understanding of religion as an ongoing human construction, however, his account of Christianity

Although Tilley grants that in some sense Jesus can be said to inaugurate the Catholic tradition, he emphasizes that "even the originating events and people of a tradition, like Jesus, are found within an already-existing stream of tradition, Judaism."[42] In this sense, and in this sense only, the Catholic tradition is "given" or "found" rather than made or invented: there is a givenness always present because we cannot make up a tradition from scratch. Tilley states, "That claims, beliefs, and symbols emerge from practices does not imply that they are 'pure human creations.' No constructions are so pure. Each construction arises out of previous practices and beliefs."[43] When certain "practitioners develop the belief that the originating events and people are the result of the creative presence and action of God," we can affirm this in the sense that the Catholic tradition's sacramental imagination always affirms God's active presence: "That human constructs can also be divine creations is an affirmation that is at the heart of a tradition that relies on and produces an analogical imagination."[44] The point, however, is that the Catholic tradition involves no strong claim of a definite founding, let alone a definite deposit of faith whose depths can be articulated doctrinally in an enduring manner.

---

lacks a place for real authority, with the result that any exercise of religious authority will be reducible in principle to arbitrary power. See also Immanuel Kant's distinction between "ecclesiastical faith" and "pure religious faith," in Kant's *Religion within the Limits of Reason Alone*, trans. Theodore M. Greene and Hoyt H. Hudson (New York: Harper & Row, 1960), 94–114, although Tilley does not fully share Kant's confidence in "the universal religion of reason." Kant, *Religion within the Limits of Reason Alone*, 113.

42. Tilley, *Inventing Catholic Tradition*, 173.

43. Tilley, *Inventing Catholic Tradition*, 173. Thus the constructions of "Christianity" will be highly diverse at all times and places, so that as Hegel puts it (in examining the issue of authority in Christianity), "Nothing has so many different meanings as the modern conception of what Christianity is, either in its essence, or in its particular doctrines and their importance or their relation to the whole." "The Positivity of the Christian Religion," trans. T. M. Knox, in *On Christianity: Early Theological Writings* (New York: Harper & Brothers, 1961), 67–181, at 174).

44. Tilley, *Inventing Catholic Tradition*, 174. See David Tracy, *The Analogical Imagination* (New York: Crossroad, 1981).

For Tilley, therefore, it would be a mistake to suppose that doctrinal "development" is fueled by something other than ever-changing practices and contexts. The practice of handing on the Catholic tradition requires great flexibility with doctrinal propositions. On this view, the faithful practitioner of Christian tradition knows that "fidelity may require even abandoning traditional formulations" because "our fidelity is constituted not by a 'what' but by 'how.'"[45] To think of fidelity in terms of an essentialist "what," a core content or deposit of faith, would be to miss the whole point. Rather, the historical practice of passing on the Catholic tradition has always involved profound doctrinal changes (ruptures and inventions) to meet the requirements of new practices and contexts, and thereby to foster authenticity among believers. This changing will not stop: we have no way of knowing what future Catholics might believe. As Tilley puts it in the conclusion of his book, "We may sing a different tune than our forebears, and our successors will sing yet differently.... Faithfully transmitting our communal memory in fidelity to our past and our future is possible only in practice, only by engaging in the ongoing, ever-changing, and multilayered practice of *Inventing Catholic Tradition*."[46]

45. Tilley, *Inventing Catholic Tradition*, 185. Compare this to Francis Bacon's view of "heathen" religion as being peaceful because it "consisted rather in rites and ceremonies than in any constant belief." "Of Unity in Religion," in *The Essays*, ed. John Pitcher (New York: Penguin, 1985), 67–71, at 67. See also Ernst Troeltsch, *The Christian Faith: Based on Lectures Delivered at the University of Heidelberg in 1912 and 1913*, ed. Gertrud von le Fort, trans. Garrett E. Paul (Minneapolis, MN: Fortress Press, 1991), at 39, 41: "We feed on the tradition, but this tradition would be a dead thing were it not for the productivity of the one who receives life from it.... all these developments and transformations should not be viewed so much in terms of perfection, but rather in terms of a living adaptation to the present environment."

46. Tilley, *Inventing Catholic Tradition*, 186. For tradition as an action, see also the philosophical reflections of Jorge J. E. Gracia, *Old Wine in New Skins: The Role of Tradition in Communication, Knowledge and Group Identity* (Milwaukee, WI: Marquette University Press, 2003). Gracia argues that "when Roman Catholics talk about beliefs as constituting a tradition, for example, they can be taken to be referring to the very actions of believing rather than to certain doctrines or to their textual formulation" (94). For an appreciation of this active sense of Tradition, without however relativizing doctrinal

In other words, the continuity is in the practice, not in the doctrine. And the continuity of practice does not mean a continuity of practices, because practices change. What stays the same is quite simply "the practice of engaging in an act of judgment or appraisal that recognizes continuity."[47] Certainly, a tradition has a history that is its givenness, but nothing in this history enables one to formulate a theory about the future development of the tradition. Tilley states that "it is not possible to devise a theory to predict future changes in *tradita* or to legitimate past changes."[48] When practices and contexts change, as they do continually and in an unpredictable way, a tradition must either change doctrinally or wither away because practices are what generates doctrines. For Tilley, the faithful practitioner of the tradition will be the one who works to "constantly invent the tradition."[49]

---

truths or their creedal formulation (the content of Tradition), see Congar, *Tradition and Traditions*, 253 and elsewhere.

47. Tilley, *Inventing Catholic Tradition*, 121.

48. Tilley, *Inventing Catholic Tradition*, 121. For his part, Lewis Ayres agrees that no theory (or set of historical and logical arguments) can fully account for the actual course of doctrinal development, but Ayres insists that this does not mean that we can or should cease offering such theories: even if the course of doctrinal development eludes rationalistic explanation, neither is it irrational. See Ayres, *Nicaea and Its Legacy: An Approach to Fourth-Century Trinitarian Theology* (Oxford: Oxford University Press, 2004).

49. Tilley, *Inventing Catholic Tradition*, 121. By contrast, Congar's presentation of the relationship of identity and change allows for both, rather than assuming rupture and sheer invention: " 'The faith which was once for all delivered to the saints' (Jude 3) is extended to a very great number of men, scattered through space and time, together with the apostolic doctrines and precepts. In this respect tradition is not in dependence on time: rather it triumphs over it, even, one might say, discounts it altogether. Tradition does not age, for to grow old is to change. It is the transmission through time, time which alters all things, of a deposit of faith; but, above and beyond the successive transmissions of this deposit, Christ the Incarnate Word, reigning as Lord above time, in giving the Church its very life, assures too the continuing identity of the truth possessed by the Church. 'Jesus Christ is the same yesterday and today and for ever' (Heb 13.8). We must go even further than this. Tradition is not the simple permanence of a structure, but a continual renewal and fertility *within* this given structure, which is guaranteed by a living and unchanging principle of identity [viz., Christ and the Holy Spirit]" (Congar, *Tradition and Traditions*, 264–65). For Congar, Tradition is both

Tilley goes on to describe a set of five "rules of grammar" for the "Catholic intellectual tradition" rather than Catholic tradition per se (although in his view there seems to be little if any difference). These five rules include an analogical and sacramental imagination, by which he means allowing for what appear to be conceptual contradictions; the Incarnation, as a sign of God's grace rather than as a logical problem, and universal hope; radical inclusivity; the worldliness and public character of the Church; and the graciousness of the Creator God and the goodness of creation. When spelled out in light of Tilley's particular understanding of "incarnation," "church," and "God," these descriptive rules show themselves to be able to encompass widely divergent content.[50]

Tilley expresses attraction to John Henry Newman's view that the "idea of Christianity" unfolds historically without being identical to that historical unfolding. For Newman, the "idea of Christianity" is not separable from a specific content, even if that content can always be unfolded more deeply.[51] By contrast, the (Schleiermachian) conclusion that Tilley draws from Newman is that "the faith, then, is not

"the transmission unchanged of a sacred deposit" and "the explanation which is made of this deposit, as a result of its being lived and defended, generation after generation, by the People of God.... What we receive in the twentieth century is always the 'faith which was once for all delivered to the saints' (Jude 3), but we cannot detach this deposit from the fellowship of the saints who have received it, preserved it and lived it from the time of the first 'saints' until our own times" (267–68).

50. Tilley justifies limiting himself to these five rules on the grounds that to include further doctrinal principles would exclude works of Catholic intellectual tradition that happen not to mention these doctrines.

51. As Terrence Merrigan observes, "Newman was absolutely committed to the idea that the Christian religion contained truths that would not have been known had they not been disclosed by God in and through the life, death and resurrection of Jesus Christ." "Revelation," in *The Cambridge Companion to John Henry Newman*, ed. Ian Ker and Terrence Merrigan (Cambridge: Cambridge University Press, 2009), 47–72, at 47; cf. 56–63. Merrigan adds that Newman also upheld "God's universal self-disclosure, at least as a sort of (ongoing) preparation for the reception of the Gospel" (47). These truths, expressed dogmatically (propositionally), can never of course exhaust the content of the revealed realities.

reducible to any one articulation of the [Christian] vision or any one way of practicing the faith. The faith is the faith, and the expressions are that by which we come to recognize and eventually to understand what it means to live in and live out that faith."[52] But the creedal, dogmatic Christianity advocated by Newman depends upon the view that the content of Christian faith can be rightly expressed, even if not exhausted, by a particular "articulation of the vision"; Newman does not separate faith and dogma in the way that Tilley does.[53] A similar problem arises when Tilley links his own approach with that Avery Dulles's *Models of Revelation*. Dulles seeks to reject the view that revelation is either "the delivery of immutable divine propositions" *or* a subjective interior feeling or intuition.[54] Tilley claims to be doing the same, but Dulles accepts, in his nuanced fashion, the unique revelation of God to Israel (culminating in Jesus Christ) and the propositional truth of dogma, while Tilley profoundly relativizes them.[55]

52. Tilley, *Inventing Catholic Tradition*, 112.

53. See, e.g., John Henry Newman, "On the Introduction of Rationalistic Principles into Revealed Religion," in *Essays Critical and Historical*, vol. 1 (New York: Longmans, Green, 1897), 30–101; idem, "Private Judgment," in *Essays Critical and Historical*, vol. 2 (New York: Longmans, Green, 1895), 336–74; idem, "Contracted Views in Religion," in *Parochial and Plain Sermons* (San Francisco: Ignatius Press, 1987), 545–51. For Newman's position on faith and dogma, see esp. Terrence Merrigan, *Clear Heads and Holy Hearts: The Religious and Theological Ideal of John Henry Newman* (Louvain: Peeters, 1991); Avery Dulles, SJ, *Newman* (London: Continuum, 2002); Jan Hendrik Walgrave, OP, *Newman the Theologian: The Nature of Belief and Doctrine as Exemplified in His Life and Works* (New York: Sheed and Ward, 1960).

54. Tilley, *Inventing Catholic Tradition*, 171.

55. Thus Tilley asks how we can speak of an "original Christian 'interpretandum,'" given that Jesus's own claims (insofar as we can know them) and the New Testament's diverse interpretations of Jesus, just as much as later dogma, can from a certain perspective only be interpreted within the developing and multifaceted streams of Second Temple Judaism(s). But what does it mean to call something "a legitimate and even permanent milestone" in an ever-changing historical movement? What does a "milestone" signify, and why would we suppose that the road has an end or goal? For Tilley, as for Troeltsch, an emphasis on praxis can obviate these problems: "While I would not advocate keeping silent about doctrines, as the editors of the *Apophthegmata* [*Patrum*] likely did, I would advocate not making them a litmus test for sharing practices and forming communities of resistance and solidarity. Doctrines divide where

Tilley's account of the relationship of practices and doctrines is shaped by various contemporary thinkers, including Kathleen Boone, Clifford Geertz, James McClendon, and Robert Schreiter. A practice involves a shared vision about the goal of the practice and its attainability, dispositions that serve the attainment of this goal, and the "grammar" or rules of the practice that suggest what actions befit the practice. For Tilley, the Christian vision involves understanding "human life as created, redeemed, and sustained by the God present and revealed in and through Jesus the Christ."[56] Tilley develops this

---

practices can unite. Let the future settle the ideological disputes whenever possible; let the present find ways to share projects and practices, to engage in mutual enrichment, to live like Christ among our neighbors, and to seek reconciliation—thus fulfilling the law of Christ that all should thrive and creating an even larger community that undertakes reconciling practices." *The Disciples' Jesus: Christology as Reconciling Practice* (Maryknoll, NY: Orbis Books, 2008), 259. Tilley's emphasis on the divisiveness of doctrines should not obscure the fact that his own claims about "the law of Christ" and about the community of reconciliation are doctrinally weighted: even if one bemoans their divisiveness, doctrines cannot be avoided. See also Tilley's point that "we cannot 'get back' to an actual man, Jesus, and certainly not to his 'self-consciousness'—for all we have are records of performances of the Jesus-movement. What we get is the historic Jesus, Jesus remembered in and through the practice of tradition, which he is also remembered as having initiated by his own powerful and empowering practices" (*Disciples' Jesus*, 57). Cf. Nicholas Lash, "Performing the Scriptures," in *Theology on the Way to Emmaus* (London: SCM, 1986), 37–46. For Tilley, "we can make arguments about which memories are accurate, which distorted. The results of those arguments can provide touchstones, if not formal criteria, for linking our present practices with those inaugurated in the Jesus-movement (which at the beginning, of course, included Jesus)" (50n2). Because Tilley considers that the Jesus movement's practices do not merely serve as a resource for Christology but in fact "*are* christology," he concludes that "Jesus" should be understood as the one "who does not reveal truths but draws out from members of the movement insights that help them to see how to live truthfully; who graces the movement not by infusing its members with something from on high but by surfacing the divine creative grace in the movement and helping shape an ongoing movement of created, creative grace; who refuses to make the disciples into wholly dependent patients who respond to God's powerful Agent in passive acceptance but empowers them to become creative and graceful reconciling agents of the commonweal divine" (70). In this reductive vision, Christianity is nothing but human practices; words such as "divine" add nothing to what Tilley is saying. See also Schillebeeckx, *Church*, 224.

56. Tilley, *Inventing Catholic Tradition*, 56.

portrait of the Christian vision even further when he construes the Catholic tradition as a "set of enduring practices" according to which believers are incorporated into Christ's body by sharing in a sacramental and moral life that builds up the kingdom of God, in accord with the tradition's "grammar" as spelled out in "scripture, creeds, confessional statements, magisterial pronouncements, catechisms."[57] He emphasizes, however, that doctrines are learned in and through practices, and more specifically that doctrines are learned in the particular context of local communities. Because there is no universal language or universal experience, every doctrine (insofar as it is a universal truth-claim) must be interpreted and adjusted at the level of the local congregation to meet the practical needs of specific believers. As an example, he states that the universal "right to life" can be spelled out in many ways, so that "no appeal to the abstract claim is sufficient (and may not be necessary) to adjudicate among competing concrete and practical uses of the claim."[58]

Because Tilley locates the significance of doctrinal truth-claims, such as those found in Scripture and the Creeds, within competing and ever changing local practices and contexts, his articulation of "human life as created, redeemed, and sustained by the God present and revealed in and through Jesus the Christ" is inevitably amorphous. Each of the terms in this phrase ("human life," "created," "redeemed," and so forth) has a variety of potential meanings that cannot be adjudicated by appeal to universal truth-claims. This situation befits the constant reimagining and remaking of doctrine that Tilley takes to belong to the practice of "tradition." Drawing upon Schreiter, Tilley sums up: "As with a language, so with a tradition; we really only have performances of the faith before us."[59] He uses

57. Tilley, *Inventing Catholic Tradition*, 58.

58. Tilley, *Inventing Catholic Tradition*, 60. For a better account of the relationship of universal and particular in moral discourse, see David Novak, *Natural Law in Judaism* (Cambridge: Cambridge University Press, 1998). See also Hadley Arkes, *Constitutional Illusions and Anchoring Truths: The Touchstone of the Natural Law* (Cambridge: Cambridge University Press, 2010).

59. Tilley, *Inventing Catholic Tradition*, 65.

the example of changes in the eucharistic liturgy (and in eucharistic piety) to argue that these performances/practices are ever changing, with corresponding evidence that profound doctrinal instability is unavoidable and indeed desirable, lest one think that "one set of theological words can be the necessary and sufficient expression of the presence of Christ."[60]

The critique of propositional truth is distilled in Tilley's six-point definition of "tradition as a set of practices."[61] The first point is that a proposition is intelligible only in terms of its practical use or application, and that since this use often changes, so does the meaning of the proposition. The second, third, fourth, and sixth points reduce to the claim that practices, which change regularly, shape, and define the ever-changing meaning of propositions/doctrines. The fifth point is that there is no way to understand a "tradition" except in terms of practices, so that the "how" has priority over the "what."

Can Catholic "tradition" understood in this way develop? Tilley claims that Catholic tradition can develop if by that we mean that it can constantly recalibrate itself so as to promote authenticity among believers. For Tilley, this authenticity, and not any other content, is ultimately the meaning of the Catholic "tradition." This is not a teleological development, however, nor is it an unfolding of the doctrinal content of God's revelation. Instead, it is a continual adjustment to the times so as to avoid withering and dying. This continual adjustment, Tilley makes clear, is not simply what he wishes would happen (although it certainly is that) but is in fact what has historically happened. Tilley rejects the idea of doctrinal progress not least on the grounds that it is arrogant: "The presumption that 'we' have made religious progress or become more religiously advanced (holier? wis-

60. Tilley, *Inventing Catholic Tradition*, 73n9. It would be helpful, however, to distinguish between the view that there are propositions adequate to expressing the reality that Christ is present and the view that a set of propositions can exhaustively describe this reality. Tilley seems to suggest that there are theologians who hold to the latter view.

61. Tilley, *Inventing Catholic Tradition*, 79.

er? more moral?) because 'we' have a more 'developed' notion of the papacy, the Eucharist, or religious liberty than our forebears cannot be sustained."[62] Catholic theories of development of doctrine have not generally claimed that we are better Christians than our predecessors. But Tilley's point is probably directed toward those who agree with him that tradition is simply "a pattern of inculturation and contextual adaptation": such persons might be tempted to think that this contextual adaptation is ever better. Tilley's commitment to tradition as an ever-changing adaptation cannot coexist with the claim that a particular adaptation, in a particular culture, expresses a *truer* doctrine (rather than a truer doctrine for that particular culture and context).[63]

But do doctrines have an ontological reference that can be more

62. Tilley, *Inventing Catholic Tradition*, 81.

63. Along similar lines, Troeltsch observes, "Allotment of truth to the different epochs of history and participation by individuals in the ultimate values of history belong to a realm that transcends history and lies beyond our knowledge. . . . A liberal and critical attitude toward history, which in its ups and downs sometimes approaches the ideal and sometimes departs from it, must free us from both skepticism and evolutionary progressivism." "Faith and History," in *Religion in History*, trans. James Luther Adams and Walter F. Bense (Minneapolis: Fortress Press, 1991), 134–45, at 143. Troeltsch's development on this point can be seen by comparing his "Rival Methods for the Study of Religion" (1916) with his "Christianity and the History of Religion" (1897), in *Religion and History*, 73–76 and 77–86, respectively. In the latter essay, Troeltsch takes an evolutionary view in which he seeks to identify a "religiosity" that gives "living embodiment to the central idea taking shape in the evolutionary process" ("Christianity and the History of Religion," 80), and he finds "in the Prophetic-Christian religion the high-point, or rather a new point of departure, in the history of religion" (84). In the former essay, Troeltsch concludes that "even an allegedly rationally-necessary scheme for the future is a palpably transparent illusion. The evolutionary goal is not, in fact, constructed from a scientifically established law of cause and effect, but every 'law' of cause and effect is itself derived from a sense for the uniqueness of the moment—however this sense may arise—and the facts are accordingly arranged in a sequence that makes the religious life (conceived more concretely or more abstractly) of the present, or even merely of the author, appear as the evolutionary goal that may be glimpsed at any point. Hence the Jew, the Christian, the Hindu, and the Chinese (regardless of how loosely each may be identified with the group)—above all, the European and the Oriental—will inevitably have a different basic framework for his or her construction of the evolution of religion" ("Rival Methods for the Study of Religion," 76).

(or less) accurately expressed? Tilley deals with this problem in his constructivist account of truth toward the end of the book. Ontological reference is not possible, except in the sense that one can measure one's truth-claim by the practical results (authenticity) that it fosters in believers. In his discussion of whether doctrine can develop, he contents himself primarily with suggesting that those who insist on ontological reference tend to become rigidly attached to an alleged "deposit of faith" with the result that they petrify Catholic "tradition" and make it "brittle and hegemonic," so that reactionary repression and narrowness result.[64] Instead, he says, we must learn "how to live the tradition."[65] To live the tradition is faithfully, and often radically, to change its doctrines and practices so as to meet contemporary needs. For Tilley, Catholic "tradition" is primarily this "how."

Παράδοσις and Catholic Tradition

Tilley does not quote from Scripture in his book. Given his account of constantly reinvented tradition, Tilley would be unlikely to be persuaded by appeal to scriptural texts. In my view, however, just such an appeal helps us to understand why it is that Catholic Tradition must be, to mediate divine revelation, something quite different from what Tilley describes. It is Scripture itself that points us toward a far deeper view of Tradition than Tilley's, and this scriptural view is precisely what Catholic Tradition claims for itself.

To make this case, I examine a selection of the New Testament's positive and negative uses of παράδοσις ("tradition").[66] While much

64. Tilley, *Inventing Catholic Tradition*, 85. The *nouvelle théologie* accused the neo-scholastics of this, but Tilley here has in view the *nouvelle théologie* (and its followers today). For background, see Jürgen Mettepenningen, *Nouvelle Théologie—New Theology: Inheritor of Modernism, Precursor of Vatican II* (London: T&T Clark, 2010). See also Tracey Rowland, *Ratzinger's Faith: The Theology of Pope Benedict XVI* (Oxford: Oxford University Press, 2008), esp. 11–14.

65. Tilley, *Inventing Catholic Tradition*, 86. Cf. Troeltsch, *Christian Faith*, 45–46.

66. I could also have included here a discussion of the multiple uses of the verb παραδίδωμι, which is often translated as "hand over," "deliver," "give over," or

more could be said regarding what Scripture contributes to the theology of Catholic Tradition—and indeed Congar adds a good deal in his *Tradition and Traditions*—my main point is that Scripture not only rules out the validity of a continually reinvented or non-doctrinal "tradition," but also provides the contours of the actual theology of Tradition that the Church recognizes to be the real alternative to the continual reinvention that Tilley advocates.[67]

At first glance, tradition does not appear to be a valued concept in Jesus's preaching. In the Gospels of Matthew and Mark, the Pharisees accuse Jesus's disciples of transgressing "the tradition (παράδοσις) of the elders" by not washing their hands before eating (Mt 15:2; cf. the parallel text in Mk 7:5–13).[68] Jesus responds forcefully to this charge. He accuses the Pharisees of obeying not God's word but their own constructions.[69] Turning their question against them, he asks, "And

---

"commit," but is in fact a verbal form of "tradition." See, e.g., Lk 1:2, Lk 10:22, Rom 6:17, 1 Cor 11:23, 1 Cor 15:3, Jude 3, and elsewhere. See Humphrey, *Scripture and Tradition*, 43.

67. See Congar, *Tradition and Traditions*, esp. 5–22. For Congar, the source of Tradition is Jesus Christ; Tradition exists because God wills for the revelation of Christ to be transmitted in the Church. "As witnesses to Christ and doctors of the new justice, the apostles *transmitted* the witness of a previous and sovereign master, greater than Moses. It is reasonable to suppose that they transmitted, from memory, not only the words of Jesus, with their simple and rhythmic oral style, but even the very inflexions of his voice. . . . Progress in the understanding of the events and words which present revelation was achieved, however, in the Christian community, just as it occurred in Israel, and it was going on even while the apostles were still making their revelation. It, too, has been incorporated into the Christian message as it has been handed down to us" (6). Ratzinger similarly observes that "within the New Testament itself" we can see "the ecclesial process of interpreting what has been handed down" ("Question of the Concept of Tradition," 61).

68. See W. D. Davies and Dale C. Allison Jr., *The Gospel According to Saint Matthew*, vol. 2, *Commentary on Matthew VIII–XVIII* (Edinburgh: T&T Clark, 1991), 520: "Because παράδοσις describes the Pharisaic tradition in Paul, in the gospels, and in Josephus, it was clearly a technical term. It probably translates the Hebrew *massôret*. The tradition of the Pharisees had a controversial status before A.D. 70. The Sadducees repudiated it. So did those responsible for composing the Dead Sea Scrolls."

69. Thus Karl Barth wished to leave room for God's continual reformation of Christian doctrine on the grounds that the fallible Church must continually be united more closely to God's free and definitive revelation, God's radical inbreaking on

why do you transgress the commandment of God (τὴν ἐντολὴν τοῦ θεοῦ) for the sake of your tradition?" (Mt 15:3). Jesus takes the "com-

---

behalf of sinners. Barth's position relativizes Church teaching with the goal of exalting divine revelation in Christ. See Karl Barth, *Church Dogmatics*, I.1, *The Doctrine of the Word of God*, 2nd ed., trans. G. W. Bromiley (Edinburgh: T&T Clark, 1975), 117–21, 248–75. Barth closely links Protestant liberalism and Roman Catholicism as instances of the idolatrous desire to make ourselves superior to the Word of God. He observes, "Though it puts tradition alongside the Bible, the Roman Catholic Church, too, has and reads and honours the Bible. But this is not the Bible in itself, the emancipated Bible, the Bible which confronts the Church as an authority. The fact that the Bible in its own concreteness is the Word of God, and that as such it is the supreme criterion of Church teaching, is not acknowledged here. What we have here is the Bible which belongs to the Church, which is understood aright and expounded aright and applied aright by its teaching office. This Bible is the Word of God by which all proclamation is to be measured. The *regula proxima fidei*, the nearest immediate plumbline of Catholic faith, is not, then, the verdict of the Bible but the verdict of the teaching office on the Bible" (257). Barth further explains the fallibility of Church dogma: "Even and especially on Roman Catholic soil, if dogma is equated with God's Word, will it not have to be understood primarily as command in accordance with the usage of the Bible which was at least possible in the fathers of the first centuries too? . . . A command is what it is only in the act of the one who gives it and the one who obeys or disobeys it. One cannot give oneself a command in the way the Church gives itself Church dogmas. . . . The material and impersonal intrinsic truth ascribed to dogma, the contemplative objectivity which is the issue in Roman Catholic theology when it emphasises the sense of doctrinal proposition in the concept of dogma, this is for us the mark of a truth which is conditioned and limited not merely by the creatureliness of man but also by his sinfulness, a truth in comparison with which the truth of God in His revelation is quite different. By the very fact that as a proposition it can only be contemplated, that it is neutral and permits neutrality, that as a theory—and who can deny that Church dogma is this too?—it bears witness itself to where it belongs, namely, to the Church, its talk, its testimonies, its proclamation, its dialogue with itself—all this with great distinction, for it is not our intention to disparage Church dogma on this its proper level—and yet still to the Church and not the Word in which God addresses the Church. We do not understand and we can never understand how the truth that is put into the hands of the Church as Church dogma can be the truth of God. What we think we know as the truth of God's Word from the witness of Holy Scripture is a very different truth, a sovereign truth" (271–72). My disagreement with Barth's dogmatic occasionalism is ultimately rooted in Scripture's testimony to the Church and its participation in Christ. Theocentricity does not require disclaiming the graced fidelity—with regard to the proclamation of the Gospel and to the sacraments—of the Church's participation in Christ.

mandment of God" to be God's own word, which Israel has received from God. In what does the "commandment of God" consist? Jesus gives as examples two commandments from the Torah: "Honor your father and your mother" (Ex 20:12) and "For every one who curses his father or his mother shall be put to death" (Lv 20:9). By contrast, the Pharisees' tradition is not supported by a commandment of God. Jesus summarizes the tradition quite negatively: "But you [Pharisees] say, 'If any one tells his father or his mother, What you would have gained from me is given to God, he need not honor his father'" (Mt 15:5). At issue is whether a son of impoverished parents is justified in giving to the temple the resources that otherwise could have nourished his parents. Jesus holds that the Pharisees' interpretation of the Torah in this regard undermines God's commandments in the Torah.[70]

Even if the practice of temple offerings can be adapted in certain ways, according to Jesus, it cannot be adapted in this way without contradicting the express content of the commandments. The reve-

70. As Humphrey comments, "Jesus . . . declares that they have 'put aside' the commandment of God, while elevating human commandments that originally were intended to *aid* in the keeping of the divine Torah. What the Pharisees call 'the tradition of the elders' has been diminished in their hands and been rendered merely 'the tradition of men,' for the Pharisees are not maintaining a continuity between these traditions and the divine Word. Their problem is not tradition itself, but that they are using lesser traditions for the purpose of eluding the demands of the ongoing Tradition of God. Indeed, in speaking specifically about the oral traditions followed by the Pharisees (later to be encoded in the Mishnah), Jesus (to the surprise of some) does not challenge them in following these: 'But woe to you Pharisees! For you tithe mint and rue and every herb, and neglect justice and the love of God; these you ought to have done, without neglecting the others' (Lk 11:42 / Mt 23:23)" (Humphrey, *Scripture and Tradition*, 56). Lest she leave the impression that Jesus leaves these traditions intact, Humphrey adds that Jesus nonetheless implies "within this discourse that if the *inside* of a person is clean the outside will take care of itself (Lk 11:41 / Mt 23:26). This is an intimation of the new covenant that he would enact, so that the oral protective laws, called by the rabbis 'the hedge around the Law,' would no longer be necessary. When it becomes possible, by the Spirit and in the new creation, for the believer to have strength inwardly to keep the Law, then it will no longer be necessary to multiply instructions to prevent him or her from breaking it" (56).

lation mediated by the Torah is not adaptable in a plastic manner; it has a content that must be respected. Put another way, the practical form taken in our lives by God's commandment to honor our father and mother will differ depending on our circumstances. But it will not differ so much as to suppose that God's commandment has no intelligibility outside the particular circumstances of those who obey it.

In short, Jesus suggests that the "tradition" of the Pharisees has here made of God's commandment a mere human construct, revisable by those who do not possess authority to revise it. As Jesus says, when we do not care for the material needs of our parents—despite the explicit meaning of God's commandments in Exodus 20:12 and Leviticus 20:9—our parents' poverty shows that we are failing to obey the laws that God has revealed. The revisable construct is not God's commandment but rather is the Pharisees' tradition by which they have sought to strengthen the temple's finances. Jesus warns them: "So for the sake of your tradition, you have made void the word of God. You hypocrites!" (Mt 15:6–7). The "tradition" involved here is an interpretation of the Torah that contradicts God's own teachings (in the Torah) about what we owe in justice to our parents.

Jesus condemns their "tradition" not simply on his own authority, but also by citing the authority of the prophet Isaiah. He quotes Isaiah 29:13 (in a version derived from, but not identical to, the Septuagint), "This people honors me with their lips, but their heart is far from me; in vain do they worship me, teaching as doctrines (διδασκαλίας) the precepts of men" (Mt 15:8–9). In the Revised Standard Version (RSV), Isaiah 29:13–14 reads:

> And the Lord said, "Because this people draw near with their mouth and honor me with their lips, while their hearts are far from me, and their fear of me is a commandment of men learned by rote; therefore, behold, I will again do marvelous things with this people, wonderful and marvelous; and the wisdom of their wise men shall perish, and the discernment of their discerning men shall be hid."

But does Isaiah 29 mean that new circumstances are leading God to *undo the truths* that Israel's "wise men" and "discerning men" have learned? Certainly, the prophetic text points to a future act of God that will vindicate God's faithfulness to Israel so that Israel will again "sanctify the Holy One of Jacob, and will stand in awe of the God of Israel" (Is 29:23). Because of this future act, says God, his people will "sanctify my name" (Is 29:23). But Isaiah makes clear that the problem is not God's previous revelation, as if God were going to change it in a way that makes it no longer authoritative. Rather, the problem is that the "wise men" of the people no longer hear the word that God has given them. God's purpose is not to show them that his word changes to meet the times, but rather to instruct them about his word, which is not a "commandment of men" but rather is the word of the awe-inspiring living God. God promises that when he accomplishes his plan for the restoration of Israel, his people "will stand in awe of the God of Israel. And those who err in spirit will come to understanding, and those who murmur will accept instruction" (Is 29:23–24).[71]

The point, then, is not to negate previous understandings, but to awaken God's people to understanding. This awakening will take place when God does something that reveals him as the living God, so that they no longer fear God only "by rote." Their fear of God should arise from the commandment of the living God rather than from "a commandment of men." They need to relearn how to hear God's word as God's, so that they respond to God interiorly, with awe and devotion, rather than treating God as though his commandment (viz., to fear God, to honor God) were merely commanded by human beings. This is the opposite of what Tilley proposes. Isaiah 29 speaks about *God* doing something that will show his people once again that God's word is the word of the living God who instructs them. Tilley treats the content of divine teaching as radically changeable by humans. All Catholic tradition, for Tilley, is made or invented by humans (even that

71. In this regard, Humphrey emphasizes that we must read Scripture as opening us to the living God, so that Scripture functions as an icon rather than a barrier or an "end in itself"; see *Scripture and Tradition*, 60–62.

which is "given," is given simply in the sense of being made by earlier humans); the same applies to the words of Scripture. When one treats the content of revelation as always in the process of being changed to fit new circumstances, then one is treating God's word simply as a human construction rather than as the word of the living God.[72]

In sum, the "tradition" that Jesus describes in Matthew 15 (and Mark 7) is a human construction that prevents the people of God from hearing and obeying the explicit content of God's word. If Catholic Tradition were what Tilley says it is—not a "what" but a "how," and a "how" that involves no enduring doctrinal and moral content (because the meaning of terms is always changing)—then it could not help but fall under the condemnation that Jesus directs toward what the Pharisees call "the tradition of the elders" (Mt 15:2). A key aspect of this condemnation consists in Jesus's emphasis that "the commandment of God" has an actual truth content that has been obscured by the Pharisees' tradition but that cannot be changed, namely, that we must care for our father and mother in need. It is also noteworthy that Jesus's distinction between a divine commandment and a human tradition could not cogently be made on Tilley's terms.

A second biblical perspective on tradition arises from Paul's use of the term παράδοσις. The Pauline letters contain various instances of the term, including Galatians 1:14, Colossians 2:8, 2 Thessalonians 2:15 and 3:6, and 1 Corinthians 11:2.[73] In Galatians 1, Paul is speaking about the Gospel that he preaches. This Gospel, he emphasizes, "is

72. This is not to deny full human agency in the Spirit-guided expression of divine revelation. Humphrey observes that "the Scriptures themselves came out of traditions and then were interpreted, within Israel and within the Church, by tradition" (*Scripture and Tradition*, 64). See also Humphrey's discussion of four instances of "modified tradition," including most notably the introduction of prayer to the Holy Spirit (138–49). She notes that these cases "are explicable by close attention to the intent and deeper meaning of the Scriptures, and by reference to the overall Christian story that finds its fulfillment in Jesus" (148).

73. Colossians and 2 Thessalonians are often considered to have been written by someone other than Paul and thus to reflect a somewhat later period of first-century Christianity.

not man's gospel. For I did not receive it from man, nor was I taught it, but it came through a revelation of Jesus Christ" (Gal 1:11–12).[74] This emphasis on truth that Paul has received, and whose origin is God (or Jesus Christ), is something to which I return below in reflecting upon the biblical portrait of Tradition. For now, we can note that Paul certainly envisions revelation in terms of doctrinal and moral content, and he denies that this content comes from human making or inventing. Paul emphasizes that he did not learn the Gospel from merely human sources but received it while still a Pharisaic Jew, through a personal revelation of Jesus Christ, a revelation that was later confirmed by the Apostles Peter and James when Paul visited them in Jerusalem. As a Pharisee, Paul persecuted the nascent Church and was "advanced in Judaism beyond many of my own age among my people, so extremely zealous was I for the traditions of my fathers" (Gal 1:14). This use of "traditions" obviously refers to Pharisaic tradition, but since Paul is writing to Gentile believers, it may also connote the entirety of the Mosaic law.[75] In referring to "the traditions of my

74. K. K. Yeo insightfully remarks on this passage, "The word 'received' (*parelabete*) has a technical meaning and refers to a body of tradition (1 Cor 11:23; 15:1, 3; Phil 4:9; 1 Thes 2:132; 4:1). Paul did not simply create his gospel out of whole cloth, he received the gospel from the risen Lord and passed it to the Galatians as something he had received—as tradition. His reception of the gospel could be described as the *apokalypsis* (revelation) of God, so that any turning away from that gospel would be a rejection of God's call (1:6) and a fall from grace (1:6, 5:4). The word 'tradition' does not mean human creation. As Paul had experienced it the apocalyptic intrusiveness of the Christ event was not a human creation. Similarly, the Torah, though received as a revelatory act from God through Moses, was in Paul's day guarded as sacred tradition and not as a human creation." *Musing with Confucius and Paul: Toward a Chinese Christian Theology* (Cambridge: James Clarke, 2008), 139. This does not gainsay Ratzinger's point that "Tradition is, of its nature, always interpretation: it exists, not independently, but as explication, as interpretation 'according to the Scriptures.' That holds true even of the proclamation of Jesus Christ himself: that it appeared as fulfillment and thus as interpretation of something, though as authoritative interpretation, of course" ("Question of the Concept of Tradition," 65).

75. See Ben Witherington III, *Grace in Galatia: A Commentary on Paul's Letter to the Galatians* (Grand Rapids, MI: Eerdmans, 1998), 104: "The phrase 'the traditions of the fathers' has been taken by Dunn and others to refer to the oral *halakah* which was an

fathers," therefore, Paul may have in view not only negative but also positive realities, even though he holds that salvation comes through Christ rather than through the law. Elsewhere he makes clear that the Jewish people (his "fathers") are the inheritors of divine revelation and God's elect people.

Colossians 2:8 contains a critique of "tradition" similar to the one that we found in Jesus's encounter with Pharisees, but this time the "human tradition" (Col 2:8) to be avoided is that which stems from pagan culture (or from a mingling of pagan culture and Judaism). Paul warns the Colossians, "See to it that no one makes a prey of you by philosophy and empty deceit, according to human tradition, according to the elemental spirits of the universe, and not according to Christ" (Col 2:8).[76] The wisdom of such human tradition is an illusion, an "empty deceit" that entraps those who accept it. The opposite of such human tradition is "Christ." For Paul, the term "Christ" here contains within it a plethora of doctrines and practices. Doctrinally speaking, Christ "is the head of all rule and authority" (Col 2:10). Christ, although a man, possesses the fullness of divine life in a unique manner: "For in him the whole fulness of deity dwells bodily"

---

extrapolation beyond the Mosaic Law though based on it, not a reference to the Mosaic Law itself. It would then be similar to the phrase found in Mk 7.5 'the tradition of the elders.' It must, however, be remembered that Paul is writing in this letter primarily if not almost exclusively to Gentiles. The phrase 'ancestral traditions' to them would have surely connoted the Mosaic Law, and perhaps also any oral extrapolations, but in any case would not have excluded the Law itself."

76. N. T. Wright comments, "'Human tradition', a phrase picked up in 2:22, recalls the polemic of both Isaiah (29:13) and Jesus (Mk 7:5*ff.*) against the transformation of true, living religion into a set of ideas and rules handed on at a purely human level. This is not to deny that there is a proper use of 'tradition' within Christianity, when Christ himself works by his Spirit to bring his truth to a new generation through the witness of the church. What Paul has in mind is undoubtedly the traditions of the Rabbinic schools in which he had grown up." *The Epistles of Paul to the Colossians and to Philemon: An Introduction and Commentary* (Grand Rapids, MI: Eerdmans, 1986), 101. Wright argues at length in favor of Pauline authorship of Colossians (see 21–34). For the opposite view, see Margaret Y. MacDonald, *Colossians and Ephesians* (Collegeville, MN: Liturgical Press, 2000), 6–15.

(Col 2:9). This doctrinal claim is certainly capable of being elaborated or developed in numerous ways, but there are also obviously ways in which one could interpret it that would evacuate it of the meaning that Paul gives it, for example, if one made the claim that the "whole fullness of deity" was not in fact embodied in Christ.[77]

Thus Colossians 2 sets up a doctrinal claim—"in him the whole fullness of deity dwells bodily"—against a merely "human tradition." The tradition that comes from God instructs us doctrinally about Christ. This instruction about Christ is related to, but distinct from, its extension in practices. With regard to the latter, Paul notes that "in him also you were circumcised with a circumcision made without hands, by putting off the body of flesh in the circumcision of Christ; and you were buried with him in baptism, in which you were also raised with him through faith in the working of God, who raised him from the dead" (Col 2:11–12). For Colossians, therefore, the tradition that comes from God, as opposed to a merely "human tradition," teaches that baptism incorporates the believer into Christ in a manner parallel to the way in which circumcision incorporated Jews into the chosen people. Faith in God's saving deeds and saving power is also mentioned as necessary for incorporation into Christ, and so is Christ's resurrection (which presumes that Christ was raised from bodily death to a glorified bodily life, so that his body did not remain a corpse). Again, there are a variety of ways of developing this doctrinal content, but there are limits as well; one can easily imagine false developments. Certainly, the divine alternative to the deceitful "human tradition" has doctrinal content that is not as

77. Rather than grounding Christology in Christ's words and deeds, Tilley argues that "christology always arises in disciples' imaginations. We start with Jesus as he is perceived and imagined on this earth. *We* start his story here even if we imagine or infer that it really began in heaven. If the 'binitarian' worship of Jesus is the community's recognizing in him the unique and profound agency of God in and through the movement God constituted as the Jesus-movement, and if this worship is quite early, then the pattern of christology charted above is also probably quite early" (*Disciples' Jesus*, 68). The references to "God" do little work in Tilley's formulation, since we can know only the products of the community's imagination.

malleable as Tilley's *Inventing Catholic Tradition* would have us suppose.[78]

In 2 Thessalonians, we find two positive references to "tradition." The first reference is perhaps the most important for later Catholic Tradition. Paul states, "So then, brethren, stand firm and hold to the traditions which you were taught by us, either by word of mouth or by letter" (2 Thes 2:15). First, it is evident that these "traditions" have a strong doctrinal content (including doctrine about the practices appropriate to Christianity). One of these doctrines has just been elucidated by Paul in this letter: the doctrine of Christ's Second Coming, which, says Paul, will be preceded by the coming of "the lawless one by the activity of Satan" (2 Thes 2:9).[79] The coming of the Antichrist, the "lawless one," reveals God's punishment for those who reject God

78. In *Disciples' Jesus*, Tilley argues that we should read such words as those found in Colossians 2 "as a score to be performed or a script to be enacted, rather than as a text to be read and interpreted" (76). But why this either/or? Do not reading and interpretation belong to performing and enacting any score or script? Tilley holds that the New Testament's central Christological texts "do not first set patterns for belief, as some christologists seem to think, beliefs that Christians may accept, reject, modify, or develop. Rather, they set patterns for practice that Christians are to reenact to be part of the 'running performances' of discipleship—performances that take widely varying forms. Believing (having faith) is carried out by engaging in those practices, but beliefs are not the 'foundations' of practice, but shorthand guides abstracted from performance practice" (76). It follows for Tilley that "christology is not to be rooted in systematic thought but in reconciling practice" (77). But the opposition here imagined between action/performance and intellectual endeavor is difficult to sustain. If intellectual work (including receptivity to Jesus's own words and deeds) does not ground practices/performances, then the latter are mere gestures, hardly human at all, to which almost any ideas can be correctly (but extrinsically) attached. Tilley's effort to suppress doctrines ends with practices that can have any meaning or no meaning. No wonder that Tilley cites with approval Wayne Meeks's suggestion that Jesus's first followers were fanatical mythologists: "We cannot ignore 'the exuberance of Jesus' followers that created in the first decades of the movement's existence, the wildest diversity of mythic portraits of Jesus'" (citing Meeks, "The Man from Heaven in Paul's Letter to the Philippians," in *The Future of Early Christianity: Essays in Honor of Helmut Koester*, ed. Birger A. Pearson et al. (Minneapolis: Fortress Press, 1991), 329–36, at 329).

79. On the "lawless one," see Luke Timothy Johnson, *The Writings of the New Testament: An Interpretation* (Philadelphia: Fortress Press, 1986), 269.

and whom God condemns and abandons to their choice. There is certainly room here for doctrinal elaboration, but again there will be a difference between abandoning Paul's claims about the Antichrist and the Second Coming of Christ on the one hand and developing them in accord with other testimony of Scripture on the other hand. The content of the "traditions" delivered by Paul is deeply doctrinal—certainly (in Tilley's terms) a "what" and not just a "how." This extends to Paul's utter rejection of metaphysical dualism: the Antichrist and the powers of evil cannot stand against Christ; rather, when the "lawless one" is revealed, "the Lord Jesus will slay him with the breath of his mouth and destroy him by his appearing and his coming" (2 Thes 2:8).

It is also significant that Paul refers to two kinds of "traditions," both of which Paul communicates to the Thessalonians in accord with his mission as an Apostle. These two kinds of traditions are those that Paul delivers "by word of mouth" and those that he delivers "by letter" (2 Thes 2:15).[80] Looked at in this way, Tradition itself can be said to encompass Scripture, insofar as Tradition (or "the traditions which you were taught by us") includes Paul's letters. Paul makes clear that the Church is to hold firmly both to his letters (later recognized as Scripture) and to what he has taught "by word of mouth." Does this mean that the content of Tradition should be now restricted to what the Apostles taught "by word of mouth" rather than by their writings? I think that the answer is no, both since Paul's use of "traditions" is broader than this, and since we do not now possess a way of knowing what, if anything, the Apostles taught orally that they did not teach in

80. See Gordon D. Fee, *The First and Second Letters to the Thessalonians* (Grand Rapids, MI: Eerdmans, 2009). Fee's commentary employs Today's New International Version, which substitutes the word "teachings" for "traditions." Fee corrects this and comments, "The use of the word 'traditions' here, which has a long history in the Judaism in which Paul was raised, is his way of indicating that his teaching at the same time belongs to the much larger community of faith, of which they themselves have now become a part. Thus, by turning aside from his prior teaching, the Thessalonians have also turned aside from the common teaching of the early believers. But his concern at this point is with *his* teaching, which they are now disregarding" (305). Fee argues that "by letter" refers to the letter that we possess as 1 Thessalonians.

their writings. Even so, Paul's words demonstrate that there is an apostolic communication that belongs to the Church as a living subject and that in some way differs from Scripture.[81] Put another way, Paul's distinction between traditions delivered "by letter" and traditions delivered "by word of mouth" enable us to appreciate that divine revelation is not communicated to the Church solely by means of Scripture. At the same time, Paul's reference to traditions communicated "by word of mouth" need not open the door to Tilley's view of the Church as inventor or maker of tradition. What Paul communicates "by word of mouth" is not, by his own testimony, anything less than the "gospel" (2 Thes 2:14) and "the word of the Lord" (2 Thes 3:1).[82] He is communicating what he has received.

81. See Thiel, *Senses of Tradition*, 13–22, with discussion of the Council of Trent's "Decretum primum: recipiuntur libri sacri et traditiones apostolorum" (April 8, 1546), which its teaching about the gospel proclaimed by Jesus Christ and handed on "in written books and in unwritten traditions which were received by the apostles from the mouth of Christ himself, or else have come down to us, handed on as it were from the apostles themselves at the inspiration of the Holy Spirit." *Decrees of the Ecumenical Councils*, vol. 2, *Trent to Vatican II*, ed. Norman P. Tanner, SJ (Washington, DC: Georgetown University Press, 1990), 663; cf. Ratzinger, "The Question of the Concept of Tradition," 67–89. On the Church as a living subject (constituted sacramentally as the Body of Christ), in connection with the idea of "tradition," see Joseph Ratzinger, "The Spiritual Basis and Ecclesial Identity of Theology," in *The Nature and Mission of Theology: Essays to Orient Theology in Today's Debates*, trans. Adrian Walker (San Francisco: Ignatius Press, 1995), 45–72, at 52–55. Drawing upon Romans, Galatians, and 1 Corinthians, Ratzinger states that "according to Paul, the Church is in no wise a separate subject endowed with its own subsistence. The new subject is much rather 'Christ' himself, and the Church is nothing but the space of this new unitary subject, which is, therefore, much more than mere social interaction" (54). Turning to the Gospel of John, Ratzinger observes that "the Spirit effects a space of listening and remembering, a 'we,' which in the Johannine writings defines the Church as the locus of knowledge. Understanding can take place only within this 'we' constituted by participation in the origin" (55).

82. Ratzinger's comments are helpful for distinguishing between invention and interpretation: "What is true of the message of Christ, that it occurs in no other way but that of interpretation, is most certainly true of apostolic proclamation and still more so of the proclamation of the Church: as 'tradition,' it too ultimately has to remain interpretation 'according to the Scriptures,' to be aware of owing something to Scripture and being closely linked to Scripture. True, it too is not interpretation

Paul's statements elsewhere further confirm the doctrinal character of Tradition. Consider, for instance, his remark to the Romans that they should avoid "those who create dissensions and difficulties (σκάνδαλα), in opposition to the doctrine (διδαχή) which you have been taught" (Rom 16:17). What is the "doctrine" that Paul has in view? It is "the gospel of God which he [God] promised beforehand through his prophets in the holy scriptures" (Rom 1:2). The doctrine is God's revelation, God's word, not an invention of Paul's. Paul, of course, emphasizes certain things in his communication of this revelation, and Paul's formulations may bear clarification and development.[83] But this development would be false if it undermined his central teachings, including the bodily resurrection of Jesus, the affirmation that Jesus is the Messiah of Israel, the affirmation that God's grace comes through Jesus and is received by faith, and so forth. This "doctrine," Paul makes clear in Romans 16:17, is not changeable in Tilley's sense of changeability (although it is changeable, in certain ways, in Newman's sense).[84] There is a real doctrinal content—a "what"—in Paul's "gospel and the preaching of Jesus Christ, according to the revelation

in the sense of mere exegetical interpretation, but in the spiritual authority of the Lord that is implemented in the whole of the Church's existence, in her faith, her life, and her worship. Yet it does remain, far more than the Christ-event that founded the Church, interpretation, linked with what has happened and what has been spoken. In this is expressed its connection with the concrete activity of God in this history and its historical uniqueness: the ἐφάπαξ, the 'once only' aspect, which is just as essential to the reality of Christian revelation as the 'forever'" ("Question of the Concept of Tradition," 65).

83. As constitutive of Tradition, Ratzinger thus identifies two principles: "'gospel' as a principle always only able to be partially converted into Scripture, and the activity of God's Spirit in the age of the Church" ("Question of the Concept of Tradition," 71).

84. Thus, in his *Essay on the Development of Christian Doctrine*, Newman states with respect to the history of a belief, "In time it enters upon strange territory; points of controversy alter their bearing; parties rise and fall around it; dangers and hopes appear in new relations; and old principles reappear under new forms. It changes with them in order to remain the same. In a higher world it is otherwise, but here below to live is to change, and to be perfect is to have changed often" (40). For discussion, see Gerald H. McCarren, "Development of Doctrine," in *The Cambridge Companion to John Henry Newman*, 118–36, at 121.

of the mystery which was kept secret for long ages but is now disclosed and through the prophetic writings is made known to all nations" (Rom 16:25–26). Again, the content of the Gospel is not something that Paul or any merely human authority vouches for or invents. Some of the Corinthians imagined themselves to be followers of a particular Apostle, but Paul rebukes them for thereby "behaving like ordinary men" (1 Cor 3:3). The Apostles, he explains, are merely servants of God who have received a mission to proclaim the truth of Jesus Christ crucified and risen: "So neither he who plants nor he who waters is anything, but only God who gives the growth" (1 Cor 3:7).

In 2 Thessalonians, Paul also invokes "tradition" to delineate the boundaries of the Christian community. He states, "Now we command you, brethren, in the name of our Lord Jesus Christ, that you keep away from any brother who is living in idleness and not in accord with the tradition that you received from us" (2 Thes 3:6). What is this "tradition"? Here, it seems to be Paul's own personal example. When he was with the Thessalonians, he reminds them, he worked for his living rather than accepting food from others. Those who wish to live a Christian life cannot suppose that it is good to live in an unnecessary dependency upon the work of others. Paul urges that the Thessalonians find "in our [Paul's] conduct an example to imitate" (2 Thes 3:9). Tradition as Paul conceives of it thus includes not only doctrines, but also practices such as hard work. Yet here again we can perceive doctrinal stability: it would not be possible for Catholic Tradition, in its development, to substitute laziness for the hard work that Paul advocates. With regard to the lazy person, Paul commands that the community not associate with him, although Paul tells the Thessalonians that they should "not look on him as an enemy, but warn him as a brother" (2 Thes 3:15). He remains a "brother" in Christ even when, by turning away from "the tradition that you received from us," he has consciously or unconsciously separated himself from the Christian community and its identifying practices.

A final place that Paul employs παράδοσις is in 1 Corinthians 11:2, where he tells the Corinthians, "I commend you because you remember me in everything and maintain the traditions even as I have delivered them to you."[85] These "traditions" surely include the practice of the Lord's Supper that he describes in 1 Corinthians 10–11. This practice requires the Corinthians not to eat food sacrificed to demons (1 Cor 10:20–21) and to avoid eating the Lord's Supper unworthily (1 Cor 11:27–30). The Lord's Supper is not a practice that should privilege the wealthy, and it is not merely another meal. In Paul's account of this practice, we find significant doctrinal content about what the Lord's Supper is. Indeed, what the Lord's Supper is determines how we should practice it.[86] Paul explains, "The cup of blessing which we bless, is it not a participation in the blood of Christ? The bread which

85. Anthony C. Thiselton comments, "In his study of tradition and tradition terminology [K.] Wegenast argues that this epistle provides the first setting within which the notion of a received and transmitted doctrine and practice arose (esp. in relation to 11:23 and 15:3–5). This is plausible in the light of the Corinthian tendency to regard their own thought and practice as a unilateral affair (cf. 1:3; 14:36; and elsewhere)." *The First Epistle to the Corinthians: A Commentary on the Greek Text* (Grand Rapids, MI: Eerdmans, 2000), 810–11. See also K. Wegenast, *Das Verständnis der Tradition bei Paulus und in den Deuteropaulinen* (Neukirchen: Neukirchener, 1962); Joseph A. Fitzmyer, SJ, *First Corinthians: A New Translation with Introduction and Commentary* (New Haven, CT: Yale University Press, 2008), 408–9.

86. From the opposite perspective, Tilley argues that practices radically determine the meaning of the Lord's Supper: "With changes in action come changes in belief; the Eucharist comes to signify a communal meal more than a sacrifice. The significance of the altar changes; it more signifies the meal table than the place of sacrifice where the human confronts the divine. No longer do only priests touch the consecrated bread; lay ministers also distribute the hosts into people's hands. As the doctrine of the Real Presence is intimately connected with the topography of the ritual space and behavior, the doctrine changes its significance. . . . If beliefs are indeed shaped by participation in practices, then as practices shift, beliefs will be likely to shift, too. Some theologians still working with the same theological concepts and doctrinal abstractions verbally unchanged from those developed when one style of practice was dominant may deplore the loss of the concept of Real Presence among the laity. But these theologians may not have noticed that the ritual practice no longer so clearly connects belief in the Real Presence as they have understood it with the belief that the Mass is the reenactment of the sacrifice made once for all on the cross. . . . [In the new context, "transubstantiation"] may even acquire a new meaning hardly connected to the traditional sense, for example, that transubstantiation refers to the transformation of the worshiping assembly into the body of Christ in and

we break, is it not a participation in the body of Christ?" (1 Cor 10:16). Because the cup and bread are a participation (κοινωνία) in Christ, our reception of the cup and bread truly unites us: "we who are many are one body, for we all partake of the one bread" (1 Cor 10:17). Paul knows what the Lord's Supper is because of Jesus's own words and deeds. As Paul says, "For I received from the Lord what I also delivered to you, that the Lord Jesus on the night when he was betrayed took bread, and when he had given thanks, he broke it, and said, 'This is my body which is for you. Do this in remembrance of me.' In the same way also the cup, after supper, saying, 'This cup is the new covenant in my blood'" (1 Cor 11:23–25). The "traditions" also include practices whose source is not directly attributed to Christ, including Paul's explanation in 1 Corinthians 11:3–16 about why women should not pray with their heads uncovered. In light of other biblical texts, the Church has judged that this practice has its meaning within a particular cultural context rather than being rooted in an enduring doctrine about women in relation to men, even if 1 Corinthians 11:3–16 does possess doctrinal import in other ways.[87]

At various points in his letters (and in those attributed to him), Paul summarizes the doctrinal content that he seeks to hand on to his congregations, and in this way, Paul gives us a sense of how Tradition is handed on. Paul reminds the Corinthians, "in what terms I preached to you the gospel, which you received, in which you stand,

---

through reception of the Eucharist. The point is that once the term *transubstantiation* is no longer connected with the ritual as traditionally performed, the meaning of the term becomes indeterminate" (*Inventing Catholic Tradition*, 69, 71–72).

87. Indebted to Dale Martin, Aline Rousselle, and others, Anthony Thiselton points out that the Roman cultural context is crucial for understanding 1 Cor 11:3–16. But he also draws upon Judith Gundry-Volf, Jerome Murphy-O'Connor, OP, Morna Hooker, and others to persuasively sketch the ongoing theological value of this passage. See Thiselton, *First Epistle to the Corinthians*, 800–809. See also Richard B. Hays, *First Corinthians* (Louisville, KY: Westminster John Knox Press, 1997), 181–91. Hays is particularly interested in how the Church might reinterpret 1 Cor 11:3–16 in light of the full scope of Scripture and doctrinal tradition. See also the helpful discussion in Humphrey, *Scripture and Tradition*, 149–50.

by which you are saved, if you hold it fast—unless you believed in vain. For I delivered to you as of first importance what I also received" (1 Cor 15:1–3). This Gospel is not something that Paul made up but rather something that he received (in his case by means of God's revelation). The central content of this Gospel is something that happened in Jerusalem, namely, Christ's death and resurrection. Paul particularly wishes to underscore Christ's resurrection from the dead. Some of the Corinthians, by denying that there will be a resurrection of the dead, have instituted a rather radical change of doctrine. Paul lets them know that the handing on of divine revelation does not permit of such doctrinal malleability. As Paul says, "Now if Christ is preached as raised from the dead, how can some of you say that there is no resurrection of the dead? But if there is no resurrection of the dead, then Christ has not been raised; if Christ has not been raised, then our preaching is in vain and your faith is in vain" (1 Cor 15:12–14).

Everything hinges, in other words, on the content of what Paul "delivered" to the Corinthians "as of first importance." If that content (the "what," in Tilley's phrase) is not true, then Paul's "preaching is in vain." Could it be that we could reinterpret the content of Christ's resurrection in such a way that it no longer matters whether the phrase refers to the dead Christ being given life in the flesh again—and not just life but glorified life? Paul emphasizes that no reinterpretation of this kind will do: either the dead Christ is now alive again in the flesh, or else Paul's entire mission is a blasphemous sham. Paul observes that if Christ has not been raised from the dead, "We are even found to be misrepresenting God, because we testified of God that he raised Christ, whom he did not raise if it is true that the dead are not raised" (1 Cor 15:15). It follows that the kind of malleability of doctrine that Tilley advocates in the name of "Catholic tradition" will not work in the case of Christ's Resurrection.[88]

88. Tilley affirms Christ's Resurrection, and he argues at length against both skeptics and literalistic believers: "The root problem is that people think of the resurrection as either a historical event or not a historical event. They think it one in a

A brief, evocative doctrinal formula is found also in 1 Timothy 3:16. Here, Paul proclaims, "Great indeed, we confess, is the mystery of our religion: He was manifested in the flesh, vindicated in the Spirit, seen by angels, preached among the nations, believed on in the world, taken up in glory." While requiring further development and clarification (e.g., what does it mean to say that he was "vindicated in the Spirit"), this passage makes clear that Jesus Christ died but is dead no longer.[89] One might also think of the promise Jesus gives in his farewell discourse according to the Gospel of John. In this promise, Jesus depicts the role of the Holy Spirit in the post-Resurrection apostolic community: "I have yet many things to say to you, but you cannot bear them now. When the Spirit of truth comes, he will guide you into all the truth; for he will not speak on his own authority, but whatever he hears he will speak, and he will declare to you the things

---

series of one damn thing after another—arrest, trial, crucifixion, resurrection. This thinking misleads them. The agents who arrested, tried, and crucified Jesus of Nazareth were human. The agent who raised him up was divine. If they're all 'events,' they're not of the same kind. The agents are as different as divine nature is different from human nature.... The question is not the event, but the agent. Were these events sustained by God or illusions in the minds of the witnesses? Could they be both? (Remember St. Joan)" (*Disciples' Jesus*, 272, 275). But it does seem as though, at the level of event, we cannot exclude the question of what happened to Jesus's corpse. In raising the dead Jesus, God could not simply have left Jesus's corpse as a corpse. At this level, the events "sustained by God" must be something much more than "illusions in the minds of the witnesses." See also Roger Haight, SJ, *Jesus, Symbol of God* (Maryknoll, NY: Orbis Books, 1999).

89. N. T. Wright comments on 1 Tm 3:16—which he terms a "puzzling little poem"—"Though we might be surprised at there being no explicit mention of the resurrection in such a formulaic statement, it is clearly some kind of poem or hymn rather than a creed (it does not mention the cross, either), and should not be pressed for details of matters about which it does not speak. However, two points of interest remain for our purposes. It is likely that 'he was justified' (*edikaiothe*) is an oblique way of referring to the resurrection: Jesus was 'vindicated' by the living God—not least as Messiah—after being condemned and killed. We have already noted the subtle and important links between resurrection and justification. The phrase 'in the Spirit' will then refer to the *agency* of the Spirit in his resurrection, as regularly in Paul, not to the supposed 'non-bodily' sphere in which this 'justification' takes place." *The Resurrection of the Son of God* (Minneapolis, MN: Fortress Press, 2003), 270–71).

that are to come. He will glorify me, for he will take what is mine and declare it to you" (Jn 16:12–14).[90] The Holy Spirit's guidance provides a principle for doctrinal change, and this principle is teleological (*pace* Tilley): the Holy Spirit will progressively lead the whole community into "all the truth." Furthermore, the unveiling of further knowledge will not involve a rupture from what Jesus has taught, since the Holy Spirit will "take what is mine and declare it to you." The doctrinal change envisioned here does not involve the radical reinvention that Tilley envisions.

Conclusion

According to the New Testament, Jesus anticipated the handing on of his Gospel. Otherwise, Jesus could hardly have said, "This is my body which is for you. Do this in remembrance of me," and many other similar things. Paul is engaged in just such a process of handing on, not least in his urgent reminder to the Corinthians of "in what terms I preached to you the gospel, which you received, in which you stand, by which you are saved. . . . For I delivered to you as of first importance what I also received." This is what we would expect of divine

90. This guidance should not be conceived solely in terms of teachings (or practices). Rather, as Vladimir Lossky emphasizes, Tradition also involves silence, our mode of receptive attentiveness to the Word. Lossky associates Tradition with the illumination brought by the Holy Spirit. Thus he notes that the "unity of the Scriptures can be recognized only in the Tradition, in the Light of the Holy Spirit communicated to the members of the unique Body of Christ." "Tradition and Traditions," trans. G. E. H. Palmer and E. Kadloubovsky, in *In the Image and Likeness of God*, ed. John H. Erikson and Thomas E. Bird (Crestwood, NY: St. Vladimir's Seminary Press, 1974), 141–68, at 155. He adds that, given the relationship between Tradition and the Fathers' rule of faith, "One cannot belong to the Tradition while contradicting the dogmas, just as one cannot make use of the dogmatic formulas received in order to oppose a formal 'orthodoxy' to every new expression of the Truth that the life of the Church may produce. The first attitude is that of revolutionary innovators, of false prophets who sin against the expressed Truth, against the Incarnate Word, in the name of the Spirit to which they lay claim. The second is that of the conservative formalists, Pharisees of the Church who, in the name of the habitual expressions of Truth, run the risk of sinning against the Spirit of Truth" (165).

revelation. It must be handed on in order to have its salvific impact. As Moses teaches in Deuteronomy 29:29, "the things that are revealed belong to us and to our children forever, that we may do all the words of this law." Earlier in Deuteronomy, Moses says, with regard to the handing on of divine revelation (tradition), "And these words which I command you this day shall be upon your heart; and you shall teach them diligently to your children, and shall talk of them when you sit in your house, and when you walk by the way, and when you lie down, and when you rise" (Dt 6:6–7). This is not an invitation to radical doctrinal change in every generation.

The issue of tradition might seem to be solved once the content of divine revelation has been written down and set forth once and for all in canonical Scripture. Tradition can then seem to be simply handing on Scripture and doing what Scripture says to do, always with openness to further correction by God's word in Scripture. But without neglecting the authority of Scripture, we can observe that Jesus devoted his earthly ministry to forming his apostolic Church rather than to forming canonical Scripture. What, then, did Jesus intend for the Church to do? Certainly to preach the kingdom, baptize, celebrate the Eucharist, give alms, love each other as he had loved us, await his eschatological return, and so forth. But he also intended his Church to proclaim the content of the good news, the content of divine revelation. This proclamation will not always be well received: "they will lay their hands on you and persecute you, delivering you up to the synagogues and prisons, and you will be brought before kings and governors for my name's sake. This will be a time for you to bear testimony" (Lk 21:12–13). After the Resurrection, he "opened their minds to understand the scriptures, and said to them, 'Thus it is written, that the Christ should suffer and on the third day rise from the dead, and that repentance and forgiveness of sins should be preached in his name to all nations, beginning from Jerusalem'" (Lk 24:45–47).

The fact that Jesus must open his Apostles' "minds to understand the scriptures" makes clear that content of divine revelation cannot be handed down, even in scriptural form, without being interpreted.

What does Jesus mean when he says over the bread, "This is my body," or when he commands, "Do this in remembrance of me"? What is the "this" that we are to do, and when, where, and by whom should it be done? When Philip says in the Gospel of John, "Lord, show us the Father, and we shall be satisfied," Jesus responds, "Have I been with you so long, and yet you do not know me, Philip? He who has seen me has seen the Father; how can you say, 'Show us the Father'?" (Jn 14:8–9). But nonetheless one feels some sympathy with Philip: what does Jesus mean by saying, "he who has seen me has seen the Father"? The precise character of Jesus's relationship to the Father is at issue. The Gospel of John indicates that Jesus was not unaware of this need for interpretation, for the handing on of the Gospel in an interpretive Tradition. Jesus tells his disciples, "I have yet many more things to say to you, but you cannot bear them now. When the Spirit of truth comes, he will guide you into all the truth; for he will not speak on his own authority, but whatever he hears he will speak" (Jn 16:12–13). Even here, however, we are faced with the question of who precisely is the "Spirit of truth" and what is his relationship to Jesus and the Father. Tradition is necessary for the handing on of the content of divine revelation, and Jesus promised to sustain this Tradition by his "Spirit of truth."

Tilley agrees that tradition is necessary, but he eviscerates both it and divine revelation of its power to communicate enduring truth about the realities of salvation. Tilley has in fact advocated the kind of ever-changing human "tradition" that Jesus and Paul, in the New Testament, are at pains to reject. Tilley's inability adequately to identify God as the source of the Gospel's doctrinal and moral teachings is one of the factors that produce his misreading of Catholic Tradition. He reduces Catholic Tradition to humanly constructed, time-bound claims about the community and its ever-changing practical authenticity, to the exclusion of divinely revealed enduring truths about the triune God, Jesus Christ, creation, the moral law, and so on.[91]

91. For further discussion of this problem, see also Leo Elders, SVD, "The Immutability of the Sense of Dogmas and Philosophical Theories," in *Faith and Reason:*

At various points in his book, however, Tilley argues that his account of tradition simply maps what has happened in the history of what we call God's covenantal people. On this view, no matter what Scripture or Platonizing theologians might have to say about it in the abstract, Christianity in the concrete continually morphs into something quite different from its earlier incarnations. In response, without conceiving of Tradition as unchanging in every sense or denying that Tradition involves the "how" as well as the "what," I have argued that Tilley is too quick to choose rupture over development of doctrine, both in Scripture and in the history of the Church. Development of doctrine can coexist with a significant degree of historical complexity with respect to the meaning and the proper relationship of biblical and ecclesiastical texts. The eyes of faith can perceive Tradition's Spirit-guided fidelity in handing on the content of divine revelation, without such a claim being rendered impossible by obvious ruptures.

Is such a reply sufficient? Tilley holds that it is not adequate to what has occurred in Catholic Tradition's efforts to hand on divine revelation. For example, in the *Syllabus of Errors* that accompanies Pope Pius IX's encyclical *Quanta Cura* (1864), Pius IX condemns as erroneous the proposition that "Every man is free to embrace and profess that religion which, guided by the light of reason, he shall consider true." Tilley cites this text and pairs it with a statement from the Second Vatican Council's Declaration on Religious Freedom, *Dignitatis Humanae* (1965): "The human person has a right to religious freedom.... In matters religious no one is to be forced to act in a manner contrary to his own beliefs. Nor is anyone to be restrained from acting in according with his own beliefs, whether privately or publicly."[92] For Tilley, it is obvious that this pairing reveals a "patent contradiction."[93] He observes that this contradiction was embodied in

The Notre Dame Symposium 1999, ed. Timothy L. Smith (South Bend, IN: St. Augustine's Press, 2001), 21–35.

92. See Tilley, *Inventing Catholic Tradition*, 116.

93. Tilley, *Inventing Catholic Tradition*, 116.

the life of John Courtney Murray, who was silenced by the Church in 1955 for teaching what *Dignitatis Humanae*, under Murray's guidance, taught a decade later. Tilley concludes that, despite the efforts of a few tendentious and "tortuous accounts" that "have attempted to show an alleged continuity between these two statements," "no convincing theory of development has accounted for the 'course of development' that allows a clear contradiction in 1965 of what the highest magisterial authority in the Church taught in 1864."[94] This conclusion does not bother Tilley, because his account of tradition argues that constant reinvention and reimagining to fit today's context and practices is the very core of Catholic "tradition."

But why, given his concern for contextualized truth in other cases, is Tilley so adamant that he has found an absolute contradiction ("reversals, fractures") of previously definitive doctrine?[95] At the very least, he has not shown that we obviously have a "patent contradiction" rather than a "development of doctrine." The development might well have occurred through a rather "tortuous" process; after all, development is not repetition or even (necessarily) a simple logical extension, but instead genuinely goes beyond earlier insights—for example, by asking and answering new questions—while retaining previous *definitive* doctrine on the subject and correcting nondefinitive teaching. To account for the development, then, may well require complex reasoning! Denial of doctrinal development with respect to the duties of persons and the state vis-à-vis divine revelation would require more than showing that the Church's view of "religious freedom" changed rapidly in the mid-twentieth century.

94. Tilley, *Inventing Catholic Tradition*, 117.
95. Tilley, *Inventing Catholic Tradition*, 119–20.

GERALD GLEESON

2 • THE INCARNATION

Debate and Development in Catholic Tradition

> Christ, the last Adam, in the revelation of the mystery of the Father and His love, fully reveals man to man himself and makes his supreme calling clear.
>
> *Gaudium et Spes*, 22

> How can you say, "Show us the Father"? Whoever sees me, sees the Father.
>
> John 14:9

All Christian tradition depends on the great, once-and-for-all *traditio* that was the "handing over" of Jesus Christ, given for us and for our salvation.[1] The mystery of Christ crucified is the Tradition that the Church exists to hand on, in word and sacrament. But *who is Jesus Christ, and what manner of person is he?* This essay is an exploration within the Catholic theological tradition, focusing on a recent proposal for rethinking the mystery of the Incarnation in terms of the "theandric" nature of the Incarnate Word, who is human in a divine way and divine in a human way. I argue that this perhaps startling claim is both a legitimate and valuable development of Catholic tra-

1. Hans Urs von Balthasar, "Tradition," in *Elucidations*, trans. Johns Riches (London: SPCK, 1975), 73.

dition, and in accord with St. Thomas's teaching on the two *esse*'s in Christ. I begin with a review of the Church's first clarifications of its faith in Christ, the Word Incarnate.

Introduction

The "318 Fathers" at Nicea (325 AD) affirmed that Christ is in no way less than God, for he is "consubstantial" with the Father, and that "he came down and became incarnate, became human, suffered and rose up on the third day." This affirmation did not *explain* the mystery of Jesus Christ as both truly divine and truly human; it simply marked the parameters of orthodoxy and thereby invited further theological development. When that development occurred in different parts of the Roman Empire, with their different cultures and in the minds of Christians with different philosophical presuppositions, diverse explanations of the identity of Christ were proposed, some more and some less successful. Further conciliar clarifications were required.

Most importantly, the Council of Chalcedon (451 AD) declared that Jesus Christ was one "person," or "subsistent being," with two "natures" (human and divine). In the words of J. N. D. Kelly, Chalcedon balanced the "essential truth which Alexandrian theology had grasped"—that the divine Word is the unique subject of the Incarnation, with the sound "theological intuition" of the Antiochene tradition—as to the full reality of Christ's human life.[2] For some, however, Chalcedon's account was too balanced—suggesting the two natures existed in parallel, as if the person of Christ was divided, with each nature the source of independent actions. As a further refinement of Chalcedon, the understanding of the unity of Christ championed by Cyril of Alexandria was endorsed at the Second Council of Constantinople (553 AD) in the affirmation that the one "person" in Christ is the divine person, the Word or Son of God. Lest even this formulation might compromise the true humanity of Christ, the Third Council of

2. J. N. D. Kelly, *Early Christina Doctrines*, 4th ed. (London: Adam & Charles Black, 1968), 341.

Constantinople (681 AD) affirmed that Christ possesses a truly human will and intellect, in addition to his divine will and intellect.

This rapid overview of the developing tradition highlights the way new questions, as well as problematic answers, prompted further insight into the mystery of faith. Our age has its own questions, and Chalcedon should be the constant foundation rather than the conclusion of the Church's Christological tradition. In the 1980s, then-Cardinal Joseph Ratzinger warned that if reflection on the mystery of Christ rests with Chalcedon, "dogmatic Christology comes to stop with a certain parallelism of the two natures in Christ."[3] Sadly, few theologians have taken up Ratzinger's challenge. A cursory survey of recent text books in Christology shows how little attention they give to developing Chalcedon: most are content simply to affirm the "one person, two natures" doctrine and then quickly move on to what are assumed to be more accessible and more interesting questions about the historical Jesus, his soteriological relevance, and the popular concerns of contemporary theologians. Yet the doctrine of Christ's person and nature is surely the most exciting theme in Christology, a theme that no reflection on Christian or Catholic tradition should ignore.

By way of some final introductory remarks, I note that in defining the faith, in clarifying the great Tradition, the Church is primarily concerned to establish limits or "rules" for what may rightly be thought and said about Christ, but not to foreclose on future development. Further, when conciliar definitions invoke various technical, philosophically derived, terms to protect the mystery of faith, they do not purport to fully explain or exhaust the mystery, nor do they exclude the later use of different philosophical and theological perspectives. For example, the teaching of Constantinople II that the union between the human and divine natures of Christ is "hypostatic" sim-

3. Cited in Aaron Riches, "After Chalcedon: The Oneness of Christ and the Dyothelite Mediation of His Theandric Unity," *Modern Theology* 24, no. 2 (2008): 199–224, at 207.

ply means it is the kind of union consistent with the existence of a single subsistent being; it does not explain how such a union is possible. "Hypostatic" marks the uniqueness of this union chiefly by way of contrast with other kinds of union that would fail to do justice to the mystery of the Incarnation (e.g., union in will or in dignity).

Accordingly, it is crucial to get behind the technical terms in conciliar definitions to determine what they sought to convey. For the present study, some brief comments on the terms "person" and "nature" are essential. *Nature* is to be understood in the Aristotelian sense as the principle that explains *what* something is and why it typically *acts* as it does. Although it is always the subject or person who acts, a being's action is in accord with the principles and capacities of its nature. If nature accords with the *essence* of a being (what it is), *person* identifies a being's characteristic *mode of existence*. Persons are not kinds of things; rather, person designates the excellence with which a being exists, namely, as individual, subsisting, and rational. Like life, personhood is not a property added on to a being. For living things, to be is *to live*. Living is the activity in and by which living things exist. Likewise, for persons, to be is *to-be-in-a-personal-way*, and clearly the term "person" is analogous because the ways in which humans, angels, and God are persons are radically different, notwithstanding the slight similarity. The terms "nature" and "person" thus mark the distinction between *what a being is* and—if a being does exist—what is the "subject" (*supposit*) that exercises existence as that kind of being. In some cases, the *supposit* is a "person," not merely an individual *something*, but rather *a someone* who subsists in their nature, whether that nature be human, angelic, or divine.

Finally, while person and nature are clearly the most important terms in Christological doctrine, one other principle is also crucial and is usually referred to by the technical term of *enhypostasia* as developed by Leontius of Jerusalem (†543 AD).[4] This principle epito-

4. Aloys Grillmeier remarks that "Leontius may be regarded as the best christological author of his time" despite "a certain exuberance which must be

mizes the orthodox faith of Chalcedon and Constantinople and will be the key to the theology developed here. The *enhypostasia* affirms that Jesus's humanity is complete as human but does not subsist in its own right; rather, the humanity of Jesus has its *subsistence* (or "hypostasis") *in* the subsistence of the divine Word. That is to say, in the case of the man Jesus of Nazareth, the principle of his personhood is nothing other than the personhood of the divine Word.[5]

The Quest for a Contemporary Christology

Given the doctrinal foundation of Nicea and Chalcedon, the contemporary challenge to elucidate the mystery of Christ as Son of God, "like us in all things but sin," is shaped by three factors in particular: modern Scripture scholarship and the attempts to understand Jesus in his first-century context; obvious changes in the meanings of key theological terms such as "person" and "nature"; and above all the loss of a genuinely metaphysical understanding that enables us to engage with both the transcendence and the immanence of God's being. All three factors contribute to the contemporary emphasis on the humanity of Jesus as "a true human person" (in the modern psychological sense of person) and hence to the crisis in Christology identified by the International Theological Commission concerning how we should understand the unity of Christ as the Word made flesh.[6]

In the quest for a contemporary Christology that seeks to be an organic development of the tradition, open to the conclusions of our best biblical scholarship, particularly the clear New Testament presentation of the humanity of Jesus, and responsive to contemporary

explained and curtailed." *Christ in Christian Tradition*, vol. 2, Part 2 (Louisville, KY: Westminster John Knox Press, 1995), 309.

5. There are only three options with respect to understanding the human nature of Christ: first, Jesus is "a human being" subsisting in his own right, yet somehow united to the divine Son (the so-called Nestorian view); second, Jesus is "a divine being" whose humanity is less than complete (the so-called Monophysite view); and third—the only orthodox position available—the *enhypostasia:* Jesus's true humanity subsists in the being of the Word.

6. See Riches, "After Chalcedon."

concerns for the unity of Christ, I examine the work of Australian theologian David Coffey, and chiefly his 1999 article "The Theandric Nature of Christ."[7] While respecting the concern for the integral humanity of Jesus, Coffey works within the tradition of the *enhypostasia* doctrine of Leontius of Jerusalem to explain what it is for Jesus Christ, the Word Incarnate, to be a divine person (the Word) having its *hypostasis* in the human nature of Jesus of Nazareth.[8] Two key questions focus this inquiry: first, what are the implications for Jesus's human nature of the truth that this nature has its being and personhood (its *hypostasis* or subsistence) in the Word of God? Second, what are the implications for the person of the divine Word of the truth that he has taken the human nature of Jesus as his very own? The term "theandric" will assist us to answer these questions.

What Is Meant by "Theandric"?

The tradition from Dionysius through St. Thomas Aquinas and beyond has been willing to speak of the theandric *actions* of Christ, but not of his theandric *nature*. Theandric action is exemplified in the case of Christ healing the sick: in virtue of his human nature, Christ is able *to lay hands on* a sick person; in virtue of his divine nature, he is able *to heal* a sick person. The one divine person thus does some things through the joint action of his two natures. Such actions are said to be "theandric": *the one action* is both human and divine, al-

7. David Coffey, "The Theandric Nature of Christ," *Theological Studies* 60 (1999): 405–31. See also David M. Coffey, "Quaestio Disputata: Response to Neil Ormerod, and Beyond," *Theological Studies* 68 (2007): 900–915; David Coffey, "De La Taille on the Grace of Union," *Irish Theological Quarterly* 79, no. 3 (2014): 197–218, where Coffey presents his most refined account of this theology.

8. What is remarkable, and what might seem alarming, in Coffey's account, is that *the Incarnate Word* has only one nature—a "theandric" human nature—and for this reason, some critics have described this theology as Monophysitism from below, if not Nestorianism, should it imply that Jesus of Nazareth was a human person (distinct from the divine person of the Word). I believe these criticisms are unfounded, and I explain why—recognizing that a detailed examination of Coffey's proposals is beyond the scope of this presentation.

though the person who performs the action is divine only.[9] But if the one action can be both human and divine, why can that one action not proceed from a nature that is at once both human and divine? The traditional objection to this idea is that in the Incarnation the two natures are not mixed or confused; each nature retains its own integrity. Christ is neither superhuman nor partly divine. Though Christ's actions are singular, and yet theandric, his two natures remain distinct as natures.

As an initial response to this objection, we may note first that, although he is *integrally* human, like us in all things (essential to being human) except sin, there is clearly a crucial way in which Christ is *not* like us—for he is not "a human person" in the philosophical and theological sense. His personhood consists in his being the *Logos*, the Son of God. Christ's human nature has its *hypostasis*—its subsistence and actuality—in the subsistence of the person of the divine Word. We are thus entitled to ask how the subsistence of Jesus's human nature in the person of the Word impacts on that human nature.[10] The traditional limitation of the theandric principle to Christ's actions alone avoids this question and remains stuck on the tracks of the parallelism of two natures against which Ratzinger warned.

How Could Christ's Human Nature be Theandric?

Progress in understanding the unity of Christ in his humanity has been assisted by important achievements in twentieth-century Catholic theology by Maurice de la Taille and Karl Rahner. Two related

9. From the Greek, *theos*, or God; *ander*, or man.

10. In raising this question, I am conscious of the criticism sometimes leveled against modern Christologies associated with Karl Rahner, viz., that they blur the distinction between person and nature that is fundamental to the definitions of Chalcedon. Critics say we should simply stick with Chalcedon's formula (one person, two natures) and eschew any ambition to further explain the mystery of the Incarnation. To exclude the possibility of progress on this question, however, is to ignore Ratzinger's warning against taking Chalcedon's formula as the end point of our theology.

insights lay the groundwork for understanding Christ's nature as theandric.[11] The first insight is quite traditional: human beings are created with a capacity for God—we are *capax Dei.* Genesis speaks of our creation in the image of God, and the Gospel promises eternal life in which we participate in the very being of God. The prayers of the liturgy are replete with the promise of our partaking in the divine nature, yet our tradition has struggled to take these promises literally.

How is this capacity for God to be understood? *What is the basis in human nature for men and women being able to share the divine nature*? The traditional answer of St. Thomas is that the human soul is a rational spiritual substance with faculties of intellect and will by which we are open to the infinite. Thomas argued that human nature "was made for attaining to the Word *to some extent by its operations,* viz. by knowing and loving Him."[12] There is a general Thomistic principle, however, that a being's actions flow from its nature. If the human *operations* of knowing and loving can attain to God to some extent, then surely this implies that human *nature* itself can attain to God to some extent. This was the conclusion Rahner drew. In Coffey's words:

> the very fact that human nature can attain God by faith and charity implies that human nature as such can attain God ontologically, not of course, by way of a natural potency but, as Rahner says, by way of an obediential potency.[13]

Thomas, however, did not draw this conclusion; accordingly, he held that the divine person could subsist in the human nature only insofar as that nature is capable of *operations* that can attain the infinite (cf. *ST* III, q. 2, a. 8). Coffey asks:

11. I believe it is possible to retain many of Rahner's insights without endorsing the tendency to transcendental idealism in his philosophy.

12. *ST* III, q. 4, a. 1. All references are to Thomas Aquinas, *Summa Theologiae*, rev. ed., trans. Fathers of the English Dominican Province (Allen, TX: Christian Classics, 1981); see also Kevin Knight's New Advent website, accessed September 23, 2018, www.newadvent.org/summa.

13. Coffey, "Theandric Nature of Christ," 416.

> To what extent could human nature thus conceived truly belong to the Word? For nature is an intrinsic mode of being. How could a nature incapable of embracing the Word by its being be an intrinsic mode of being of the Word? . . . Aquinas's view of human nature as capable of God by its action but incapable by its being seems indicative of . . . [his] failure [noted by Henri de Lubac and Joseph Komonchak] to reconcile the Aristotelian concept of a finite nature possessing an immanent, proportionate end with the patristic concept of the "image of God," openness to the absolute.[14]

Coffey argues that "the thesis that Christ's human nature is theandric becomes inevitable once human nature is defined in terms of orientation to God."[15] Taking the step Thomas did not take: the human openness or orientation to God allows the idea of a theandric human nature to emerge, that is, of a nature that is truly human but also able to be divinized (the very possibility that constitutes our Christian hope). In the words of the International Theological Commission, "deification is the truest and ultimate hominization of man."[16] On this account, although Christ's human nature remains integrally human and so is not capable of strictly divine actions, it is nonetheless changed from how it would otherwise be by virtue of its hypostatic union with the Word of God. (Coffey explains this "change" quite simply as the "sanctification" of Christ's humanity.) One might wonder: What greater change or difference could there be than for human nature to have its subsistence in union with the personal subsistence of the divine Word? Before exploring this question, we should note a second Rahnerian insight as to God's self-communication.

God offers us not merely gifts but his very self; not merely created graces but the Uncreated grace of the divine life itself. So we ask again: What is human nature if we can be recipients of *God's self*-communication, if we can become adopted sons and daughters in the very Son of God? More crucially, what is human nature if the

14. Coffey, "Theandric Nature of Christ," 417.
15. Coffey, "Theandric Nature of Christ," 413.
16. Quoted in Riches, "After Chalcedon," 202.

Son of God, the person of the Word, can assume human nature *as his very own*?—for that is what our faith professes. The Incarnation reveals not merely one among many possibilities for human nature, but the defining potentiality of humankind for divinization. Hence we can speak of Christ as the "uniquely highest case of the perfection of human reality."[17]

At this point, some crucial qualifications are needed, which Coffey has explored under the theme of "the Whole Rahner on the Supernatural Existential."[18] Rahner's theology of grace was initially developed in response to the debate over the nature/supernature relationship and the teaching of *Humani Generis* (1951) in response to the *nouvelle théologie*. To preserve the gratuity of divine grace—that is, to avoid the tendency of de Lubac to "supernaturalise created nature"—Rahner argued that the truth that human nature always in fact has God as its supernatural end is grounded not in creation as such (as implied by de Lubac), but in that gracious act by which God not only creates human nature but also constitutes God in himself as the supernatural end of that concrete human nature. This constitution is "ontological" and "existential"—it entails something real about human nature that is prior to the exercise of human freedom; it is a certain "restructuring" of human nature as the basis for the subsequent offer and acceptance of sanctifying grace. What Rahner famously termed "the supernatural existential" does not modify the "substance" of our nature, nor is it a habitual, "accidental" quality of our nature. But it truly affects our nature by assigning a new supernatural end (God in himself) as a new and higher mode of our natural end (God as creator). This *existential* disposition to the offer of grace grounds both the gratuity of grace and the unity of the divine economy, for it involves not merely the new supernatural destiny as such, but also a real enhancement of human nature, whereby it is

17. Coffey, "Theandric Nature of Christ," 412.

18. David Coffey, "The Whole Rahner on the Supernatural Existential," *Theological Studies* 65 (2004): 95–118.

now capable of receiving God's self-communication (in grace and in the Incarnation).

It is not enough to highlight the "narrative" unity of nature and grace owing to God's personal providence for each human being, as Guy Mansini does in his otherwise helpful examination of de Lubac.[19] According to Mansini, in many cases at least, prior to the actual offer of saving grace, we should assume in a person nothing more than the misery of fallen nature, a "blank page" that is receptive to the words of the Gospel but is otherwise untouched by grace.[20] For Rahner, by contrast, the offer of saving grace presupposes someone affected by that prior gracious act by which God constitutes his very self as the only actual end for that person.

Rahner did not, however, explain exactly how God's act of gracious constitution affected human nature; he did not, that is, explain what the "supernatural existential" actually is (and this may have invited the criticism that Rahner unduly "naturalises the supernatural"). On this point, Coffey offers a persuasive development of Rahner's account. First, he explains why sanctifying grace must be understood as being given in two stages: initially, at the creation of every human being, there is the grace of being constituted with the supernatural end of God in himself. Human nature does not demand this supernatural vocation—although it is capable of being so elevated, and yet God does graciously create us with a supernatural vocation.[21] This initial "grace" is the supernatural existential that "entails exposure to 'the permanent dynamism of grace.'"[22] Subsequently, at the moment of justification (by faith), this supernatural destiny is actualized in habitual sanctifying grace.

19. Guy Mansini, OSB, "The Abiding Theological Significance of Henri De Lubac's Surnaturel," *The Thomist* 73 (2009): 593–619.

20. See Mansini, "Abiding Theological Significance," 516.

21. De Lubac's mistake was to make the supernatural destiny a created aspect of our human nature itself.

22. Coffey, "The Whole Rahner," 103, citing Karl Rahner, "Concerning the Relationship between Nature and Grace," *Theological Investigations* 1 (1961): 301.

> the supernatural existential . . . is the beginning of God's self-communication in grace. God then awaits our free decision of faith, which is at the same time the product of the permanent offer of grace and our own authentic act. This beginning of grace is fulfilled, partially in the grace of justification, and ultimately in the beatific vision.[23]

The reason for this two-stage understanding of grace is that, as spiritual beings, humans must attain their end through their freely chosen actions. God imparts our ultimate end in two stages: "in the first as an existential, prior to freedom, and in the second through their free cooperation, that is, through justification by faith and perseverance in the life of grace."[24]

Second, Coffey has clarified the outstanding question of what the supernatural existential is by recalling the scholastic fourfold analysis of causality. The existential can be understood in terms of material causality by which human nature is disposed for receiving the self-communication of God.[25] As such, the supernatural existential is not God himself but the receptivity to God's self-communication, the ultimate prerequisite for the quasi-formal causality of divine grace.[26]

> Such "obediential" restructuring [of human nature] is a possibility for the subject because it is ordered by nature already to the same one, true God, though only through the humbler relation of creature to creator.[27]

23. Coffey, "The Whole Rahner," 109.

24. Coffer, "The Whole Rahner," 116.

25. "Material," of course, concerns potentiality not physicality. By identifying the supernatural existential at the level of material causality, it becomes clear that it does not imply that a person has indeed begun to live the life of faith or has begun to be justified by grace. We might well, with Mansini, suppose that the apologist will often not know whether the addressee "is already animated by the supernatural and ready to understand the gift of God" and hence might proceed along the Augustinian lines he recommends (Mansini, "Abiding Theological Significance," 614). The supernatural existential, however, explains why the apologist can always be assured that the person addressed can find their true end only in the beatific vision.

26. Quasi-formal causality is explained further below.

27. Coffey, "The Whole Rahner," 116.

On this account, the relation between the purely natural human end and the supernatural end is best understood in terms of "sublation"—the natural end is thus preserved in its integrity but is taken up into the higher supernatural end (thus avoiding de Lubac's unsatisfactory conclusion that I would not be the same person if I did not have the supernatural end).

Against this background, it follows that there is a third instance of what is essentially the same grace of divine self-communication, namely, the grace of hypostatic union given only to Christ.[28] While Christ's human nature is created with the same supernatural destiny we all share, in his case—in virtue of the grace of union that sanctifies his humanity—this destiny is actualized uniquely as that of the Son of God. It is thus valid to say that "in Christ we see what is possible for human nature," provided we recognize that we are referring to what is only possible *under grace*—for we are not dealing with a potentiality that is naturally attainable. This account accords with the teaching in *Humani Generis* in two ways: first, this possibility is supernatural in the sense that it is not given with human nature as such but only with nature as graced with a supernatural destiny, and second, whereas for us the supernatural existential is completed by the grace of adoption and the beatific vision, for Jesus uniquely, it is completed by the grace of hypostatic union. There is a difference of kind, not degree, between the two forms of divine self-communication in grace and incarnation.

As Coffey explains:

> hypostatic union is not a natural potency of human nature. It is a supernatural potency, one that would allow a human nature, God so willing, to be borne by grace beyond its natural limits to an absolute fulfillment. On the part of Christ's human nature it is this transcendence of natural limits along with its unsurpassable outcome in hypostatic union that justifies my use of the word "theandric" in its regard. For the rest of us there remains a destiny beyond our natural limits and one indeed not extraneous to hypostatic union: participation in Christ through grace. Hence we can say that

28. See Coffey, "De La Taille on the Grace of Union."

human nature as potentia obedientalis for hypostatic union is realized absolutely in the case of Christ, and relatively in the case of others.

It follows that there are two ways of being divine—the simply given divinity of God as such and the divinity achieved by grace in human nature; in traditional terms, we may speak either of the "substantial" divinity of Christ, in contrast to the "accidental" divinity of other human beings by habitual grace (to use the Scholastic terms), or of personal and hypostatic divinity in the case of Christ, by contrast to participation in divinity in the case of others (to use the patristic terms).[29]

How Could the Infinite God Be United to Finite Human Nature?

To further explain this account, it is necessary to address another traditional objection by noting a second key development of twentieth-century Catholic theology that marks a seismic shift with respect to our understanding the union between God and humankind in the three properly supernatural mysteries of incarnation, grace, and the beatific vision.

Classical theology understood these three unions as indirect: for example, grace was understood as a modification of the human being (an accidental quality of the soul) whereby a person is joined to God so as to be able to live and act in a Godlike way. This traditional understanding of God's gracious action upon us assumed the commonsense view that because of its limitations, human nature needs first to be changed in some way to become capable of sharing in the divine life or of seeing God face to face. On this commonsense view, sanctifying grace is the created effect of God's action that is prior to our union with God, who is uncreated grace. On this account, even the human nature of Jesus required prior sanctifying grace to prepare it for hypostatic union with the Word.[30]

A revolutionary insight in the work of Maurice de la Taille—and

29. Coffey, "Theandric Nature of Christ," 413.

30. See Coffey, "De La Taille on the Grace of Union."

subsequently, albeit independently, in that of Rahner—overturns this seemingly commonsense presupposition and enables us thereby to take at face value the numerous scriptural texts that speak of our direct union with God, for example, "the love of God has been poured into our hearts by the Holy Spirit" (Rom 5:5). It is now possible for us to accept the more biblical view that sanctifying grace is the created effect that *follows on from* our direct union with God in grace.

The traditional view could not accept any immediate union between God and creature because it focused on the infinite distance between God and creature, between Pure Uncreated Act and the actualization of a finite potential in the creature (e.g., in the gift of grace). De la Taille, however, saw that in the case of properly supernatural realities we do indeed have "created actuation by Uncreated Act"—that is, a finite reality (the grace of union, sanctifying grace, the beatific vision) is a finite actualization, not by its proper finite act but by God himself, who is Infinite Act.[31] In the supernatural cases, there is a radical disproportion between Infinite Act (God) and the creaturely potential that God actualizes. Less radical but similar disproportions are found in nature, most clearly in the case of the human soul. The soul is the act of the body it informs and actualizes, but the soul is more than the act of the body (for it can survive death); the soul does not merely inform the body. As de la Taille put it, actuation is not equivalent to in-formation in cases where the act and the potential are not correlative.[32]

This idea can be further explained in terms of Rahner's account of quasi-formal causality. The soul is the formal cause of the living human being; it in-forms and actualizes the bodily potential such that there is just one being, a human person; soul and body, form and mat-

31. M. de la Taille, SJ, *The Hypostatic Union and Created Actuation by Uncreated Act* (West Baden Springs, IN: West Baden College, 1952).

32. For further philosophical defense of this principle, see Kevin G. O'Connell, SJ, "The Philosophy of Actuation Distinct from Act," *Science et Espirit* 20 (1968): 223–45, and 383–408. See also P. De Letter, SJ, "Created Actuation by the Uncreated Act: Difficulties and Answers," *Theological Studies* 18 (1957): 60–92.

ter, together constitute the one being. Rahner speaks of divine grace as a *quasi*-formal cause because, like a formal cause, it shapes and transforms the creature, but unlike a natural formal cause, it does not become one in being with the creature.[33] That is to say, God himself, Uncreated grace, acts immediately upon the creature just as a formal cause would, but without becoming one entity with the creature.[34]

These theological developments by de la Taille and Rahner overcome the objection that the infinite distance between God and created human nature precludes their direct union. It follows that the "hypostatic union" can be understood directly as the union of the human nature of Jesus with the person of the divine Word (through the grace of sanctification, the Holy Spirit).

A Key Distinction

At this point, a key distinction emerges to further facilitate our inquiry: the distinction between what it is to speak of the Word as such and what it is to speak of the Word Incarnate. This distinction allows us to hold that, with reference to the Word as such, it is true to say that *the Word* has two natures (divine and human). With reference to the *Incarnate* Word (hereafter "the Christ"), however, it is true to say that the Word has only one nature—namely, the human nature assumed.[35] This distinction enables a crucial transformation of traditional Christological thinking.

33. As it happens, Rahner here echoes John of St. Thomas (*Eighth Disputation on Part III of the Summa*, no. 18) whom de la Taille rightly cites in support of his position (see de la Taille, *Hypostatic Union*, 68, and Coffey, "De La Taille on the Grace of Union").

34. For an apposite discussion of these issues in another context, see R. Jared Staudt, "Substantial Union with God in Matthias Scheeben," *Nova et Vetera*, English ed., 11, no. 2 (2013): 515–36. See also Matthew Lewis Sutton, "*Mysterium Christi:* The Christologies of Maurice de la Taille and Karl Rahner," *International Journal of Systematic Theology* 10 (2008): 416–30.

35. The more familiar distinction is between what it is true to say of Christ "in his human nature" (e.g., that he died on the Cross) and what it is true to say of Christ "in his divine nature" (e.g., that the Son does not suffer death). This distinction is valid from the perspective of a descending Christology; the new distinction being

With reference, first, to the Word as Incarnate, our concern is simply the assumption of a human nature by the Word of God; the Word becomes what we are in all things but sin. Thus in meeting the Christ, Jesus of Nazareth, we are meeting the Word made flesh, the Word who now subsists in union with the human nature of the man Jesus. In so speaking, we do not refer to the divine nature of the Word precisely because we are talking about the Word *as Incarnate*.

By contrast, second, the traditional "two natures" Christology was focused on the Word in himself. That traditional (descending) Christology remains always valuable for the light it sheds on the Incarnation with respect to the Word as such. For example, in defending and explaining the mutual coordination of the two wills in Christ, the classical approach shows how it can be true that the will of Jesus is one with the will of God (as exercised by the Word or Son).[36] But the traditional "two natures" approach does not shed light on the quite different question about the nature of the *Word Incarnate*, the Word subsisting in union with the human nature of Jesus. Here, the concern is simply to understand the relationship between the person of the Word and the human nature he assumes. It would be a category mistake to invoke a two natures approach to address these questions. As Thomas Weinandy puts it, "Everything concerning the Son of God within his human state as man must be conceived and articulated within that incarnate state, and, thus not in relationship to his own divine nature."[37]

It follows that a complete Christology acknowledges two complementary perspectives, corresponding to Christology from above (the Johannine perspective) and Christology from below (the Synoptic

---

recommended here is valid from the perspective of an ascending Christology and is crucial to the development of a contemporary Christology.

36. See, e.g., Thomas Joseph White, "Dyotheletism and the Instrumental Human Consciousness of Jesus," *Pro Ecclesia* 27, no. 4 (2008): 396–422.

37. Thomas G. Weinandy, OFM Cap., "The Beatific Vision and the Incarnate Son: Furthering the Discussion," *The Thomist* 70 (2006): 605–15, at 614. There are other aspects of Weinandy's approach that I would not endorse.

perspective). The former perspective will speak of the two natures of the Word, the latter perspective will speak of just one nature, the theandric (human) nature of the Word Incarnate. The International Theological Commission takes the latter perspective when summarizing the teaching of Constantinople III in terms of our salvation being willed by a divine person through a human will.[38]

Is This Theology Consistent with the Conciliar Teaching about the Communication of Properties?

A close reading of the texts shows that the traditional conciliar definitions implying that Christ possessed two natures are indeed open to the interpretation being developed here. While the conciliar definitions do not consistently distinguish between the Son of God in himself and the Son incarnate—that is, the Christ—they are suggestive of this distinction. Thus Chalcedon speaks of Christ being "made known (to the intellect) in two natures"—it does not speak of Christ *being* "in two natures," and in the latter part of the definition, it is as the divine Word that Christ is the subject of the definition: "one and the same only-begotten Son, God, Word, Lord Jesus Christ."[39] It is *the Son and Word as such* (not the Word Incarnate) who is "made known in two natures"; that is, we now know that the Son who is consubstantial with the Father is also, in virtue of the Incarnation, consubstantial with us in all things but sin. But understanding how Christ is consubstantial with us does not involve claims about the divine nature of the incarnate Son.

Constantinople III (680–81 AD), however, might seem to require a two natures understanding of Christ: "Believing our Lord Jesus Christ, even after his incarnation, to be one of the Holy Trinity and

38. International Theological Commission, "Select Questions on Christology" (1979), #7, available at the website of the Holy See, accessed September 23, 2018, http://www.vatican.va/roman_curia/congregations/cfaith/cti_documents/rc_cti_1979_cristologia_en.html. Likewise, St John Paul II said that Christ "acted with a human will, and with a human heart he loved" (*Redemptor hominis*, 8).

39. As quoted by Coffey, "Theandric Nature of Christ," 410n16.

our true God, we say that *he has two natures shining forth in his one subsistence*."[40] The background to this text was the theological principle of the *communicatio ideomatum*—the principle that, by virtue of the Incarnation, properties true of Christ in his human nature are true of the divine Son, just as properties true of the Son in his divine nature are true of the Christ. For example, Mary is the "Mother of God" because she is the mother of the one who is the Son of God.

As St. Thomas notes, Nestorians tried to resolve puzzles about incarnational predication by dividing properties so that some were true of Jesus as a human being, others were true of Christ as Son of God, and others again were true of Christ as both human and divine. "Catholics on the other hand maintained that words which are said of Christ either in His Divine or in His human nature may be said either of God or of man. . . . since there is one hypostasis of both natures, [i.e.] the same hypostasis is signified by the name of either nature" (*ST* III, q. 16, a. 4). Although this claim is traditionally taken to support the "two natures" understanding of Christ, Thomas warns us always to consider "the reason" for our statements, whether they are based on the divine nature or the human nature.[41]

Accordingly, if we reflect further on the reason for the sharing of properties, we will note an asymmetry in their application. The attribution of human predicates to the divine person is straightforward—we are speaking of the Word Incarnate. By contrast, the attribution of divine properties, such as "is omniscient," to the *Incarnate* Word requires us to ask the prior question whether what is true of the Son in himself, precisely as Son of God, is necessarily true of the Son as incarnate. An a priori argument that because Jesus is the Son of God he must possess *all* the properties that the Son possesses in himself *as*

40. Third Council of Constantinople, in *Decrees of the Ecumenical Councils*, ed. Norman P. Tanner, available at Papal Encyclicals Online, accessed September 23, 2018, www.papalencyclicals.net/Councils/ecum06.htm. (Emphasis added.)

41. Hence "we say that the Son of God suffered, yet we do not say that the Divine Nature suffered" (*ST* III, q. 16, a. 5, ad 1).

divine simply begs this question[42] and flies in the face of the Gospel evidence.

Clearly, there is a tension between (human to divine) attribution of properties on the basis of the Gospel evidence and (divine to human) attribution of properties on the basis of theological assumptions. The reason for this tension is that, on the one hand, it is true that a complete divine person assumes a human nature, with all its properties, whereas on the other hand, it is not the case that a complete human person assumes the divine nature, with all its properties. This is not to say that no divine properties are true of Jesus of Nazareth; it is simply to caution against the (descending) assumption that has controlled Christology for so long—namely, the assumption that to affirm that Jesus Christ is the Son of God is to affirm that he possesses the divine nature *in itself*, rather than the divine nature as *incarnate* in a human nature. Recall that St. Thomas did not hesitate to say that, by reason of the union of natures in Christ, "the Divine Nature is said to be incarnate and the human nature deified" (*ST* III, q. 16, a. 5, ad 2). At this stage, we should leave open the precise character of the distinction between the divine nature in itself and the divine nature as incarnate. With this question left open, we can simply hold that "to speak of Jesus Christ is to refer to the existence and operation of the Divine Word in the human nature rather than the divine [nature]."[43]

Ontological Communication between the Two Natures

Moreover, and most importantly, the interchange or communication between attributes cannot be merely a matter of predication, of what it is true *to say*—statements that in any case require qualifications (e.g., *the Son as divine* did not die on the Cross). As Coffey emphasizes, the predications must be supported by *an event* of communication,

42. In the traditional and correct sense of "beg the question"!

43. Coffey, "Theandric Nature of Christ," 410.

that is, "an ontological communication between the natures" that underlies the predication.[44] This "ontological communication between the natures" explains the impact on the human nature of Jesus of its personhood in the Word, and hence of what it means for the Word to have its subsistence in that nature. Because by virtue of the Incarnation the Word assumes a human nature, we may legitimately ask: What must be communicated between the divine person and the human nature for that nature to be both integrally human *and* the Incarnation of one who possesses the divine nature? In answering this question—that is, in seeking to understand the ontological communication of attributes—we should be guided by a priori as well as a posteriori principles.

A priori, "the divine nature must communicate to the human nature whatever the latter requires for its integrity as a human nature"—for example, that Christ know who he is—namely, the divine Son—even though he will know this in a human way.[45] Likewise, the divine person must communicate to the human nature whatever the latter requires for it to be the hypostasis of the divine person *in a human nature*—for example, the divine will, such that Jesus's will is the (incarnate) will of the divine Son, and so may be called a theandric will. A posteriori, we must look to the Gospels, and subject to appropriate biblical criticism, to discover what exactly God chose to communicate to the human nature of Christ. Under this heading, an obvious attribute is the power to heal and to forgive sin.

Further reflection on a priori theological principles as well as a posteriori study of the Gospels will reveal more about the communication between divine and human natures. What we should not do during such reflection is simply assume that *all* divine attributes true of *the Word as such* are necessarily communicated to the theandric nature of *the Word Incarnate*.

The point being made here is common among spiritual writers,

44. Coffey, "Theandric Nature of Christ," 419.

45. Coffey, "Theandric Nature of Christ," 420.

when they remind us that in seeing Jesus (in his life, death, and resurrection), we see what God "looks like" when God reveals himself outside the Trinity. We need to do justice to the full force of the statement in John's Gospel: "Whoever has seen me [in my human nature] has seen the Father" (Jn 14:9, New Revised Standard Version). Jesus does not mean "whoever sees me sees someone who—as it happens—shares the divine nature with the Father." What Jesus is saying, surely, is that the Father's divine nature is fully revealed—well, as fully as is possible outside the Trinity—in the human being that he is (and a fortiori in his life, death, and resurrection).[46]

At this point, an objection needs to be stopped in its tracks. This account of Christ's theandric nature is not to be equated with either the single (divine) nature view advocated by the Monophysites of the sixth century, nor with a Monophysitism "from below" as if Christ's nature was *merely* human. Christ's nature is *integrally* human, albeit as the human nature of the Word elevated by the grace of union, and so as actualized by the divine Word.[47] Nonetheless, this account means we need to ask a question that Rahner did not ask: What kind of distinction is there between the simply divine nature of the Word and the theandric nature of the Word Incarnate (i.e., the human nature of the Word as elevated by the grace of union)? This cannot be a real distinction, for the person is the same, nor can it be a merely logical distinction, for the natures are distinct. It is best understood as a virtual distinction—that is, a logical distinction with a foundation in reality (viz., in the distinction of the two natures). That is to say, the distinction is logically implied by the two different and complementary ways in which we engage in our theological exploration, namely, by understanding and affirming of the Word as such two natures—his simply divine nature and his assumed human nature—and by understanding and affirming of the Word as Incarnate a human nature

46. The sense in which Jesus is "a human being," albeit not "a human person," will become clear shortly.

47. On this issue, see also the earlier discussion of the supernatural existential.

rendered "theandric" by the grace of union, a nature that is human in a divine way, or divine in a human way.[48]

Renewing the Tradition

In conclusion, I note how compatible this theology is with an often neglected teaching in St. Thomas. As David Coffey emphasizes, the most fundamental communication from divine to human concerns not properties, but "the communication of the divine *esse*, the divine act of existence, whereby [Jesus] is constituted in human existence as the only-begotten Son of God."[49] Coffey's approach accords with Thomas's argument that in a sense there are two *esse*'s in Christ: "a single *esse* corresponding to his single divine personhood. . . . But in so far as [the divine *esse*] founds Christ's human nature in existence, it is received as a human *esse* . . . [which] founds the unique person who is both human and divine." Hence, as incarnate, Christ's *esse* "is neither simply divine nor simply human, but . . . is theandric."

> If . . . one regards Christ as the realization of the divine person in the human nature, then . . . one should say that there is in him a single theandric nature and a single theandric act of existence.[50]

Christ had a concrete human nature, which was "theandric" in this sense: it was essentially human but also divine in that, by grace and in the same act as that by which it came into existence, it achieved the full potential of humanity for divinity.[51]

48. A corollary that Coffey has recently drawn is that, whereas for Thomas, Christ's simply human nature needed sanctifying grace as an "accidental" modification to enable his human nature to participate in the being of the Word, on this account in which the *substantial* grace of union ensures Christ's theandric nature subsists in the Word, sanctifying grace is not required. Moreover, Thomas's idea of Christ possessing the fullness of sanctifying grace suggests the dangerous idea that Christ differs from us only in degree! Coffey's argument also finds support in the somewhat different approaches of Felix Malmberg and Maurice de la Taille. See Coffey, "De La Taille on the Grace of Union."

49. Coffey, "Theandric Nature of Christ," 421.

50. Coffey, "Theandric Nature of Christ," 422.

51. Coffey, "Quaestio Disputata," 911. It is important to recall Coffey's explication of the supernatural existential which distinguishes the way the grace of hypostatic

Support for this position is found in St. Thomas, as noted by James Reichmann, SJ, one of the most "traditional" of Thomistic interpreters (whose critique of transcendental Thomism in the late 1970s has been of enduring significance for me). As Reichmann writes, explaining Thomas:[52]

> Although the Eternal Word was not perfected in any way by having assumed the individuated human nature, the eternal supposit [person] is "substantialized" (*substantificatur*) by the human nature assumed, *in that the Word is this man.*[53]

Because the Word is a single person, there is strictly speaking only one divine *esse*, that of the Word possessing the divine nature, but insofar as the Word exists in time, he has a secondary *esse* in his assuming a human nature that also exists but is not joined to the Word as its proper suppositional nature. In technical terms, the human nature does not exert formal causality on the divine *esse.*

> In this unique instance of the Incarnation, the human nature is actualized by the divine esse of the Word, [but] does not in any way determine or limit that esse ... this secondary esse is not an esse distinct from the divine esse of the Word which actualizes the human nature.... [But] The human nature can be said to have esse, for it does indeed exist. Yet the actuality by which it is, is not, properly speaking, its own actuality.[54]

As Reichmann shows, and as Coffey had noted independently, this teaching of St. Thomas in his *De Unione Verbi Incarnati* is to be found in the work of Johannes Capreolus in the fifteenth century and

---

union divinizes Jesus from the way sanctifying grace divinizes his adopted brothers and sisters.

52. James B. Reichmann, SJ, "Aquinas, Scotus, and the Christological Mystery: Why Christ Is Not a Human Person," *The Thomist* 71 (2007): 451–74. See also Victor Salas Jr., "Thomas Aquinas on Christ's *Esse*: A Metaphysics of the Incarnation," *The Thomist* 70 (2006): 577–603.

53. Reichmann, "Aquinas, Scotus, and the Christological Mystery," 469, emphasis added.

54. Reichmann, "Aquinas, Scotus, and the Christological Mystery," 469. Hence the qualified sense in which Jesus "is a human being."

in the early twentieth century in the work of de la Taille referred to above. What Coffey shows, in addition to Reichmann's account, is that this somewhat isolated Thomistic insight has been recovered in our times because of the seismic shift in Catholic theology in the twentieth century with respect to our understanding the union between God and humankind in the three properly supernatural mysteries of incarnation, grace, and the beatific vision.

Conclusion

The claims and arguments presented in this essay require more defense than has been offered here, and they presuppose a metaphysical tradition in Christology that is no longer fashionable. By way of conclusion, I identify the following four themes as crucial to the proposal, themes that may be summarized in nontechnical ways as follows. First, human beings have been created with a capacity for God, for deification, and, uniquely, for incarnation. Second, when this capacity is actualized in the three properly supernatural mysteries (incarnation, grace, and beatific vision), God's action is direct and immediate, a created actuation by Uncreated Act. Third, in the Incarnation, the Word of God takes human nature to himself as his very own, sharing his own subsistence, in what is then a secondary existence (*esse*) of the Word.[55] Fourth, in reflecting on this mystery, theological precision requires us to distinguish between what we affirm of the Word as such (the two natures) and what we affirm of the Word Incarnate (his theandric human nature).

Of these four themes, the last is the crucial development that allows us to emphasize the unity of Christ's as a divine person subsisting in an integral human nature. Although the traditional "two na-

55. The major theme in David Coffey's theological writings is that of grace as the Gift of the Holy Spirit; the approach to Christology outlined here should be complemented by a developed "Spirit Christology" and theology of the Trinity. See David M. Coffey, *Grace: The Gift of the Holy Spirit* (Sydney: Catholic Institute of Sydney, 1979); idem, *Deus Trinitas: The Doctrine of the Triune God* (New York: Oxford, 1999); and articles such as "The Incarnation of the Holy Spirit," *Theological Studies* 45 (1984): 466–80.

tures," descending Christology remains valid with respect to claims about the Word as such, it is a category mistake to apply that way of thinking to the Word as Incarnate for it implies the parallelism between the natures that Ratzinger warned against. The development of the theological tradition recommended here enables Christology to focus simply on what is true of the Word Incarnate, the Word who has a secondary existence in the humanity of Jesus of Nazareth. It might be objected that this proposal requires us to think of the Word apart from the divine nature, in which case we are not referring to the Word at all. The reply is that incarnation is the unique instance of deification, whereby in virtue of the grace of union, human nature is elevated to be the proper nature of the Word *as incarnate*—namely, divine in a human way, and human in a divine way. To be human as Jesus was is just what it is for the divine Word to have a secondary existence in the otherness of creation.[56]

56. I am grateful to David Coffey for numerous clarifying discussions in the course of writing this essay. I alone am responsible for the way his theology is presented here with a view to a wider, less specialized audience.

RENÉE KÖHLER-RYAN

3 • KEEPING TRUTH IN STYLE

Tradition and Scandals in Roman Catholic Ecclesiastical Architecture

Tradition relies on scandals for its endurance. Indeed, scandals are essential to the notion of what it means to be Christian. With this I refer to St. Paul's idea, in Galatians, that everything that a Christian does becomes meaningless the moment he or she is no longer preaching the scandal of the Cross of Christ.[1] There are many ways of preaching or, as I reflect in what follows, of giving witness to that scandal, and traditional architecture within the Roman Catholic tradition is a stunning example. Such architecture exhibits that tradition remains alive through continual change, and it relies on continual shocks—echoes of that first scandal—to do so. I offer a model, inspired by the thought of such diverse yet interconnected figures as St. Augustine, T. S. Eliot, and Joseph Ratzinger, through which to understand this claim and thereby argue that the keepers of Tradition know, respect, and refer to what has come before. At the same time, though, they remain of the Tradition only when they can and do actively express their comprehension of what is at stake—and so at risk—in Tradition, by introducing developments to its articulation. It is only in this way that Tradition can resist one of its major threats, its vulnerability to what I will call traditionalism. It may well be the

1. Gal 5:11.

case that Tradition is even more at risk to this than to what is new. For Tradition can survive novelty far more vigorously than it can put up with unthinking repetitions of what has been accepted as traditional and therefore unchangeable in any detail of its expression.

Three thinkers, two Roman Catholic and one Anglo Catholic, all from different points in history, are my guides in what follows. I begin with some considerations from Joseph Ratzinger, who consistently reminds that we must always turn to Truth, not Custom.[2] This generates the possibility of being shocked in new ways by the beauty of art and architecture in the Roman Catholic tradition. Our relationship to God, expressed in the spaces in which we worship together, cannot rely solely upon Custom. With this Augustine, our second guide, agrees, for God's Beauty is both "so ancient" and "so new."[3] If and when artistic expressions of our relationship to God stand still, it is evidence that we have forgotten the way that Tradition is grounded in a *development* of the human appreciation of truth. Augustine thus emphasizes that Tradition is something handed down, adopted, but also adapted, to various circumstances—primarily cultural—by its many stewards. The third guide, T. S. Eliot, speaks about works of art in ways that I think can readily include church architecture. In his seminal essay "Tradition and the Individual Talent,"[4] he states that no creative genius exists outside of Tradition, and theorizes that Tradition can grow only when that genius introduces something into Tradition proper that be considered a development, a refinement, and a complication of the content that has always been there, living and enabling artistic expression and endeavors.

After speaking of the main insights of these three regarding Tradition, I finally return to Ratzinger and to two examples of church architecture—the Gothic and the Baroque—that at their inception

2. Joseph Cardinal Ratzinger, *Introduction to Christianity*, trans. J. R. Foster (San Francisco: Ignatius Press, 1990), 97.

3. St. Augustine, *The Confessions*, trans. Maria Boulding (New York: New City Press, 1997), Book X, 27, 28; 203.

4. T. S. Eliot, "Tradition and the Individual Talent," *Perspecta* 19 (1982): 36–42.

were entirely new but proved to be of the Tradition. Drawing from these three thinkers, one finds that Tradition, as something handed down or over, operates on two levels, which I call the vertical and the horizontal dimensions. At the horizontal level, works from within the Tradition stand in relationship to each other, in what Augustine and Eliot both think of as a dynamic order of development (which is not to be confused with simple progress, or progression). On the vertical level, the individual artist, in conversation with previous and current artists and artworks, at the same time receives stimuli from personal experience, from surrounding culture, and, particularly in the case of sacred architecture, from a personal—what we would most often call religious—encounter with the divine. In speaking of churches, I specifically refer to spaces set aside for what Roman Catholics believe to be the ultimate sacrament of encounter, the Eucharist. The celebration of that sacrifice means that there are certain constancies within a church structure. In particular, the centrality of the altar will be one of these—an unchanging point around which all else develops and moves.

Joseph Ratzinger: Truth, Not Custom

This focus on the altar, according to Ratzinger, essentially necessitates one of the most important continuities within this tradition of architecture, which is its emphasis on beauty, but of a unique kind, because it engages in transformation of the space in which the great drama of the Eucharist takes place. Church architecture cannot deal with any simple kind of beauty because it needs constantly to refer to what is ultimately mysterious and beyond any single artistic rendering. Such spaces perpetually have the difficult task to indicate that there is something more, beyond what is being seen, and they can do so by intensifying the visible to its most piercing possibilities. Benedict XVI's[5] address to artists in 2009[6] is particularly helpful for

5. I refer to Ratzinger as Benedict XVI whenever he is declaring a philosophical-theological position from his office as pope.

6. Benedict XVI, "Meeting with Artists Address," Sistine Chapel, November 21,

understanding this point. There, he says that beauty brings about a kind of "shock" that is in keeping with the importance of art to what he called a "new humanism," thereby invoking Paul VI and also John Paul II. In particular, relates Benedict, Paul VI asked artists "for a newer and deeper journey in mutual acquaintance and dialogue in order to arrive at an authentic 'renaissance' of art in the context of a new humanism." Such newness is precisely what is at stake when speaking of beauty as Benedict does, for without it, depth of both understanding and vision, and the dialogue that leads to these, are lacking. Drawing closer to the sense of beauty of which artists need constantly to be conscious, Benedict goes on to state that:

> an essential function of genuine beauty, as emphasized by Plato, is that it gives man a healthy "shock," it draws him out of himself, wrenches him away from resignation and from being content with the humdrum—it even makes him suffer, piercing him like a dart, but in so doing it "reawakens" him, opening afresh the eyes of his heart and mind, giving him wings, carrying him aloft . . . Beauty pulls us up short, but in so doing it reminds us of our final destiny, it sets us back on our path, fills us with new hope, gives us the courage to live to the full the unique gift of life. The quest for beauty that I am describing here is clearly not about escaping into the irrational or into mere aestheticism.[7]

Such beauty is forever new when it speaks to each and every person, across the ages, and it can work upon the human soul to such an extent that one can rise up above the merely "humdrum," only because it comprehends the ultimate significance of the everyday. Within this same speech, Benedict reflects upon the space of the Sistine Chapel, dominated by the scene of the Last Judgment, which "[invites] us to raise our gaze to the ultimate horizon." Behind the altar, this masterpiece in the space of the chapel draws us both forward and upward. On a horizontal level, one finds that the horizon has a limitless reach, leading to what finally transcends.

2009, http://www.vatican.va/holy_father/benedict_xvi/speeches/2009/november/documents/hf_ben-xvi_spe_20091121_artisti_en.html.

7. Benedict XVI, "Meeting with Artists Address."

Development within Tradition, according to Ratzinger, relies on the perennial possibility of such an intense realization. At the same time, it demands that artists and architects not complacently deliver more of the same. Benedict reminds us of the painter Georges Braque, who said that "art is meant to disturb," unlike science, which "reassures."[8] Such agitation is necessary, as what T. S. Eliot refers to as a *refinement* is also a *complication* of what has always been inherent within Tradition. Within the tradition of church building, I argue that such disturbances or shocks are necessary scandals. That is, they confront us with at least one aspect of reality that may not previously have concerned us. Such shocks are vital because they perform a test both for artists and architects as well as for us, the receivers who encounter the resulting artwork. The artist is tested for whether he has translated the content of Tradition into a style that can transport us while at the same time expressing our relationship to God; but we too are tested, for our capacity to recognize whether something new is still of the Tradition.

In *The Spirit of the Liturgy*,[9] Ratzinger writes that the church structure can be considered something functional. After all, Christians need a place to meet. But the term *church* also stands for "living community,"[10] and so some of what we say about a church building can also reflect the disposition of that community, so that the building and the communal character of the church inform each other. The Catholic understanding, according to Ratzinger, places Christ at the center of his people; he incarnates himself in our worship. Christ's centrality, though, cannot negate the way that Jewish worship and places of worship are already in continuity with Christian churches.[11] Perhaps most significant is Ratzinger's indication that in the synagogue, worship reaches its climax with the communal recitation of the Kiddush, which draws on prayers spoken by angels in the Books

8. Benedict XVI, "Meeting with Artists Address."

9. Joseph Cardinal Ratzinger, *The Spirit of the Liturgy*, trans. John Saward (San Francisco: Ignatius Press, 2000).

10. Ratzinger, *Spirit of the Liturgy*, 62.

11. Ratzinger, *Spirit of the Liturgy*, 62–63.

of Isaiah and Ezekiel. In saying this prayer, the worshipers make it their own, so that "the congregation does not offer its own thoughts or poetry but is taken out of itself and given the privilege of sharing in the cosmic song of praise of the cherubim and seraphim."[12] Crucially, this repetition is only meaningful if and when those speaking know what they are doing and why. The Christian development of this truth becomes represented in the way that we start to orient our churches, no longer toward Jerusalem and the earthly temple but toward the rising sun, which symbolizes Christ. The whole church and the people it represents thus become at one with the cosmos, which like them is oriented and transformed by Christ's incarnation, death, and resurrection. Yet this is not the only change that the Christian church brings about. The breach between Judaism and Christianity is evident in that the Roman Catholic church now contains an altar, and the sacrifice of the Mass:

> brings heaven into the community assembled on earth, or rather it takes that community beyond itself into the communion of saints of all times and places. We might put it this way: the altar is the place where heaven is opened up. It does not close off the church, but opens it up—and leads it into the eternal liturgy.[13]

The altar, toward which the church is now focused, because the whole cosmos is oriented toward Christ, operates along both the horizontal and the vertical dimensions. It brings community and world together along a horizon, but at the same time it takes everyone upward, toward God.

While everything in the church surrounds and emphasizes the place of the altar, there is for Ratzinger the need for development, rather than progress, in the way that liturgy expresses that centrality. There can, he says, "be a thoroughly living kind of development in which a seed at the origin of something ripens and bears fruit."[14] Ratzinger might well say the same about the tradition of art and ar-

12. Ratzinger, *Spirit of the Liturgy*, 67.
13. Ratzinger, *Spirit of the Liturgy*, 71.
14. Ratzinger, *Spirit of the Liturgy*, 82.

chitecture that presents cosmic space for the liturgical event. His considerations are in keeping with Augustine's and T. S. Eliot's reflections upon Tradition. All three of these thinkers enable us to articulate a model for understanding and perhaps also bringing about communal spaces for the worship particular to Eucharistic celebration. All three thinkers maintain an essential difference between progress and development such that, while progress obscures and denies its source of change, development touches upon what was there at the beginning, waiting to be revealed in not just one but a variety of ways. Development brings with it hope that is present because of a trust in what has been given, while progress depends upon leaving behind the past and relying on human powers alone. One might add regress to this list, which relies inordinately upon the past so that it loses all possibility of saying something genuine. This is the risk that traditionalism, rather than Tradition per se, takes, at the same time endangering that which it seeks overbearingly to preserve.

Augustine: Tradition and Truth

Turning to Augustine, one finds that certain points about Tradition come to the fore. Augustine thinks of Tradition primarily as that which comes from Christ, who has handed down Truth, through Creation from the beginning of time, and continues to do so now, through the apostolic ministry of the Church. Crucial to that handing down are the celebration of the Eucharist and infant baptism, with the authority that validates these sacraments in each case coming from Christ through the Apostles.[15] Furthermore, something of the Tradition, according to Augustine, is handed down with the acknowledgment both that the one who gives and the one who receives are stewards of the same Truth. For instance, we are assured that the words of Scriptures that we receive remain intact, because they have always been taken care of by the custodians of Tradition.

15. G. R. Evans, "Tradition," in *Augustine through the Ages: An Encyclopedia*, ed. Allan D. Fitzgerald (Grand Rapids, MI: Eerdmans, 1999), 842.

As G. R. Evans reminds, though, tradition for Augustine is about more than written records.[16] The content of the records, that of which Scripture speaks, the communal relationship between us and God and through God with each other, in all its aspects, is what is at stake in Tradition. This, which is far more difficult to convey from one person or one age to the next, is the life and meaning of Tradition. Thus Augustine muses that there is something obscure about the traditional Law of Moses—a content that cannot be completely described and so could be deemed fragile.[17] This Law depends upon Tradition for its life as well as for its stability; but this example from Augustine also indicates what he sees to be the problematic nature of Tradition, which is that it makes tough demands. Truly to live the Tradition, for Augustine, means being able to manifest in one's current age what was embodied previously differently. Augustine's forebears in the Tradition lived in a variety of times and places, and more importantly they were unique persons. Thus he can never live the Tradition in exactly the same way as anyone else. He is, nonetheless, only of the Tradition when he substantiates the Truth he shares with them. It is unsurprising that Augustine thinks like this, given his insistence that Tradition is more than a historical affair. Instead, it has to do with the work of evangelization, with going out into the world to make known the Good News. But that work of evangelization can only occur if and when the Gospel message, the life of faith and grace, flourishes within the heart of the witness, who lives what he understands in community with others.

It is from that secure foundation, where individuals live out the Gospel together in their daily lives, that vibrant original forms of Tradition's expression are possible. Augustine, defender of the content of the Faith against heresy, held this point dear: that every Christian is called upon to incarnate fresh, sometimes surprising, instances of

16. Evans, "Tradition," 842.

17. "Augustine speaks of the *aliquid obscurum* in the traditional Law of Moses (*en. Ps.* 102.14)." Evans, "Tradition," 842.

what Christ demands. Faced with the Pelagian heretic Julian, for instance, Augustine argues vehemently in his own voice for what he has been handed by others before him. Augustine's argument throughout the work now known as *Contra Julianum* is helpful in several ways to our understanding of Tradition.[18] There, he argues about Original Sin, which is something inherited but not literally from the Tradition. Instead, from one generation to the next, extending to the sin of the first parents of humankind, we have suffered the same fate. But Tradition is not precisely this kind of undergoing. Instead, it is the labor of working against the grain of sin, which happens in the order of grace. When of the Tradition, believers can fight against the inheritance of original sin by embodying Christ's salvific action. Thereby a Christian manifests a Tradition that constantly speaks from, transforms, and also reveals the meaning of that first sin.

But how do we know this? Augustine's certainty comes from having tested his arguments against those of his predecessors in the Tradition. They become both his conversationalists and judges. Living in different times, fighting different philosophical and theological battles, thinkers such as Irenaeus, Cyprian, Hilary, Ambrose, Gregory, Innocent, John, Basil, and Augustine's contemporary Jerome are neither simple friends nor enemies of Augustine.[19] Precisely because of this impartiality, he can count on them to judge both him and Julian. One by one, Augustine calls up his forebears, reviewing and analyzing their arguments, drawing from these what speaks most to him and the concerns of his current age. He finds their words pertinent not just to the past but also to his own time. Augustine discovers that he is the child of a family of thinkers extending back to the early Church. So it is that he can describe Tradition, saying of the early Church Fathers: "They held what they found in the Church;

18. See in particular the following section: St. Augustine, "The Struggle against the Law of Sin," Book II in *Answer to Julian*, vol. I/24, *The Works of Saint Augustine*, trans. Roland J. Teske (New York: New City Press, 2003), 330–35.

19. St. Augustine, "Struggle against the Law of Sin," 10.33; 331.

they taught what they learned; they handed on to their children what they received from their forebears."[20] This helpful definition is not enough to flesh out what he is saying, and so he goes on to declare to Julian that all of those named: "knew neither you nor us, and yet we read their decisions against you in our favour. We were not yet in conflict with you, and we were victorious by reason of their decisions."[21] It is as though Augustine and Julian stand in a law court. Even though their judges have long since passed away, the words those same judges have made available in Augustine's present age still convey truth and proffer judgment. Augustine claims to make that same truth known once more. Simply receiving is not enough to constitute Tradition, however. So Augustine challenges Julian: "wherever you are, wherever you may be able to read these words, I bring you before [the] judges in your heart."[22] Augustine makes this appeal for inward action, where in a quiet moment, truth is looked at squarely and honestly appraised. No Christian can rest content to simply take what is handed to him solely because of the identity of the giver. The content of Tradition must be located, recognized, assented to, and lived. The community of believers constitutes a community of the heart, which is to say of the shared internal realization of truth, externalized through lives lived in common pursuit of the same.

Crucial to all this is the moment of interchange. As forebears hand over the content of Tradition to their children, the precious message, or matter, of that same Tradition can easily be misunderstood, misinterpreted, rejected, and in any of these ways lost. Josef Pieper in this regard, also drawing on Augustine, warns that the meaning of a tradition can die out when those who should receive cannot, at least in part because of the way they have been asked to receive. Handing down can only occur when the children spoken of actively accept what is being given. There is no transfer without such

20. St. Augustine, "Struggle against the Law of Sin," 10.34; 332.
21. St. Augustine, "Struggle against the Law of Sin," 10.34; 332.
22. St. Augustine, "Struggle against the Law of Sin," 10.34; 332.

receptivity. But, equally, the one who conveys needs to communicate what is to be accepted, precisely by getting across to the potential recipient why what is being given is valuable. That is, the delivery can only happen when what is conveyed is in a communicable form. Pieper observes that a tradition can only remain alive if its importance is not explained in terms of being traditional. As soon as a parent tells a child that the only reason something is to be done is because it is traditional, that tradition's death knell is already sounding. Thus Pieper insists that:

> "old truths," if they are really true [must] be kept really alive and present—for example and before anything else, by means of a living language; through creative rejuvenation and sloughing off of the old skin like a snake, so to speak; through a continual confrontation with the immediate present and above all with the future, which in the human realm is the truly real. When you do this, you will see clearly what a demanding business the act of tradition is.[23]

Tradition, then, carries with it all the strangeness involved when past, present, and future merge to bring about something new. Such action is only possible if something of the past is present in the artist or architect (in our case), who at the same time accurately assesses the goodness within as well as the needs of the surrounding culture, and then articulates a surprising embodiment of truth. What is thereby produced glimmers, like the body of the snake, its skin newly sloughed away, emerging as what has always been there underneath, but now more ready to find its way into the future. Certainly, a continual confrontation with what has yet to come is not easily realizable. Neither is it always possible to say what will ultimately survive to become a full member of a still living tradition.

In light of these observations, Augustine's definition loses any sense of being completely straightforward, that is, of being simply linear. The bearers and the receivers of tradition have a difficult task.

23. Josef Pieper, *Tradition: Concept and Claim*, trans. E. Christian Kopff (South Bend, IN: St. Augustine's Press, 2010), 15.

It is essentially that of translation, but not only in words. The truth content of tradition is to be lived and reflected upon and brings with it a vertical dimension. Any handing down relies on what T. S. Eliot refers to as the receiver's "great labour,"[24] which is to say that every receiver must give birth anew to the content of tradition if Tradition is to continue. When this link in the chain of Tradition is an artist, we are in the context of a necessary scandal.

Eliot: Depersonalization and the Great Labor of Tradition

That scandal, Eliot theorizes, relies upon the ability of the artist (in Eliot's case, the artist is primarily a poet) to find what is universally true through one's particular experience of the world. Augustine appealed to the heart of the philosopher-theologian to adequately respond to, represent, and live the truth; likewise, Eliot requires that the artist locate the way that his own pulse keeps time with the rhythmic beating of his age, as well as ages gone, so that past and present can remain alive into the future. For this to happen, what Benedict XVI has referred to as the "shock" of beauty must be ever on the horizon. In speaking of the Tradition of literature, specifically of poetry, Eliot is very much aware of the work of the poet who must labor both to know his Tradition and then speak it in his own way. This double task requires that the poet should not be so filled with a sense of self-importance that he thinks he owes nothing to Tradition. Equally, Eliot's poet needs to recognize that just because he comes after others in a historical sense, he has not superseded them. For Eliot, all works of Tradition, together with those who make them, comprise an order that depends upon and yet transcends time. The poet who enters and engages that order has a formidable task: he must remain reflective and truly himself, and simultaneously undergo a *depersonalization*, because what he must convey in his poem concerns not him alone. It is of universal human concern and so needs to manifest that communal dimension.

24. Eliot, "Tradition and the Individual Talent," 37.

In essence, Eliot's depersonalization is the corollary to Augustine's insistence on the impartiality of the one who receives and conveys truth. One might even question whether "depersonalization" is the best term for what Eliot is trying to express. After all, John Casey[25] has suggested that it is exactly Eliot's work within and with tradition that enables him to find the "self" so necessary to the work of the poet. It seems that what Eliot wants to suggest is not that the poet negates all that is particular to him, in the act of creation, but rather that the emotions that would separate him from the possibility of the poetic act need to be somewhat subsumed as he undertakes his task. This depersonalization is not to be understood as dehumanizing, but instead separating out what properly belongs in poetry, from what can only be his own.

Eliot's striking analogy, taken from the seemingly objective world of chemistry, describes what he means. The artist, Eliot muses, is like a

> bit of finely filiated platinum . . . introduced into a chamber containing oxygen and sulphur dioxide. . . . the analogy [is] that of the catalyst. When the two gases...are mixed in the presence of a filament of platinum, they form sulphurous acid.[26]

Eliot goes on to explain that without the presence of the platinum, nothing would happen. Inert gases would remain unchanged. The platinum enters the chamber and thereby brings about a change without itself being affected. The platinum is the mind of the poet, says Eliot. The poet can create because he does not insert too much of what is idiosyncratic or private into his work. He needs to articulate what is true of *every* human person. The better the poet can separate out his personal life from his art, the better his work will be and the more ability he has to contribute something to the Tradition. Eliot observes:

25. John Casey, "T. S. Eliot: Language, Sincerity, and Self," *Proceedings of the British Academy* 63 (1977): 95–125.

26. Casey, "T. S. Eliot," 37–39.

> one error . . . of eccentricity in poetry is to seek for new human emotions to express; and in this search for novelty in the wrong place it discovers the perverse. The business of the poet is not to find new emotions, but to use the ordinary ones and, in working them up into poetry, to express feelings which are not in actual emotions at all.[27]

The only actual emotions that the poet can know are his own, but these are not the ultimate source of the feelings that he represents. Instead, what he expresses comes from something deeper, his integration and participation within humanity. So, in presenting a truth about the human condition, the poet increasingly finds that what he writes is not only and certainly not most importantly about himself. Instead, he identifies something worthy of expression, and the resulting work asserts that what is personal is also not personal at all. The artist can only sincerely re-present the content of what he expresses when he realizes that what he says transcends him, and that it is for this reason that he can speak and be heard and understood by anyone else. In the case of the poet, this content is emotion. Part of the possibility of depersonalization comes from the artist's attitude to Tradition, for if he does not listen to those who have come before him, what he creates has no chance of being communicable to those seeking and living the content of Tradition. At the same time, though, Tradition cannot survive without the artist's work of development.

The difference between Eliot and Augustine is clear. Augustine is concerned with truths handed down from Christ. Eliot speaks of the truth of the human condition, specifically in the way that humans reflect upon and experience emotions. Both, however, consider Truth and Tradition similarly. Eliot, like Augustine, thinks of works from those of the past as impartial judges of anything that looks new in the Tradition. The parallel here is that just as the artist who is truly of his age and yet of the Tradition is doing something both old and new, Augustine the philosopher-theologian rearticulates and at the same time reorients the thoughts of those preceding him.

27. Casey, "T. S. Eliot," 42.

Traditional Space: A Model for Interpreting Artworks

Ratzinger's description of a community of worship, Augustine's of an interior law court where the judges are philosopher-theologians of the past, and Eliot's experimental chamber, when brought together, enable us to formulate a kind of model that helps to understand how Tradition works. Let us imagine that the artist, with his artwork, enters into a space where other artists, with their artworks, are already in conversation. To take some Eliot mentions, Homer, Shakespeare, and Dante are all there, each with his masterpieces and each quick to perceive something new, and yet recognizable, because it is true. A further statement from Eliot is instructive. "What happens," he describes,

> when a new work of art is created is something that happens simultaneously to all the works of art which preceded it. The existing monuments form an ideal order among themselves, which is modified by the introduction of the new (the really new) work of art among them. The existing order is complete before the new work arrives; for order to persist after the supervention of novelty, the whole existing order must be, if ever so slightly, altered; and so the relations, proportions, values of each work of art toward the whole are readjusted; and this is the conformity between the old and the new.[28]

So far, we have seen that the tenuous nature of introducing anything into an already existing tradition involves a complex relationship between past, present, and future. Simply stated, something of the tradition is both temporal (in the order of history) and timeless. For a new work of art to succeed in the tradition, it must convey something of what is true and thus eternal. What is most interesting, though, about the model we might work with here, for how works enter into and become *of* the tradition, is that each new work brings about an inner transformation, or reordering, within an ideal realm. This is no static realm of Platonic forms, but a vibrant and on-

28. Casey, "T. S. Eliot," 37.

going conversation, seemingly about what is substantially important concerning the commonly held concerns and aspirations of humankind. In this space of tradition, with all speaking together, the old does not have complete authority over the new. For, while in a way the new is judged by the old, if the new really is of the Tradition, then old and new become measures of each other. One might think here of Ratzinger's observation that Christian worship does not obliterate that of the Jews but reorients it, and with this orientation comes a whole new way of imagining sacred spaces.

The new, Eliot describes, is not an improvement of the Tradition, but instead a "development," a "refinement," and certainly a "complication"[29] within the Tradition. Another way of bringing these terms together is by illustrating that all of them can be applied to Augustine's work in refuting heresies; this again tells us something of the picture of truth, or reality, with which we are dealing. Augustine develops the arguments of those who have come before him, refining them to meet the philosophical and theological needs of his own time. But he also introduces a complication in that he wants to discover in previous thinkers particular themes and arguments, introduced previously in a different context, to support his claims. Only then can Augustine's writings become a measure of those that precede him: inasmuch as a work makes assertions coherent and consistent with others of the Tradition, it measures up. At the same time, those previous appraise Augustine: only when he has really listened to, understood, lived, and properly communicated, in his own way, what they have said, has he proved himself a worthy child and also forebear of Tradition.

For now, then, we have a working model of Tradition—a kind of scaffold upon which to build some affirmations for ecclesiastical architecture. We find that Tradition involves handing down of universal truths capable of various expressions. Those of the Tradition are characterized by their carefulness for, knowledge of, and reflection

29. Casey, "T. S. Eliot," 38.

upon what precedes them, but they are unafraid to speak in new ways of the content of the Tradition. Finally, to be of the Tradition is to be of an order in which one is both judged and a judge. This judgment is impartial—although it might also be mistaken.

Tradition and Ecclesiastical Architecture: Tertullian Revisited

What implications does this model of organic development have for Roman Catholic church architecture? We might, for a moment, again think of Ratzinger, who states in his *Introduction to Christianity* that "The Christian position ... is put emphatically by Tertullian when he says with splendid boldness: 'Christ called himself truth, not custom.'"[30] This, Ratzinger reflects, is:

> the struggle of the early Church, and the abiding task with which the Christian faith is confronted if it is to remain itself ... Christianity ... put itself resolutely on the side of truth and turned its back on a conception of religion satisfied with mere outward ceremonial which in the end can be interpreted to mean anything one fancies.[31]

In his own way, Ratzinger is speaking of the great labor carried out both by Augustine and by Eliot, of knowing the Tradition so as to speak it anew. The currency that is called for will always be demanding. If it is truly novel, then perforce it will seem strange and may not at first be recognized as of the Tradition. By the same token, if one is too intent upon accepting whatever is presented *because* it is new, one runs the risk of accepting what is sheer nonsense for a revelatory moment within the tradition. Even so, our model suggests strongly that such problems are good to have—for the other option is the stagnation that can set in with traditionalism. Traditionalists, far from being bearers of Tradition, make us incapable of speaking in our own voices. Without the daring artist, we run the risk of arguing like a traditionalist revivalist who claims that the absence of anything Gothic means the

30. Ratzinger, *Introduction to Christianity*.

31. Ratzinger, *Introduction to Christianity*.

absence of a church. Richard Kieckhefer, critic of this stance, sums it up pithily: "No gargoyles, no churches."[32] To say that one or several peripheral architectural elements are the essence of Tradition is dangerous. For when artists dare not venture into new expressions of truth, none of us can be at home in our churches, speaking with our forebears as the Jews in their synagogues can sing with angels.

All the foregoing has constituted an argument for the necessity of scandal to the tradition of Roman Catholic church architecture. I now briefly illustrate my point by examining aspects of two cases of style in architecture: the Gothic and the Baroque. I concentrate on two examples of these styles: the Abbey Church of St. Denis for the Gothic and St. Peter's Basilica and square for the Baroque. My main point here is to show that these styles were shocking when they first appeared, that they retain some of this startling nature if we allow ourselves to be receivers of the truths they embody, and finally that what was once a scandal has become incorporated into the canons of our Tradition. Both examples, I argue, can now act as judges or measures of other styles that might yet still come, which at the same time means that they should not stifle genuine developments in sacred architecture.

I speak of the Abbey Church of St. Denis because of its position as reputedly the parent of the Gothic style. This church is also intriguing in that Abbot Suger, who arranged for its renovation and thus the beginnings of what we now associate with the Gothic, has done us the singular favor of reflecting upon the difficulties of his own great labor. Suger's sanctuary was transformative, and art historian Otto Von Simson claims with some justification that in particular Suger's stained-glass windows within it began the Gothic style.[33] Abbot Suger wrote several works outlining why he chose to renovate a much revered church, and how he did so, and his writings are punctuated with an obvious sense of gratitude for the graces received in his work

32. Richard Kieckhefer, *Theology in Stone: Church Architecture from Byzantium to Berkeley* (Oxford: Oxford University Press, 2004), 267.

33. Otto Von Simson, *The Gothic Cathedral: Origins of Gothic Architecture and the Medieval Concept of Order* (Princeton, NJ: Princeton University Press, 1988), 100.

as well as astonishment at the beauty of what he has facilitated. He proves to be of the Tradition because he brings about an expression of Truth already contained within the thought and buildings of those who precede him. He acknowledges what he receives, reflects upon it, and at the same time brings about something new. The result challenged a view prevalent at the time, particularly within the thought of Bernard of Clairvaux, that sacred art and architecture should not be too ornate or distracting. Excess could only lead believers away from God, whereas for Suger it was precisely through the overwhelming nature of the beauty that his architecture conveyed that the glory of God could be in any way imitated or approximated. Erwin Panofsky observes that in his account of rebuilding the church,

> Time and time again Suger interrupts his enthusiastic descriptions of gleaming gold and precious jewels to counter the attacks of an imaginary opponent who is in fact not imaginary at all but identifical with [St. Bernard] who had written: "But we who, for the sake of Christ, have deemed as dung whatever shines with beauty, enchants the ear, delights through fragrance, flatters the taste, pleases the touch—whose devotion, I ask, do we intend to incite by means of these very things."[34]

Bernard and others like him at the time may have found the beginning of the Gothic excessive, but by now the Gothic has lost so much of its shock value that it has become a kind of standard for those who want a church to look as much as possible like a church. The Gothic is in that jury room, judging what our artists and architects might make today. The question remains as to what may still enter that room and shift, or stir, its order.

One of the details most helpful in conveying Suger's role within the Tradition of church architecture is that when he began his reconstruction of the dilapidated church in his care, he needed to pull apart the walls of the nave. The church in its Carolingian form, tra-

34. Erwin Panofsky, "Introduction," in *Abbot Suger on the Abbey Church of St.-Denis and Its Art Treasures*, ed. and trans. Erwin Panofsky (Princeton, NJ: Princeton University Press, 1979), 15.

dition said, had been blessed by Christ himself, and Suger makes note of this in passing.[35] Suger took care to preserve as much of the material of those original walls as possible, but at the same time he performed an act of transformation by using the same to build up higher and further apart.[36] Suger's vision for what he was facilitating is even more intriguing given that his inspiration came from at least one church that he had never seen. Informed by Christian Neoplatonic theories of light and of grace, he listened to descriptions of pilgrims returned from Jerusalem, of the Byzantine church of Hagia Sophia.[37] So strong was his sense that something new could emerge in what are now the outskirts of Paris that he challenged Bernard of Clairvaux's claims for austerity in church architecture and decoration, by choosing beauty that would transport those who entered into his new space. He wanted to excel in this grand enterprise, fueled by the conviction that art and architecture should seem to resemble the beauty of heaven as much as possible. His Abbey Church should spark the imaginations of those who entered it, so that they could become increasingly aware of the interrelationships between our world and what lies beyond, as well as between the people of God on earth and the heavenly city above. The abbot remained ever concerned that his church be at least on a par with those churches mentioned, which in all their luster he had personally known only by hearsay but that formed part of an ideal order to which he aspired.

The second illustration of a scandalous style is the Baroque, a form of ecclesiastical architecture that embodies the Roman Catholic response of the Council of Trent to the Protestant Reformation.

35. "The noble church consecrated by the Hand Divine." Panofsky, "Introduction," 45.

36. "We tore down a certain addition asserted to have been made by Charlemagne on a very honorable occasion . . . and we set our hand to this part. As is evident we exerted ourselves incessantly with the enlargement of the body of the church as well as with the trebling of the entrance and the doors, and with the erection of high and noble towers." Panofsky, "Introduction," 45.

37. Panofsky, "Introduction," 65.

The Baroque evokes and embraces the senses in a full-bodied form. Almost garish in its gold and marble, deliberately tricking the senses, playing with perception and one's sense of space, the Baroque also traps and transforms as much light as possible, making everything radiate. It can all feel a bit too much, but this seems to be the point. Robert Harbison has recently written of the Baroque as "disruptive," as "annoying [to] purists" because its buildings "strive after the impossible, aiming to suggest to viewers that they are watching an unfolding process rather than a fixed and finished composition."[38] Perspectives keep changing in a Baroque space, so that everything has several aspects, challenging us to broaden our scope of meaning. At once lighthearted and serious, I suggest that the Baroque asks us to play with possibilities and impossibilities alike, to see truth from a multiplicity of different angles. It challenges us to stretch ourselves into and then beyond the horizon that it offers, just as Michelangelo's *Last Judgment* challenges us to reflect profoundly upon realities known yet not entirely seen. Its disruption, in its own time, was a revelatory shock, only possible because of the initial scandal that Christianity undertakes to live and to make known.

An exterior Baroque space, this time of Bernini's Piazza of St. Peter's, rather than the basilica itself, facilitates an appreciation of how the baroque can transform in various ways, thereby conveying something of its horizon of vision. Originally, there was no grand causeway to this square. Instead, the visitor would travel through a jumble of medieval streets and then be surprised by columns and an open space. "Once inside," Harbison describes, "you watch the space expand around you, its 'walls' individualized by the columns into something like a promenading throng."[39] Dominating the square is the tremendous obelisk, possibly dating from the time of Moses and probably

38. Robert Harbison, "The Case for Disruption," chap. 1 in *Reflections on Baroque* (Chicago: University of Chicago Press, 2003), 1.

39. Harbison, "Case for Disruption," 2. This theme of disruption could be considered together with Kingwell's discussion of the importance of rupture to democracy, in chapter 7 of this volume.

viewed by St. Peter as he died crucified on a cross, like Christ, but upside down. Baroque architecture, exterior and interior, is theatrical, complete with its own smoke and mirrors, appropriate to a stage production. Within a Baroque church, the altar is still center stage. Tricks of the eye and of proportion have the participant in liturgy enter into a domain that is so extraordinary as to transport, to elevate, and at the same time to illuminate. Such devices might have been too much even for someone like Suger, and I have heard many a tourist complain that the interior of St. Peter's basilica is excessive. Such bombardment of the senses in any event calls upon us to assess the Tradition and the story that it continues to convey of what is now and what lies beyond.

New Truths in Style

Above, I quoted T. S. Eliot as saying that "for order to persist after the supervention of novelty, the whole existing order must be, if ever so slightly, altered and so the relations, proportions, values of each work of art toward the whole are readjusted; and this is the conformity between the old and the new."[40] *Supervention* is an appropriate key, or note, on which to end this exploration of the complexities of Tradition. A supervention comes after something that precedes it, as a consequence and at the same time as a contrast to its forebear. This reminds that the Tradition relies upon a series of readjustments that only manage conformity by maintaining a delicate balance. The whole process or development of Tradition relies upon the ability, as Augustine points out, to know, with that very human knowledge that includes the heart, what it means to live in relationship to truth, and then to convey that understanding to others who will live and hand over in turn. If the artists and architects involved in building churches are to realize this, then they must remain aware of Ratzinger's warning, itself a restatement of Tertullian's, that to be Christian is to live in accord with Truth before Custom. Eliot's considerations provide a starting point from which to engage further the intricacies involved in

40. Casey, "T. S. Eliot," 42.

judging whether something is of the Tradition. All these thinkers are more afraid of stagnation within the tradition than they are of something entirely new emerging, no doubt because if something really is traditional, then there is actually no risk of its being completely novel. Truth does not change, but it can reveal itself differently, so as to allow for various expressions of its inner core. Any new work in the tradition will instead prove to be a true child of the parents of many generations before it, and bring with it the hope of life for ages to come.

The natural question now is what style might come next in ecclesiastical architecture, to shock and perhaps dismay. With this question comes a problem, which is that, when dealing with an ideal order, one can often become confused by instances that *seem* like the Tradition but do not quite conform. Conformity here is a double problem, for it first demands that something new in the tradition not look exactly like what has come before; we are not dealing with a simple relationship of identity. Second, the new member of a tradition cannot be so different that it is not in the family at all. Our new Gothic or new Baroque will depend upon artists and architects who understand and can convey what they have received as well as what their ages, and the future, require. There have doubtless been attempts at new styles of church architecture that might only be explained by a denial, or else misinterpretation, of Tradition. Possibly there exist, too, styles that are of the Tradition but have not quite gone through the slow and cautious probing and so have not been acknowledged as of the ideal order. Like T. S. Eliot's poem "The Wasteland," a child of the tradition must be recognizable for all its novelty. This capacity to be discovered stems not from some kind of abstract theory or historical chain of events. In poetry, it derives from the universal human condition. Ecclesiastical architecture adds another dimension, as it develops along the contours, present as they are in every age but in a variety of styles, of what it means to be humans in conversation with each other, because in presence of God.

PART II

LIVING THE CATHOLIC TRADITION

Morality

MOST REVEREND ANTHONY FISHER

4 • CATHOLIC MORAL TRADITION

The Idea of a Sacred Moral Tradition

Secrets of a Vatican Chapel

Like a Dan Brown novel, let's begin in a "secret" Vatican chapel and try to decode its hidden meaning. It's the only survivor of several chapels painted in the 1440s by the Dominican Blessed, Fra Angelico, for Old St Peter's and the renewed Vatican Palace. Though close to the Capella Sistina and the Stanze di Raffaello, most tourists miss it; all too often, it is closed when they arrive. It is said to have survived various Vatican renovations only because the key was lost for two centuries and it was forgotten. No self-respecting detective novelist would believe that excuse.

Angelico was retained for the Vatican upgrade by Popes Eugene IV and Nicholas V. The latter was founder of the Vatican library and wanted a chapel dedicated to St. Lawrence, patron saint of booklovers, librarians, and archivists. The series opens during the persecution under Valerian. Pope St. Sextus II, attended by the clergy of Rome, ordains Lawrence as deacon. Angelico used Nicholas's portrait for Sextus, which set a precedent for such flattery elsewhere in the Vatican. The pope hands over or, in ecclesiastical usage, *traditions* the chalice, declaring: "Behold whose ministry is handed on (*traditor*) to you; therefore I admonish you to comport yourself that you may please God."

In the next scene, in an act of more secular traditioning, Sextus hands over to Lawrence all the treasure of the Roman Church. According to the *Golden Legend*, the deacon sold the treasure and distributed the proceeds to the poor so that, when Valerian's troops came to plunder the treasury, Lawrence could point to the poor and say, "There is the treasure of the Church." He is also shown preaching to his interrogators and converting his jailer, who became St. Hippolytus of Rome, putative author of the treatise *The Apostolic Tradition*. The series ends with Lawrence being barbecued and famously taunting his executioners, "You can turn me over as I'm cooked now on this side."

There is much going on in this pictorial narrative, and a parallel cycle on the life of St. Stephen with St. Peter and the Apostles is on the walls immediately above the Lawrence cycle. On the ceiling, Angelico painted the four Evangelists. Then, coming down from them, the "doctors," or greatest theologian-saints of the Church, including Jerome, Ambrose, Augustine, Chrysostom, and Gregory. Rather daringly, he also included Fra Thomas Aquinas of his order, who had not yet been canonized: the special pleading would not have been lost on the pope. Aquinas holds open his *Summa contra Gentiles* with its opening verse from Proverbs: "My mouth proclaims the truth, wickedness is hateful to my lips."[1]

Beneath the Scriptures, the apostolic generation, and the great voices of the Tradition are the popes, bishops, and clergy. As Angelico understood and painted, those entrusted with speaking the tradition must first be hearers of it; they do not receive revelation direct from God but mediated by the community of believers and the succession of teachers that preceded them. There will be development, as we see in the progress of vesture and architecture between the Stephen cycle and the Lawrence cycle. Thus the chapel is *a painted lesson in Sacred Tradition*: the Word of God above all, the apostolic generation next, the

1. Prov 8:7.

Fathers after that as the most reliable interpreters, beneath them the popes and clergy staunchly guarding and explaining the tradition, and finally the faithful, as the ultimate recipients and further transmitters of that tradition by their active witness. *Truth* it is that must be uttered and heard, believed and lived. In the words of the Second Vatican Council's *Constitution on Divine Revelation* (*Dei Verbum*):

> The teaching office is not above the word of God, but serves it, teaching only what has been handed on, listening to it devoutly, guarding it scrupulously and explaining it faithfully in accord with a divine commission and, with the help of the Holy Spirit, it draws from this one deposit of faith everything which it presents for belief as divinely revealed.[2]

In this chapter, I explore this idea of a sacred moral tradition, that is, the truth(s) about morality handed down within the Catholic faith tradition and received, believed, lived, and transmitted to others. I first trace the Catholic idea of "Sacred" or capital-T Tradition and its application in the moral sphere; the contemporary allergy to tradition, its effects and potential remedies; and some recent philosophical reflections on the idea of tradition that might enrich Catholic moral theology. I then consider the common view that tradition is inherently opposed to new situations, insights, and thus development, using slavery as a test case, and conclude with some thoughts on what tradition means for moral theology.

"The Blessed Tradition" in Premodernity

"What I received from the Lord I also handed over to you: that on the night He was handed over the Lord Jesus took bread."[3] So Paul begins his teaching on the Eucharist that proved so momentous for subsequent Christian thinking, not only on the Eucharist but on tradition and authority in teaching. Heir, though not uncritically so, to

2. Vatican Council II, *Dei Verbum: Constitution on Divine Revelation* (1965), 10.

3. 1 Cor 11:23*ff*.

the Jewish Law[4] and traditions,[5] and to Greco-Roman wisdom and customs,[6] already Christianity was beginning its own process of *paradidōmi* (handing over, traditioning). The story of the things that God had said and done in Jesus Christ was conveyed by the apostolic generation to those who "had not seen firsthand and yet believed."[7]

4. Paul was heir to the Law and the Prophets, and after his conversion, he insisted on his continuing Jewishness: "Are they Hebrews? So am I. Are they Israelites? So am I. Are they descendants of Abraham? So am I" (2 Cor 11:22). Reception of "the traditions of the fathers" was crucial to Israel's unity and sense of identity. And so was passing on that tradition: they taught it diligently to their children and spoke of it day and night (cf. Dt 6:4–9). Paul explores the continuities and discontinuities with Israel in many places, e.g., 1 Cor 7; Rom 2, 3, 9, and 15:8–9; Gal 2, 5:2–12, and 6:12–6; Phil 3:2–10. On the question of how Scripture and Tradition function in Paul's ethics, see James Dunn, *The Theology of Paul the Apostle* (Edinburgh: T&T Clark, 1998); Victor Furnish, *The Moral Teaching of Paul: Selected Issues*, 3rd ed. (Nashville, TN: Abingdon Press, 2009); R. B. Hays, *The Moral Vision of the New Testament: A Contemporary Introduction to New Testament Ethics* (Edinburgh: T&T Clark, 1997); Brian Rosner, "Paul's Ethics," in *Cambridge Companion to St Paul* (Cambridge: Cambridge University Press, 2003), 212–23; J. P. Sampley, *Walking between the Times: Paul's Moral Reasoning* (Minneapolis: Fortress, 1991); Alan Segal, "Paul's Jewish Presuppositions," in *Cambridge Companion to St Paul*, 159–72.

5. Matthew Levering discusses the ambivalence of early Christianity to "tradition" in "Catholic Tradition: Invented or Received?," chap. 1, in this volume. Already in his lifetime, Jesus's disciples were accused of breaking with "the tradition (*paradosis*) of the elders" (Mk 7:1–23, *et par*), to which Jesus responded by distinguishing divine law from human custom, warning against too readily claiming the authority of the former for the latter and pointing out how human traditions can subvert divine ordinances. Various glimpses of the debate in the early Church over the continuing force of Jewish law and tradition are given in Acts (e.g., chaps. 10, 11, and 15). Though the early Church vacated large parts of the Torah, its Jewish heritage was nonetheless mined for moral teaching (e.g., 1 Cor 9:9–10; Gal 4:30), the Decalogue was presumed to be of perennial import and Scripture functioned as an overarching proleptic vision of God's plan.

6. Examples of Paul quoting or presuming Greco-Roman philosophy and customs include among others: Acts 17:24–29; Rm 7:22–23, 12:4; 1 Cor 9:24, 13:12, 15:33; Ti 1:12; 2 Tm 4:6. But Paul also contrasts human traditions and philosophies with divine wisdom (e.g., 1 Thes 2:13; Col 2:8). The Christ event is something "altogether new" and breaks with both Jewish Law and Greco-Roman philosophy; it was "first person testimony" he offered, not somebody else's Gospel (e.g., Gal 1:11–16).

7. Jn 20:29.

The Gospels were offered as accounts of what eyewitnesses saw and evangelists handed over.[8] The Christian was one who received this "deposit" of teachings and its power.[9] Paul was especially clear that only this Gospel would save and that Christians must receive it with humility, guard it, and hold fast to it.[10] And it already included a moral content that Christians lived and to which they thus gave witness.[11]

The notion of the "blessed" Tradition, "handed down from the apostles," was prominent in the patristic period. It became clear that to be an incarnational religion, a *historical* and not merely mythologi-

8. The Gospel of Luke begins with the author explaining that he is compiling a narrative of the things that were *delivered* to him by "eyewitnesses and ministers of the Word" and that he in turn passes on to "the most excellent Theophilus" (Lk 1:1–4). In the Gospel of Matthew, Jesus "hands over" to those who are his own what he has received from the Father (Mt 11:27).

9. In his second volume, Luke identifies Christians as those who *receive* the word of God from the Apostles, believe it, and are baptized or confirmed in it (Acts 2:41, 8:14–17, 11:1, 17:11). In the Gospel of John, some *receive* the Word of God (or the name, light, grace, or truth of Christ), while others do not, but to reject Jesus's word is to renounce eternal life (e.g., Jn 1:11–18, 17:9; cf. 1 Jn 12:24–52). In Colossians, the Christians are told to eschew merely human traditions, but to receive the Christian proclamation and way of life (Col 2:6–8).

10. Thus Paul repeatedly calls his communities to stand fast to what they have received from him, and he warns them against receiving any contrary teaching (e.g., 1 Cor 15:1–4; 2 Cor 11:1–4; Gal 1:9; Col 2:8). He praises the brethren in Thessaloniki, e.g., for so readily receiving, clinging to, and in turn "sounding forth" the word of God (1 Thes 1:5–8, 2:15) and instructs them to shun those whose conduct does not accord with "the tradition received from us" (2 Thes 3). He tells those at Philippi: "What you have learned and received and heard and seen in me, do; and the God of peace will be with you" (Phil 4:9). And he commands young Timothy to entrust to faithful men what he has heard so that they will pass it on to others (2 Tm 2:2). Jude likewise appeals to his readers "to contend for the faith which was once for all delivered to the saints" (Jude 3). The writer to the Hebrews describes those who have fallen away from the word they formerly received (Heb 4:6) and the angel of the Apocalypse recalls the Church in Sardis to "remember what you received and heard: keep that and repent" of any deviation (Rev 3:3; cf. 2 Pt 2:21).

11. E.g., in the teaching about what parts of the Old Law would still apply. When Paul uses the language of traditioning with the Corinthians (1 Cor 11:23*ff.*), he is not merely retelling the Institution narrative: he is proposing eucharistic mores and criticizing partaking of the Eucharist unworthily.

cal faith, is to insist that something important really did happen, that it can be reliably known, and that there is a reliable source for knowing it.[12] Despite heated debates over orthodoxy, "Sacred Tradition" in this period was rich and creative and far from closed or nostalgic.[13]

The great medieval theologians practiced their science by thinking in symbiosis with all Tradition—philosophical, scriptural, dogmatic, liturgical—with an attitude of constant hearing or receptivi-

12. In the postapostolic and patristic periods, the notion of received tradition played a crucial role as Christians contended with new philosophical currents, heated controversies, and changing political and social circumstances. Already around 120 AD, Papias of Hierapolis insisted that the "received sayings of the Apostles," and the stories of Christ and the apostolic generation preserved with them, were authoritative (Fragment in Eusebius, *Church History* III, 39). Later in that century, St. Eusebius of Caesarea (*Church History* IV, 21) and St. Irenaeus (*Against Heresies* I, 10.2; III, 3:1–2) both sought to demonstrate that what they taught they had received from a bishop, who had received it from another who had received it from the Apostles; they called this "the apostolic tradition." Also in the second century, Clement of Alexandria (*Miscellanies* I, 1) spoke of "the blessed tradition . . . derived directly from the holy apostles." In the third century, Origen (*Fundamental Doctrines* I, 2) asked how else we who are at such a remove from the days of Christ can hope to know, with any confidence, what Christ did and said, except that we have the apostolic tradition. Thus he could declare that "That alone is to be believed as the truth which is in no way at variance with ecclesiastical and apostolic tradition." Belief that the Incarnation, Passion, and Resurrection of Christ actually took place—and all that follows—is at stake, he said, and apostolic tradition is the key to knowing what really took place and what it meant. So too St. Cyprian of Carthage (*Letters* 75:3), St. Athanasius (*Festal Letters* 2:7 and 29), St. Basil the Great (*On the Holy Spirit* 27:66), St. Augustine of Hippo (*On Baptism—Against the Donatists* V, 23), and St. John Chrysostom (*Homilies on 2Th*) after him.

13. David Yeago, "Modern but Not liberal," *First Things* 224 (June/July 2012): 25–30, at 27, points out that classical theology was marked by "a certain optimistic boldness . . . Alien cultures, threatening bodies of thought, and historical cataclysms only provided new opportunities to discover once again [the treasures in Christ and the Christian tradition up to that point] . . . This meant that when Roman civilization collapsed or when the dangerously 'secular' thought of Aristotle burst in on the mediaeval world, an Augustine or an Aquinas was able to respond without panic, confident that no contingencies, however disturbing, could overwhelm the interpretative potential" of Christian belief. Yeago's Lutheranism makes him cautious about speaking of Tradition here but his argument clearly supports it. See also Thomas White's response in the same journal: "Love's Greater Freedom," *First Things* 224 (June/July 2012): 35–37.

ty.[14] Even that which could be known "naturally," by people of other religions or none, was said to be confirmed, clarified, and applied best within what St. Thomas Aquinas called "the family tradition of the Apostles."[15] It has been argued that the entire *Summa* is intended as a guide to moral formation within a Christian community, not a series of arguments to be used apologetically with outsiders.[16] Tradition plays a crucial role in Aquinas's moral vision, mediating customs that are often more immediately useful than moral theories or principles,[17] proposing various virtues, and assisting in their cultivation. Natural reason (including the natural moral law) and sacred tradition (including revealed morality) need one another: *ratio* inter-

14. Giles Emery, OP, *Trinity in Aquinas* (Ave Maria, FL: Sapientia Press, 2006), xxiii; cf. 83. Likewise, Jean-Pierre Torrell, OP, *Saint Thomas Aquinas*, vol. 2, *Spiritual Master*, trans. R. Royal (Washington, DC: Catholic University of America Press, 2003), 2, says that for Aquinas, *Sacra doctrina* includes "every activity through which Christian truth comes to us."

15. When exploring the Catholic doctrine of the sacraments, Aquinas talks of those things "habet tamen ea Ecclesia ex familiari Apostolorum traditione" (*ST* III, q. 25, a. 3, ad 4; q. 64, a. 2, ad 1; q. 72, a. 4, ad 1). This family tradition is recorded in the Scriptures, interpreted most reliably by the Fathers and carried forward by magisterial decrees, liturgies, sainted lives, and approved authors.

16. Mark Jordan, *Rewritten Theology: Aquinas after His Readers* (Oxford: Blackwell, 2006), at 52, argues that the entire *Summa* was written for the *Secunda Pars* (the moral section) and that the *Secunda Pars* was written as a text to assist a community of moral formation, not for a public debate by people of various backgrounds, religious beliefs, and mores. It is only because his text is so rich and persuasive that people have sought to take some of his arguments into "the public square." But the natural place for reading these texts, as indeed for the Scriptures, is in the moral community—the family—of the faithful.

17. Aquinas notes that many human laws are supported as much by custom and usage (*consuetudo*) as by reason (*ratio*) and that it is often best to follow a human tradition against the counsel of pure reason because of the "greater reason" that is served by preserving continuity and community (*ST* I-II, q. 97, a. 2). In due course, a tradition may become positively burdensome or die out by desuetude. The essence of what that tradition sought to preserve can be threatened by being overgrown with concrete forms that would kill the tree underneath if allowed to continue unchallenged. See Josef Pieper, *Überlieferung: Begriff und Anspruch* (Munich: Kösel, 1970); English translation by E. C. Kopff, *Tradition: Concept and Claim* (South Bend, IN: St. Augustine's Press, 2010), 40–41.

rogates and evaluates *auctoritas*, but it accepts and builds on Sacred Tradition.[18] Aquinas challenges his readers to balance attention and innovation "by practice of active inheritance."[19]

Sacred Tradition in Modernity

In the nineteenth and twentieth centuries, John Henry Newman and Yves Congar wrote the classic treatments of the idea of tradition in response to modernity's doubts about it. For both of them, Scripture and Tradition constitute the single source of the continuing life and thought of the Church under the guidance of the Holy Spirit. Newman identified many developments in the doctrine of the Church that corroborated and perfected rather than undermined or reversed the body of the thought from which they proceeded.[20] Development of doctrine, he thought, was rather like the way a child's beliefs mature, or a good poem is found to contain far more than its author appreciated, or a plant unpacks what is already in the seed, or the way

18. Josef Pieper, Über den Begriff der Tradition (Cologne: Opladen, 1958), 24*ff.*; *Guide to Thomas Aquinas* (San Francisco: Ignatius Press, 1991), 51, notes that Aquinas never cited "traditional" sources, as if their names or age gave their arguments extra gravity. He did explore and cite the Tradition—what has been handed down—but not because of an antiquarian interest or an overblown reverence for what was old: his interest in the Tradition was on the basis that it ultimately derived from the Word of God.

19. Jordan, *Rewritten Theology*, 194, rails against Thomisms that are so often either "fantastic mimesis" or else "the manufacture of a police badge to be pinned on the current uniform." For a more optimistic view of the various Thomisms, see Roman Cessario, OP, *A Short History of Thomism* (Washington, DC: Catholic University of America Press, 2003); Fergus Kerr, OP, *After Aquinas: Versions of Thomism* (London: Blackwell, 2002). Also important here is Alasdair MacIntyre, "Aquinas and the Rationality of Tradition," in *Three Rival Versions of Moral Enquiry: Encyclopaedia, Genealogy and Tradition* (London: Duckworth, 1990), chap. 6.

20. John Henry Newman, *An Essay on the Development of Christian Doctrine* (1845, revised 1878; most recently republished by Assumption Press, 2013). See also Newman's *Apologia pro vita sua* (1864; most recently republished by CreateSpace Independent Publishing Platform, 2013). The development of Christological and Trinitarian doctrines in the face of controversy were, Newman thought, particularly apposite examples.

life and identity are passed between generations. So, the Church's doctrine of today is in an important sense the same yet in another sense, not literally the same as the Church's doctrine of yesterday and in both ways faithful to her Founder.

In *La Tradition et la vie de l'Église*, Congar, building on Newman, characterized capital "T" Tradition as the soul or life force of the Church.[21] This "soul" is generally recognized in the tension between, on the one hand, conserving the deposit of faith laid down once and for all and, on the other hand, addressing present concerns with the help of contemporary insights and in contemporary language.[22] Sacred Tradition is always found concretized in the body of ideas, formulas, and practices—lowercase "t" traditions—that are handed down. They are for the Church what language is for a national culture—and, for a Frenchman like Congar, national language is a serious matter. Traditions, like language, are the bearers of spirit and identity.[23] "Real reform is an appeal made by a shallower tradition to a more profound one; it is a return to the principle itself whose recent expression or realisation is alone questioned or judged obsolete."[24]

21. Yves Congar, OP, *La Tradition et la vie de l'Église*, 2nd ed. (Paris: Éditions du Cerf, 1984); English translation by A. Woodrow, *The Meaning of Tradition* (San Francisco: Ignatius Press, 2004), 157: tradition is something "ever fresh and alive; using its inherited riches, it answers the unexpected questions of today. It advances through history toward its final consummation, its development coinciding with that of believing and Christian humanity itself. It is borne by living men who succeed one another, and at the same time it is borne within them by a subject who transcends them: the Holy Spirit, the principle of communion." See also Yves Congar, OP, *La Tradition et les traditions*, vol. 1, *Essai historique* (Paris: Fayard, 1960); and vol. 2, *Essai théologique* (Paris: Fayard, 1963); English translation by Michael Noseby and Thomas Rainborough *Tradition and Traditions* (London: Burns and Oates, 1966).

22. Congar, *Meaning of Tradition*, 159: tradition is both changeless and up-to-date, conforming with what has been received and yet always dynamic and relevant. "Tradition is equally continuity and progress, conservation and development." Its opposites then are two: a *traditionalism* that would freeze tradition at some point and isolate it from new ideas, and an *anti-traditionalism* that abandons the deposit of faith because of dissatisfaction with some traditions or past or recent expressions of the Tradition.

23. Congar, *Meaning of Tradition*, 157–58.

24. Congar, *Meaning of Tradition*, 159.

Only the Holy Spirit can guarantee the authenticity of the Tradition handed down or of any extension or progress of it.[25]

Newman's and Congar's idea of tradition as the work of the Holy Spirit was taken up by the Second Vatican Council in *Dei Verbum*. Here, the Sacred, Apostolic, or Living Tradition *is* the Church, in her teaching, life, and worship, perpetuating and transmitting her very substance, as a "mirror" to see the God from whom she has received all.[26] The Spirit of Truth "pours out" the Tradition in the life and practice of the Church, making it key to interpreting the Scriptures and guiding those entrusted with the teaching office of the Church.[27]

Joseph Ratzinger, later Pope Benedict XVI, was one of the drafters of *Dei Verbum*. He described the Church as "the seat of Tradition," purifying human traditions of the damage of sin by proposing the "one saving Tradition . . . of Jesus, who lives his life from the Father, who receives himself from the Father and continually gives himself back to the Father."[28] The Blessed Trinity is three persons *tradition-*

25. Thus Congar developed a rich pneumatology to underpin his theology of revelation, ecclesiology, and tradition, and arguably there is much work still to be done on situating moral traditioning within a theology of the Holy Spirit and of providence. See *Je crois en l'Esprit Saint*, 2nd ed. (Paris: Cerf, 1997); English translation by David Smith, *I Believe in The Holy Spirit*, 3 vols. (New York: Crossroad, 1997). On Congar's pneumatology, see Elizabeth Groppe, *Yves Congar's Theology of the Holy Spirit* (Oxford: Oxford University Press, 2004).

26. Vatican II, *Dei Verbum* 7–10, talks of the "Sacred Tradition" (*Sacra Traditio*), the "Apostolic Tradition" (*ab Apostolis Traditio*), the "living Tradition" (*Traditionis vivificam*), that "which has been handed down from the Apostles" (*traditum, verborum traditorum, doctrina Apostolorum*), "that which has been received and firmly held to" ("ita ut in tradita fide tenenda, exercenda profitendaque"), including "the traditions learned either by word of mouth or by letter" ("traditiones quas sive per sermonem sive per epistulam didicerint").

27. Vatican II, *Dei Verbum* 10: "It is clear, therefore, that Sacred Tradition, Sacred Scripture and the Magisterium of the Church, in accord with God's most wise design, are so linked and joined together that one cannot stand without the others, and that all together and each in its own way under the action of the one Holy Spirit contribute effectively to the salvation of souls."

28. Joseph Ratzinger, *Theologische Prinzipienlehre* (Munich: Erich Wewel Verlag,

ing, giving, and receiving their substance from each other, and so the Church is at her most Trinitarian when she does so also. The Sacred Tradition is thus the "whole, ever up-to-date reality of Jesus' gift" and the "transmission of the goods of salvation which, through the power of the Spirit makes the Christian community the permanent actualization of the original communion" of the People of God.[29]

Tradition Allergy

In the early days of his pontificate, Pope Francis was described by the BBC as "The Pope who is allergic to papal tradition." The proof was that he wore black shoes and a simple white habit and did not sit in a golden throne. Those more expert in ecclesiastical haberdashery and furnishing than I assure me that his wardrobe choices are hardly avant-garde: John XXIII, who enjoyed all the pomp he could get, added gold buckles to his shoes; Paul VI removed the buckles but stuck to red; John Paul II switched from red to brown; Benedict XVI returned to red; and now Francis is wearing black. Some revolution that! As for the papal sit-upon, it looks exactly the same to me. And that simple white habit—what can I, a Dominican, say? Ever since Blessed Innocent V and St Pius V decided to keep wearing their white Dominican habits as pope, it has stuck, and so even Jesuits with Franciscan names wear modified Dominican habits. What is interesting to me here is how the tradition of the papacy is reduced, even by the BBC,

---

1982); English translation by M. F. McCarthy, *Principles of Catholic Theology: Building Stones for a Fundamental Theology* (San Francisco: Ignatius Press, 1987), 93, on which see Tracey Rowland, *Ratzinger's Faith: The Theology of Pope Benedict XVI* (Oxford: Oxford University Press, 2008), 55, and idem, *Benedict XVI: A Guide for the Perplexed* (London: T&T Clark, 2013), 48. Other important writing by Ratzinger / Benedict XVI on tradition includes: *The Nature and Mission of Theology* (San Francisco: Ignatius Press, 1995); *Handing on the Faith in an Age of Disbelief* (San Francisco: Ignatius Press, 2006); *Christianity and the Crisis of Cultures* (San Francisco: Ignatius Press, 2006); *Values in a Time of Upheaval* (San Francisco: Ignatius Press, 2006); *God's Word: Scripture, Tradition* (San Francisco: Ignatius Press, 2008).

29. Benedict XVI, *Communion in Time: Tradition*, General Audience, Wednesday, April 26, 2006, cited in Rowland, *Benedict XVI*, 53.

to such relative trivia, how any change in minutiae is presumed to signal abandonment of the whole box and dice, and how this is presumed to always be a good thing.

There are much more serious tradition allergies. Ratzinger argues that differing attitudes to the phenomenon of tradition mark "a deep rift that runs through the modern age," with those who count tradition as the prerequisite to humanity on one side and those who count modernity's abandonment of tradition essential to rationality and progress on the other.[30] Jeffrey Stout has observed that "Many modern moral philosophers have viewed tradition as, at best, an ultimately dispensable aid to fallible human reason and, at worst, a repository of superstition and a threat to autonomy."[31] Abandoning traditional precepts and their underpinnings, modern moral and political thinking turned instead to intuitions, balancing acts, and space for doing your own thing. Of course, even these approaches draw upon certain traditions and admit a limited role for custom, as for virtue, but in public rhetoric and action, the traditional is treated as prima facie irrelevant or worse.

Michael Walzer describes the state of contemporary agents unfettered by tradition:

> We liberals are free to choose, and we have a right to choose, but we have no criteria to govern our choices except our own wayward understanding of our wayward interests and desires. And so our choices lack the qualities of cohesion and consecutiveness. We can hardly remember what we did yesterday; we cannot with any assurance predict what we will do tomorrow.

30. Ratzinger, *Principles of Catholic Theology*, 86, on which see Rowland, *Ratzinger's Faith*, 86–90, and *The Theology of Pope Benedict XVI* (Oxford: Oxford University Press, 2008), 54–55. Other important writings by Ratzinger/Benedict XVI on tradition include: *The Nature and Mission of Theology* (San Francisco: Ignatius Press, 1995); *Handing on the Faith in an Age of Disbelief* (San Francisco: Ignatius Press, 2006); *Christianity and the Crisis of Cultures* (San Francisco: Ignatius Press, 2006); *Values in a Time of Upheaval* (San Francisco: Ignatius Press, 2006); *God's Word: Scripture, Tradition* (San Francisco: Ignatius Press, 2008).

31. Jeffrey Stout, "Tradition in Ethics," in *A New Dictionary of Christian Ethics*, ed. James Childress and John Macquarrie (London: Westminster Press, 1986), 629–31, at 630.

> We cannot give a proper account of ourselves. We cannot sit together and tell comprehensible stories, and we recognize ourselves in the stories we read only when these are fragmented narratives, without plots, the literary equivalent of atonal music and nonrepresentational art.[32]

Yet these human nonrepresentational artworks are, Walzer thinks, mostly happy, and liberal societies have proven resilient. They are, as it were, the worst sort of individuals and societies except for all the others.

Others are less sanguine. In a fascinating series on the future of liberalism in *First Things* in 2012, writers from various traditions observed that the democratic experiment in ordered liberty requires a heritage of anthropological and moral assumptions; even live-and-let-live toleration is impossible without them, let alone a fuller flourishing of individuals and communities.[33] As "gratitude to the past and obligations to the future are replaced by a near-universal pursuit of immediate gratification"[34] the postmodern self (especially the young self) is left rudderless, with no basis for ordering passions, rationality, and will, and so for choosing amid the smorgasbord of high-sugar-low-nutrition options offered by modernity. Without traditions, the same individual or community can demonstrate both anarchic-nihilist and despotic-ideological tendencies. As sociologist-philosopher Theodor Adorno observed, "when every tradition has been erased, so begins the descent into barbarism."[35] Meanwhile, the social agenda of liberalism becomes "ever more strident, uncompromising and moralistic" yet increasingly unable to

32. Michael Walzer, "The Communitarian Critique of Liberalism," *Political Theory* 18 (1990): 6–12, at 8.

33. Robert George, Yuval Levin, Wilfred McClay, James Rogers, and George Weigel.

34. Patrick Deneen, "Unsustainable Liberalism," *First Things* 225 (August/September 2012): 25–31, at 29.

35. Theodor Adorno, "Thesen über Tradition," *Ohne Leitbild* (Frankfurt: Suhrkamp Verlag, 1967), 35. Reflecting perhaps upon the daring and deadly experiments of various twentieth-century totalitarianism to tear down all previous traditions, Gerhard Krüger said, "The only reason we are still alive is our inconsistency in not having actually silenced all tradition" (quoted in Pieper, *Tradition*, 67–68.)

argue for its "reforms" and increasingly inclined to various forms of bullying.[36] The current push to impose a redefinition of marriage on the West seems to me to be an example of this. The failure to grasp the need for a long-evolved heritage of ideas and practices to sustain liberal democracies is also behind the tragedy of the attempt to quickly transpose Western liberal institutions to the Middle East and Afghanistan.

Even that supposedly most traditional of institutions, the Catholic Church, was not immune to the anti-traditionalism of modernity. The Second Vatican Council prescribed a return to the sources for all theology, a renewal of moral theology in particular by revisiting Scripture and Tradition, received in faith and interpreted by the *magisterium*, and a restoration of the connection of moral theology to sacramental and spiritual theology and to pastoral practice.[37] But the "new morality" that came soon thereafter the council took a different turn.

In his monumental *Les sources de la morale chrétienne*, Servais Pinckaers observed that many postconciliar moralists effectively cut ties with Scripture, Tradition, and the *magisterium*, regarding the traditional as unhelpful in the humanization of morality and the dialogue with modernity. These "revisionists" developed what Pinckaers called "an allergy to tradition" as "love of truth yielded to a taste for novelty, variety, relativity, adaptation."[38] Thus they sought to rewrite moral theology more "horizontally," drawing upon "experience," the human sciences, and the philosophies in vogue.[39] Radical openness to the world and hostility to Tradition and authority yielded a kind of "Secular Christianity." Proponents of "the new morality" used the adjective *traditional* as equivalent to closed, static, and absolutist—and therefore

36. Shalom Carmy, "Judaism and the Limits of Liberalism," *First Things* 224 (June/July 2012): 33–35.

37. Vatican Council II, *Optatum Totius: Decree on the Training of Priests* (1965), 15.

38. Servais Pinckaers, OP, *Les sources de la morale chrétienne* (1985); English translation by M. T. Noble, *The Sources of Christian Ethics* (Washington, DC: Catholic University of America Press, 1995), 304–5.

39. Pinckaers, *Sources of Christian Ethics*, 308–9.

benighted, implausible, and pious (now another scare word). Though borrowing concepts such as conscience and proportion, they repudiated the surrounding tradition that gave those concepts meaning as they accommodated the morality of the age.[40] Soon there were no moral absolutes and few almost absolutes.

In 1993, John Paul II demonstrated in *Veritatis Splendor* that such approaches and conclusions are irreconcilable with the Sacred Tradition and with the vocation of the Catholic theologian.[41] But by then the damage had been done, among pastors, ordinary faithful, and many in the surrounding culture. The abiding objection seems to be: *Catholic Tradition is just too static and restrictive in the moral sphere; it doesn't allow enough wiggle room for individuality, creativity, progress.* It is to that objection that I address the remainder of this chapter.

Some Recent Philosophers of Moral Tradition

A German Neo-Thomist Looks at Moral Tradition

The German Neo-Thomist philosopher Josef Pieper once suggested that "No one that wants to hand down a tradition successfully should talk about 'tradition.'"[42] Talking about tradition is often a sign it's too late. Yet in recent years, some philosophers have explored the idea afresh, not least Pieper himself, and not simply as intellectual archeology. Here I identify eight points about tradition that are explicit or at least implicit in his *Überlieferung*.

First, tradition is more verb than noun, a process of transmission down a line of persons.[43] *Traditio* (traditioning) is not an exchange of ideas because it operates in one direction only. The recipient is not

40. E.g., in Charles Curran and Richard McCormick, eds., *Readings in Moral Theology*, vol. 1, *Moral Norms and Catholic Tradition* (New York: Paulist, 1979), and subsequent volumes.

41. John Paul II, *Veritatis Splendor: Encyclical on Fundamental Catholic Morality* 4.

42. Pieper, *Tradition*, 15.

43. Pieper, *Tradition*; he also explored these ideas in *Muße und Kult* (Munich: Kösel-Verlag, 1948); English translation by A. Dru, *Leisure: The Basis of Culture* (London: Faber & Faber, 1952), esp. Part II, "The Philosophical Act"; see also his works on the seven virtues.

entirely passive, however; reception requires openness to receiving and internalizing what is received by pondering, interpreting, critiquing. As the recipient becomes in turn a transmitter, there is further selection, choice of rhetoric, re-expression, and so on.

Second, *traditum* (that which is transmitted) is a trust received, not just the plaything of the recipient. Traditioning *preserves* something—a doctrine, institution, or practice—incorporating the receiver and promising future recipients that what they receive will be "unadulterated and unmixed with anything foreign or inappropriate through the passage of time from the beginning."[44] This "closeness" or "fidelity" to the original inspiration gives tradition its authority.

A third point that follows from the second is that traditioning only occurs when it is received. If the process is resisted, then traditioning, in the strict sense, has not really taken place. This reception, Pieper argues, is like believing. "It *is* belief, since belief means accepting something as true and valid not on the basis of my own insight, but by relying on someone else."[45]

Fourth, a sign of genuine reception of a tradition is making it concrete in action. *Moral* traditions offer a framework, principles, virtues, and norms to make choices easier, almost automatic. Instead of having to think through every next action, we often rely upon convention.

Fifth, custom unburdens individual conscience (though without relieving it of responsibility); it also eases social interaction. "Our common life can run along with less friction and human energies can be turned . . . to their real goals, when it is taken for granted . . . that, for example, people say hello to one another on the street." Of course, customs vary and change. "Hi" replaces "Hello"; in America, you acknowledge people by effusing about how pleased you are to see them, in France by kissing them on both cheeks, and in Britain by looking away and pretending not to notice them! "It would be an unendurable burden on our common life if every decision about everything that

44. Pieper, *Tradition*, 21.
45. Pieper, *Tradition*, 18.

has to be done were decided from case to case on the basis of critical reflection."[46]

Sixth, people need reasons to receive traditions. It is quite useless, Pieper points out, to tell a young inquirer to be receptive to something because "it's just tradition" or "it's always been that way." Such evasion is often a sign that a convention is moribund or irrational.[47]

Furthermore, the seventh point is that part of the responsibility of bearing a tradition is a willingness when appropriate to pass it on. That which is received is not only for the benefit of the recipient but also for those to whom he or she will transmit it.

Eighth and finally, Pieper suggests that real traditioning requires "a living language; through creative rejuvenation and sloughing off the old skin like a snake, so to speak; through a continual confrontation with the immediate present and above all with the future."[48] Traditioning is dynamic; as a verb, it cannot be inert. Museums are valuable, but they are *not* true traditioning.

An English Wittgensteinian-Marxist-Thomist on Moral Tradition

This idea of traditions giving us patterns of life that free us from constant decision making while providing a context and instrument for living was further explored by the great Wittgensteinian-Marxist-Thomist philosopher Herbert McCabe. Like other animals, man changes amid the challenges and opportunities of his physical environment: this is called *evolution*. But as "the linguistic animal," he also changes in response to the challenges and opportunities of the cultural environment: this is called *history*. These nongenetic inheritances that account for the linguistic animal's behavior are *traditions*.[49] The linguistic animal interprets the world linguistically and so relies upon a grammar

46. Pieper, *Tradition*, 37–38.

47. Pieper, *Tradition*, 14–15, 35.

48. Pieper, *Tradition*, 15.

49. Herbert McCabe, OP, "Sensation, Language and Individuals," in *On Aquinas* (London: Burns & Oates, 2008), 29–40, at 34.

and vocabulary inherited rather than created by him. Being initiated into a tradition is like being initiated into a craft: the person receives a certain syllabus of information, skills, or customs; becomes interested in the syllabus and the goods internal to the craft; imitates great practitioners; and eventually masters it sufficiently to enter critically into the craft, even influencing its future direction.[50]

You don't teach someone how to make violins by giving them some wood and tools and telling them to get on with it. You don't even give him or her a violin-makers' handbook. Rather, "you show him how violins have been made—and this is part of showing him what a violin is. He will copy the work and techniques of skilled men of the past and, after several years or nearly a lifetime of this, he may be ready to add to and modify the tradition into which he has been introduced." Now, "the craft of making human beings, or human becomings," is *morality*, and it is unlikely to come more easily than violin making.[51]

The intimate connections between language and learning, craft and character, led McCabe to conclude that tradition "is a matter of identity, so that to have lost touch with tradition . . . is to be as crippled as an amnesiac who just doesn't remember who he is."[52] A legacy is received as a gift and requires a certain humility, patience, and self-criticism in the recipient. Moral traditioning also requires a moral community of trust and loyalty rather like an Aristotelian *polis*.[53] The process of traditioning is not, in McCabe's view, doomed to be the mere repetition of ancient forms and formulae: a culture, institution, or church must continually rewrite its own story—though not reinvent it—rewriting not so as to change its inheritance so much as to find new significance in it.

50. Herbert McCabe, OP, "The Role of Tradition," in *God Still Matters* (London: Continuum, 2002), 199–211, at 200–204.

51. Herbert McCabe, OP, "Teaching Morals," in *God Still Matters*, 187–98, at 198. There are clear parallels in Alasdair MacIntyre, "Too Many Thomisms?," in *Three Rival Versions of Moral Enquiry* (London: Duckworth, 1990), chap. 3.

52. McCabe, "Role of Tradition," 199.

53. McCabe, "Role of Tradition," 206–10.

A Scots-American Communitarian on Moral Tradition

The leading contemporary philosopher of tradition is McCabe's friend Alasdair MacIntyre. In his *After Virtue* trilogy, MacIntyre argues, against contemporary liberalism, that the self must find its moral identity in and through communities such as family, neighborhood, church, and nation, and their traditions of practice, without necessarily accepting all the moral limitations of those communities and traditions. "*What I am* is in key part *what I inherit*, a specific past that is present to some degree in the present. I find myself part of a history . . . whether I like it or not, whether I recognize it or not, one of the bearers of a tradition."[54]

By tradition, MacIntyre means

> an argument extended through time in which certain fundamental agreements are defined and redefined in terms of two kinds of conflict: those with critics and enemies external to the tradition who reject all or at least key parts of those fundamental agreements, and those internal, interpretative debates through which the meaning and rationale of the fundamental agreements come to be expressed and by whose progress a tradition is constituted.[55]

It seems to me that McCabe and MacIntyre's dialectical conception of how traditions are defined and modified is somewhat overstated: some traditions may have inherent tendencies to express and develop in particular ways without requiring the Hegelian catalyst of internal or external tension. Nonetheless, as discussed below, such forces can be important.

What traditionalists and modernists have in common, MacIntyre suggests, is the belief that a binary choice must be made between tradition(s) and reason. The traditionalist seeks unchanging customs

54. Alasdair MacIntyre, *After Virtue*, 3rd ed. (Notre Dame, IN: University of Notre Dame Press, 2007), 220; see also his *Three Rival Versions* and *Whose Justice? Which Rationality?* (London: Duckworth, 1988).

55. MacIntyre, *Whose Justice?*, 12.

when in fact part of what keeps a tradition alive is its ability to "develop" through critique and innovation; a healthy tradition is always in a state of becoming and is partly constituted by the ongoing argument about what that tradition and the institution that bears it are about.[56] The modernist, however, wants to be liberated from traditions altogether.[57] MacIntyre, like McCabe, argues that this is impossible: all reasoning and discussion take place within traditions of thought, language, and practice. Some are more successful than others in making sense of the past or responding to current challenges; liberals think this of their own tradition. But once we recognize the place of traditions in constituting self and community, we will also realize that they are essential to even the most "radical" argumentation and to genuine creativity.

A Polish Philosopher-Pope on Moral Tradition

In a trilogy of encyclicals in the 1990s, the now-sainted John Paul II hoped to kick-start the renewal of moral theology that had stalled in the postconciliar revisionist experiments.[58] In particular, he sought to clarify and recover Catholic conceptions of freedom in truth, informed conscience, natural law, authority, and tradition.

In *Veritatis Splendor* (1993), he proposed that the Catholic moral tradition is part of the patrimony of humanity, offering an unparalleled richness of reflection on sexuality and family life, bioethics, and social, economic, and political life. Identifying cul-de-sacs down which Catholic morality had gone in recent decades, the pope developed an ecclesiological and pneumatological foundation for the idea

56. MacIntyre, *After Virtue*, 221–22: "Traditions, when vital, embody continuities of conflict"; whereas traditions that have everything all worked out and neat are ossified, they engage in memorial enshrinement and repetitions of past formulas and try in vain to keep those dead or dying practices alive by self-consciously glorifying them.

57. MacIntyre, "Liberalism Transformed into a Tradition," in *Whose Justice?*, chap. 17.

58. See "Tradition Allergy" above.

of a living moral Tradition that "comes from the Apostles"; is mediated by Fathers and Doctors; is crystallized in Scripture, liturgy, and the lives of the saints; and is authentically interpreted by the *magisterium*.[59] Moral theories that purport to justify behavior contrary to the divine and natural law "cannot claim to be grounded in the Catholic moral tradition."[60]

In *Evangelium Vitae* (1995), John Paul took his project further by identifying the destructive—indeed lethal—effects of emancipating freedom from tradition and authority. Thus "subjective and changeable opinion or, indeed, selfish interest and whim" replace objective truth in determining moral choices, and "the culture of death" thrives.[61] But the Catholic moral tradition opposes direct killing of the innocent, and John Paul was ready to define three moral "dogmas" in that area (regarding the intrinsic wrongness of intentionally killing the innocent, of abortion, and of euthanasia). Thus the Tradition *crystallizes* before our very eyes, as monuments of its wisdom become crucial markers of fidelity and identity.

In *Fides et Ratio* (1998), John Paul noted that, from birth, human beings "are immersed in traditions which give them not only a language and a cultural formation but also a range of truths in which they believe almost instinctively." As they mature, they question, criticize, and even reject some of this inheritance and also recover other parts, but mostly they take it for granted. But we cannot verify everything for ourselves and so must accept much of what has been handed on to us. This makes the human being, John Paul says, a being that lives by tradition, "the one who lives by belief."[62] Aware of currents in contemporary philosophy, the pope judged the recovery of tradition as especially significant:

59. John Paul II, *Veritatis Splendor* 4–5, 27, 37.
60. John Paul II, *Veritatis Splendor* 76; cf. 80.
61. John Paul II, *Evangelium Vitae: Encyclical on the Inviolability of Human Life* (1995), 19.
62. John Paul II, *Fides et Ratio* 31.

> The appeal to tradition is not a mere remembrance of the past; it involves rather the recognition of a cultural heritage which belongs to all of humanity. Indeed it may be said that *it is we who belong to the tradition* and that it is not ours to dispose of at will. Precisely by being rooted in the tradition will we be able today to develop for the future an original, new and constructive mode of thinking. This same appeal is all the more valid for theology.[63]

I have written elsewhere of the range of resources for traditioning in contemporary moral theology, including new approaches to the Scriptures, Fathers, Scholastics, and *magisterium*; competing and mutually enriching traditions of practical reason; various moves to recover virtue, community, beauty, and liturgy in ethics; and a clearer sense of the distinctively "Christian" and "Catholic."[64] With the recovery of tradition in some moral and political philosophy, Catholic moral theology has been given a new impetus.

Is Moral Tradition Static or Developing? Slavery as a Test Case

Can Moral Traditions Admit Change?

Those suffering from tradition allergy commonly allege that Tradition is an essentially stagnant and restrictive legacy, and best renounced in the name of progress, rationality, and freedom. One test of this claim would be the ability of a tradition to develop. A leading scholar of Catholic moral tradition, John T. Noonan, claims that while Catholic morality might sometimes gradually "evolve" or "unpack" its inheritance, at other times it progresses by radically contradicting itself.[65] He offers several examples of abrupt reversals in Church

63. John Paul II, *Fides et Ratio* 85, emphasis added. John Paul concluded (at 105) by asserting that "The intimate bond between theological and philosophical wisdom is one of the Christian tradition's most distinctive treasures in the exploration of revealed truth."

64. Anthony Fisher, OP, "Context: Challenges and Resources for a New Millennium," in *Catholic Bioethics for a New Millennium* (Cambridge: Cambridge University Press, 2012), chap. 1.

65. John T. Noonan, "Development in Moral Doctrine," *Theological Studies* 54

teaching: regarding interest taking on deposits and loans and the sin of usury, regarding the indissolubility of marriage and the range of the so-called Pauline privilege, and regarding rights of conscience and religious toleration. Other examples might be given,[66] of which the most challenging is surely that of slavery.[67] If there has been no coherent Catholic tradition with respect to slavery, or if that tradition was essentially stuck in a pro-slavery position for most of Christian history and then radically contradicted by the *magisterium*, then the modernist claim that Sacred Moral Tradition is a grave obstacle to progress, rationality, and freedom would seem to be supported.

Rupture in Catholic Teaching on Slavery?

In what follows, I refer especially to *chattel slavery*, where persons are treated as property of others, with few personal rights, their labor and obedience required without recompense. In the ancient world, chattel slavery was generally confined to people captured in war, some convicted criminals and debtors, those who sold *themselves* into slavery, and the children of slaves. Attenuated forms of servitude, such as serfdom and "servile labour" may or may not be warranted

(1993): 662–77; idem, *A Church That Can and Cannot Change: The Development of Catholic Moral Teaching* (Notre Dame, IN: University of Notre Dame Press, 2005).

66. Others have suggested that Catholic teaching on mutilation (including castration), torture, just war, capital punishment, democracy and human rights, the relative value of virginity and marriage, the positive values of sexual intercourse, attitudes toward women and children, the preferential option for the poor, and the notion of structures of sin all amount to dramatic developments, even about-faces. See Marciano Vidal, "Progress in the Moral Tradition," in *Readings in Moral Theology*, vol. 13, *Change in Official Moral Teachings*, ed. Charles Curran (New York: Paulist, 2003), 319–34.

67. Noonan, "Development in Moral Doctrine," 664: "the Church taught that it was no sin for a Catholic to own another human being; to command the labour of that other human being without paying compensation; to determine where he or she lived and how much he or she was fed and clothed; to restrict his or her education; to pledge him or her for a loan, forfeit him or her for a default, sell him or her for cash; to do the same to his or her offspring; and to discipline him or her by physical punishments if he or she were rude or boisterous or slack in service." Laennec Hurbon, John Maxwell, and others have also claimed that the Catholic Church was pro-slavery until modern times.

within the Catholic tradition, but the arguments are different in significant respects.

Noonan points out that Jesus said not a word against slavery as a social institution, and New Testament authors even exhorted slaves to obey their masters.[68] The problem seems to have been an inadequate moral language or imagination.[69] No society made up entirely of free human beings was known to the world in which the Church grew up; many social factors fostered slavery, and many institutions relied upon it; it did not occur to people that the abolition of slavery was possible, let alone desirable. Only as social structures changed and slavery proved destructive for both masters and slaves did "moral mutation" become possible.

So it was, on Noonan's account, that for nearly two millennia the Apostles, Fathers, popes, and bishops all failed to oppose slavery. The Bible took it for granted. The postbiblical *magisterium* defended it. Slaves were excommunicated for escaping, and abolitionism was associated with the Manichean heresy. Some popes even owned slaves themselves. Augustine, John Chrysostom, Gregory Nazianzen, Gregory the Great, Aquinas, Luther, and Calvin all thought slavery undesirable but not absolutely forbidden in a sinful world.[70] Pro-celibacy synods from the seventh century onward threatened to enslave clergy wives and children, and popes and councils directed enslavement of the Saracens and those who assisted them. In 1488, Pope Innocent VIII received a hundred Moorish slaves from King Ferdinand II of Aragon and distributed them as gifts to his favorite cardinals and aristocrats.

68. 1 Cor 7:21; Eph 6:1–9; Col 3:22–25; 1 Tm 6:1; Ti 2:9–10; Phlm 11–19; 1 Pt 2:18.

69. Noonan, "Development in Moral Doctrine," 673: "Human beings do not reach moral conclusions in a vacuum apart from the whole web of language, custom, and social structure surrounding them."

70. On the Fathers, see: C. L. de Wet, "Sin as Slavery and/or Slavery as Sin: On the Relationship between Slavery and Christian Hamartiology in Late Ancient Christianity," *Religion and Theology* 17 (2010): 26–39; Eric Denby, "The First Abolitionist? Gregory of Nyssa on Ancient Roman Slavery," May 9, 2011, www.academia.edu/1485109. On the Scholastics, see, e.g., Aquinas, *In octo libros Politicorum Aristotelis expositio*, I, lect. 3 and 4; *ST* II-II, q. 57, a. 3, ad 2.

Like other European sovereigns, the popes powered their ships with galleys of Muslim slaves. Paul III decreed that anyone who caught the heretic King Henry VIII of England might enslave him.[71] Church leaders were often mute or more actively complicit in the Atlantic slave trade.[72]

Only in the nineteenth century, according to Noonan, did Catholic teaching start to crystallize around the position that slavery is immoral. Even then, some American bishops before the civil war[73] and the Holy Office after it affirmed that slave trading was permitted under certain conditions.[74] According to Noonan, it was not until Vatican II and the *magisterium* of John Paul II that slavery was excoriated in Catholic teaching as intrinsically evil. The Tradition proved highly resistant to any progress, and the eventual about-face by the Church in its moral teaching could not be more dramatic.

Rival Strands of the Sacred Tradition on Slavery

Yet is talk of "mutation," "rupture," or "about-face" regarding slavery accurate here? Several writers have contested that claim.[75] They point out that no magisterial source ever supported or tolerated all that goes by the name of slavery. Already the Old Testament regulated slavery so as to ensure humane treatment and, where appropriate, ultimate

71. J. F. Maxwell, *Slavery and the Catholic Church* (London: Barry Rose, 1975); David Davis, *The Problem of Slavery in Western Culture* (Oxford: Oxford University Press, 2008).

72. Hugh Thomas, *The Slave Trade: The Story of the Atlantic Slave Trade, 1440–1870* (New York: Simon & Schuster, 1997).

73. Maria Caravaglios and Ernest Unterkoefler, eds., *The American Catholic Church and the Negro Problem in the 18th and 19th Centuries* (Charleston, SC: Caravaglios, 1974); John McKivigan and Mitchell Snay, eds., *Religion and the Antebellum Debate over Slavery* (Athens: University of Georgia Press, 1998).

74. Maxwell, *Slavery and the Catholic Church*, 78–79.

75. Avery Card Dulles, SJ, "Development or Reversal?," *First Things* 156 (October 2005): 53–61; Joel Panzer, *The Popes and Slavery* (New York: Alba House, 1996); Rodney Stark, "The Truth about the Catholic Church and Slavery," *Christianity Today* (July 2003): www.christianitytoday.com/ct/2003/julyweb-only/7-14.53.0.html; Lawrence Welch, "John T. Noonan's *A Church That Can and Cannot Change*: An Evaluation," *Nova et Vetera* 4, no. 3 (2006): 697–708.

freedom.[76] Early Christian writers such as Paul tolerated slavery but made no general defense of the institution, apparently regarding it as an intractable part of a corrupt social order that was, in any case, passing away. Christians were not only commanded to treat slaves justly and kindly but also to regard them as their equals before God—a radical, almost treasonous claim in the ancient world. *The First Epistle to Timothy* condemned slave traders along with murderers and perjurers.[77] Paul exhorted Philemon to manumit Onesimus and reminded the Galatians that "in Christ there is neither slave nor free."[78] In the postapostolic period, Christian morality played out in other ways to ameliorate the situation, for example, by forbidding enslavement of fellow Christians, trafficking and sexually abusing slaves, and allowing slaves Christian baptism, Eucharist, marriage, ordination, and burial. So, the slavery "tolerated" by the early Church was already more benign that that generally known in the ancient world.

Noonan himself admits that it was long-established "Catholic moral doctrine that slaves should be treated humanely . . . that it was good to give slaves freedom . . . [and] that slaves should be allowed to marry."[79] Origen favored the Jewish practice of liberating slaves after seven years, and St. Gregory of Nyssa denounced slavery in the strongest terms.[80] Pope St. Pius I, Pope St. Callixtus, and the bishop St. Patrick were, like many clerics, former slaves: to have been able to rise to such ranks suggests, again, that Christianity was subverting the order presumed in the ancient world with respect to slavery.

76. E.g., Ex 21:1–11; Lv 25:11, 25:47–55; Dt 23:15–16; Patrick M. O'Neil, "A Response to John T. Noonan Jr. Concerning the Development of Catholic Moral Doctrine," *Faith and Reason* (Spring/Summer, 1996): 56–79.

77. 1 Tm 1:10; Mark Brumley, "Let My People Go: The Catholic Church and Slavery," *This Rock* (July/August 1999): 16–21.

78. Gal 3:27–28.

79. Noonan, "Development in Moral Doctrine," 665.

80. Origen, *Homilies*, on Gn 16:1; Gregory of Nyssa, *Homilies on Ecclesiastes* IV. See Trevor Dennis, "Man beyond Price: Gregory of Nyssa and Slavery," in *Heaven and Erath: Essex Essays in Theology and Ethics*, ed. A. Linzey and P. Wexler (Worthing: Churchman, 1986); Denby, "First Abolitionist?"

Some early Christians liberated their slaves and redeemed others. By the Middle Ages, many Christians doubted the justice and charity of enslavement: Anselm the great bishop-philosopher, for instance, opposed it.[81] Trinitarians, Mercedarians, and other religious offered themselves as ransom for slaves. Even those such as Aquinas and Bonaventure, who thought slavery contrary to the natural law but tolerable in a sinful world, so reduced the circumstances in which it might be allowed and the "rules of engagement" between masters and servants that it became more like feudal serfdom than "slavery" as understood in the pre- and postmedieval world.

In fact, by Aquinas's time, chattel slavery had all but disappeared in the West. But in the Age of Discovery, as Europeans encountered Muslim slave traders and American Indians, a new type of *racial* chattel slavery emerged, and the argument had to be made all over again. And indeed it was. In 1435, Fra Angelico's first papal patron, Pope Eugene IV, condemned the enslavement of peoples in the newly colonized Canary Islands.[82] Noonan dismisses this as half-hearted and

81. Stark, "Truth about the Catholic Church and Slavery," notes that "As early as the seventh century, Saint Bathilde (wife of King Clovis II) became famous for her campaign to stop slave-trading and free all slaves; in 851 Saint Anskar began his efforts to halt the Viking slave trade. That the Church willingly baptized slaves was claimed as proof that they had souls, and soon both kings and bishops—including William the Conqueror (1027–1087) and Saints Wulfstan (1009–1095) and Anselm (1033–1109)—forbade the enslavement of Christians."

82. Eugene IV, *Sicut Dudum* (1435): "They have deprived the natives of their property or turned it to their own use, and have subjected some of the inhabitants of said islands to perpetual slavery (*subdiderunt perpetuae servituti*), sold them to other persons and committed other various illicit and evil deeds against them. . . . Therefore We . . . exhort, through the sprinkling of the Blood of Jesus Christ shed for their sins, one and all, temporal princes, lords, captains, armed men, barons, soldiers, nobles, communities and all others of every kind among the Christian faithful of whatever state, grade or condition, that they themselves desist from the aforementioned deeds, cause those subject to them to desist from them, and restrain them rigorously. And no less do We order and command all and each of the faithful of each sex that, within the space of fifteen days of the publication of these letters in the place where they live, that they restore to their pristine liberty all and each person of either sex who were once residents of said Canary Islands . . . who have been made subject to slavery

only really concerned to protect Christians from enslavement.[83] But the text itself complains that the colonists "have subjected some of the inhabitants of said islands to perpetual slavery, sold them to other persons and committed various other illicit and evil deeds against them" and commands that this practice desist, that the slavers be rigorously restrained, and that every slave be immediately restored to liberty and compensated. While it is true that the next pope—Nicholas V, whose chapel I considered above—condoned the enslavement of Moors in a just war,[84] it was Eugene's text that passed into the Tradition as an authoritative act of moral teaching.

In his bull *Sublimis Deus* in 1537, Pope Paul III applied the same principles as Eugene to the newly encountered inhabitants of the West and South Indies. Again, Noonan dismisses this as too little, too late, and as demonstrating a concern only for Christians.[85] But, given its importance in the developing tradition, we might consider carefully what Paul III actually said: that Christ directed the Church to preach to all nations, without exception, since all are capable of faith; that the Devil stirred up his allies, out of avarice, to enslave the Indians and treat them like brute animals or worse; that the Indians are true men and not beasts; and that the pope, by his apostolic authority, decrees that reducing Indians or anyone else, "even those outside the Faith" to slavery, is "null and void."[86] Anyone purporting

(*servituti subicere*). These people are to be totally and perpetually free and are to be let go without the exaction or reception of any money."

83. Noonan, *A Church That Can and Cannot Change*, 243.

84. Noonan, *A Church That Can and Cannot Change*, 62–67.

85. Noonan, *A Church That Can and Cannot Change*, 72–73.

86. Paul III, *Sublimis Deus* (1537): "Truth Himself, who can neither deceive nor be deceived, when He destined the preachers of the faith to the office of preaching, said: 'Go, make disciples of all nations.' 'All,' He said, without exception, since all are capable of the discipline of the faith. Seeing this and envying it, the enemy of the human race . . . has thought up a way, unheard of before now, by which he might impede the saving word of God from being preached to the nations. He has stirred up some of his allies who, desiring to satisfy their own avarice, are presuming to assert far and wide that the Indians of the West and the South who have come to our notice in these times be reduced to our service like brute animals, under the pretext that they

to enslave another was declared excommunicate.[87] Despite backsliding by some ecclesiastics thereafter, the teaching of Eugene IV and Paul III increasingly became the official position of the popes and was restated by Gregory XIV in 1591, Urban VIII in 1639, Innocent XI in 1686, and Benedict XIV in 1741.[88] Missionaries in the New World and academics in the old—especially the Salamanca Dominicans—increasingly opposed the practices of the conquistadors and slaveholders.[89] Noonan admits that Bartolomé de las Casas was a case of "a Christian conscience awakening in America, making mistakes, and

---

are lacking the Catholic Faith. And they reduce them to slavery, treating them with afflictions they would scarcely use with brute animals. Therefore, We, . . . noting that the Indians themselves indeed are true men and . . . capable of the Christian faith . . . and wishing to provide suitable remedies for them, by our Apostolic Authority decree and declare by these present letters that the same Indians and all other peoples—even though they are outside the faith—who shall hereafter come to the knowledge of Christians have not been deprived or should not be deprived of their liberty or of their possessions. Rather they are to be able to use and enjoy this liberty and this ownership of property freely and licitly, and are not to be reduced to slavery, and that whatever happens to the contrary is to be considered null and void."

87. In another document, *Pastorale Officium*, accompanying the bull.

88. Gregory XIV, *Cum Sicuti* (1591); Urban VIII, *Commissum Nobis* (1639); Benedict XIV, *Immensa Pastorum* (1741). Bld Innocent XI approved the Holy Office, *Response 230* (1686), which declared enslavement immoral and obliged the slavers to emancipate and even compensate their slaves.

89. Dominican missionaries and theologians argued both in the New World and in the academies and courts of Spain and Rome that chattel slavery was morally abhorrent and must be abolished, e.g., Pedro de Córdoba and Antonio de Monetesinos, friars and missionaries in Hispaniola (now Haiti and Dominican Republic); Bartolomé de las Casas, Dominican friar, missionary, historian, social reformer, and Bishop of Chiapas, who first campaigned against the enslavement of the American Indians and only later came to oppose negro slavery as well; Alonso de Montúfar, Dominican friar and second Archbishop of Mexico; Tommaso de Vio Cajetan, Dominican friar, philosopher, cardinal, and campaigner against slavery; and Francisco de Vittoria, Dominican friar, philosopher, and theologian of the Salamanca School and the first great theorist of international law. Noonan regards some of these, e.g., Vittoria, as apologists for slavery (*A Church That Can and Cannot Change*, 73–74), yet Vittoria argued *against* slavery in *De Jure belli Hispanorum in barbarous* (1532) and *Relectiones Theologicae* (1557). See, e.g., David Davis, *Inhuman Bondage: The Rise and Fall of Slavery in the New World* (New York: Oxford University Press, 2006).

developing,"[90] but most biographers credit him with a much greater role in the campaign against New World slavery, first with respect to the Amerindians and later the negroes.[91]

Without doubt, many Church leaders were weak or half-hearted in the face of powerful slaveholding interests and sometimes complicit with them. Nonetheless, a clear and consistent teaching against chattel slavery emerged in the Age of Discovery and came to prevail in the Catholic Church.[92] Secular liberalism did *not* do the heavy lifting in the fight against slavery any more than it did with respect to segregation; those like Granville Sharp, Thomas Clarkson, William Wilberforce, Harriet Beecher Stowe, John Brown, Charles Finney, and even Abraham Lincoln were much more likely to appeal to religious arguments like those increasingly commonplace in the papal *magisterium* on slavery.[93] Thus by the time of the condemnations of slavery by Pius VII in 1815, Gregory XVI in 1839, Leo XIII in 1888 and 1890, the *Code of Canon Law* in 1917, the Second Vatican Council in 1965, and John Paul II (in many places) there was already a long tradition backing them.[94] As the Church's ancient teaching about the dignity and

90. Noonan, *A Church That Can and Cannot Change*, 70–77.

91. E.g., Lawrence Clayton, *Bartolome de las Casas and the Conquest of the Americas* (London: Blackwell, 2011); Juan Friede and Benjamin Keen, eds., *Bartolomé de las Casas in History: Toward an Understanding of the Man and His Work* (DeKalb: Northern Illinois University Press, 2008); Lewis Hanke, *Bartolomé de Las Casas: Bookman, Scholar and Propagandist* (Philadelphia: University of Pennsylvania Press, 1952); Helen Rand-Parish, Maria Concepta Maciel, and Gustavo Gutiérrez, *Bartolomé de las Casas: Liberation of the Oppressed* (Berkeley: University of California, 1984).

92. Panzer, *Popes and Slavery*.

93. On the role of Christian faith in the abolitionist movement and emancipation, see works of Christopher Brown, Eric Foner, Paul Goodman, William Hague, Keith Hardman, Adam Hochschild, Michael Johnson, Eric Mataxas, John McKivigan, Helmut Meier, James Oakes, Molly Oshatz, Derek Peterson, David Reynolds, James Stewart, Douglas Strong, and Joe Wheeler.

94. Pius VII at the Congress of Vienna in 1815 sought to have the victors over Napoleon outlaw slavery. See Gregory XVI, *In Supremo Apostolatus Fastigio* (1839), on which, see John Quinn, "Three Cheers for the Abolitionist Pope! American Reaction to Gregory XVI's Condemnation of the Slave Trade, 1840–1860," *Catholic Historical Review* 90, no. 1 (2004): 67–93; Leo XIII, *In Plurimis* (1888) and *Catholicæ Ecclesiae* (1890);

basic equality of all human beings was clarified and repeatedly restated, it was clear that there was no place for chattel slavery.

Conclusions on the Catholic Moral Tradition on Slavery

My conclusion, then, is that Noonan's claim that the Catholic moral tradition was pro-slavery and essentially stagnant for more than eighteen centuries until it was overturned is not made out. On the contrary, the development of Catholic teaching about slavery illustrates some of the points made in my paper about Sacred Moral Tradition: Catholic moral tradition articulates principles of natural and revealed morality and denounces behavior contrary to human dignity, justice, and charity. The application of those principles to questions such as slavery is clarified gradually in the evolving Tradition, inherited from the Scriptures, Fathers, and popes. Pressures external to Catholic tradition and tendencies inherent within it move it to develop in certain ways. External factors may include changed social conditions—such as the advent of effective alternatives to slavery for containing enemies or criminals, or the encounter with racial chattel slavery in the Age of Discovery, or the ambivalent experience of communities built on slavery—which can render questions previously thought theoretical much more urgent. Whereas lack of moral imagination or vocabulary can slow progress toward clarity on an issue such as slavery (which many presumed inevitable and at best only regulated benignly), new experience and controversy can expand moral imagination and assist clarity on the matter at issue. Other

Code of Canon Law (1917), can. 2354; Vatican Council II, *Gaudium et spes: Constitution on the Church in the Modern World* 27 and 29; *Catechism of the Catholic Church* (1993), 2414; John Paul II, *Veritatis Splendor* 80; *Evangelium Vitae* 3 and 31, and in many other documents of his magisterium. The teaching of Gregory XVI has been construed by Noonan and others as opposing the slave trade but not slaveholding itself. Yet the text is clearly opposed to placing or holding anyone in servitude. Panzer, *Popes and Slavery*, demonstrates that this misreading of Gregory goes back to the Catholic apologists for slavery in antebellum United States.

factors internal to the tradition that can be major drivers of development are the contemplation, study, and action of believers (e.g., theologians, lay abolitionists) and the teaching of pastors (e.g., Las Casas, Paul III, Leo XIII, Vatican II, John Paul II).

Until clarity is achieved, competing arguments and claims will be made, and powerful interests may long resist development as best they can. Under the guidance of the Holy Spirit, the Tradition nonetheless eventually "crystallizes" around some authoritative declarations (such as that against chattel slavery). Development of moral doctrine takes time, and its course is only evident in retrospect. Once clarified, handed down, and received, the moral tradition requires action (such as the efforts to abolish slavery). Even after it crystallizes with some authoritative teaching, further development may be required (e.g., regarding what we should regard as slavery).

The rival strands in the Tradition that vied for attention and the see-sawing of pastors between abolitionism and tolerance of *chattel slavery* has parallels with the early Christian controversy over Arianism—a heresy that recurred and, in different forms, was authoritatively condemned, yet continued to be advocated or tolerated by some Church leaders, and was eventually and repeatedly condemned by the *magisterium*. As with the divine nature of Christ, so the teaching against slavery seems now to be secure, but it was only clarified after long argument and is likely to meet further challenges in the future: future generations might, for instance, regard the debt bondage that miners endure in Brazil, the prostitution into which women are sold in Thailand or the laboratory manufacture and exploitation to which human embryos are subjected in Australia, as varieties of slavery that our generation wickedly tolerated.[95]

Like the evolution of Catholic teaching on capital punishment or war, the development of moral doctrine on slavery was not a movement from "all slavery is good" to "all slavery is evil," as Noonan sug-

95. On the varieties and endurance of slavery, see works of David Davis, Stanley Engerman et al., Peter Kolchin, Milton Meltzer, and Christopher Schmidt-Nowara.

gests, but rather a movement from "only some of what people call slavery can be tolerated" to "almost none of what people call slavery is just" and to increasing clarity that *chattel slavery* is in the "never just" category. This seems to me a rather more consistent trajectory than Noonan and some others have allowed, what fifth-century St. Vincent of Lerins characterized as "an authentic progress of faith, not a change of faith."[96]

Conclusion

In an era in which the Church is consecrated to a new evangelization, the recovery of a deep sense of tradition will be essential. Some seek to reinvent rather than transmit the Christian supernarrative and its mores; whatever trappings they maintain, they have in fact abandoned the Sacred Tradition. But those who stick to it need not experience the Catholic moral tradition as inhibiting, creativity dulling, or authoritarian. Traditioning engenders a grateful faith in the One from whom the moral tradition derives and in those who have struggled to articulate and live it along the way; a confident hope that this moral inheritance has a future, something worth living and developing and passing on to others in preaching, witness, and moral education; and a loving service to those presently struggling for a moral compass and ultimate happiness.

Acknowledgments

The author thanks Annie Sandrussi, David Collits, and Hayden Ramsay for their assistance with this essay.

96. St. Vincent of Lerins, *Commonitorium* 23.

CHRISTIAN BRUGGER

5 • REASON'S "WAX NOSE"

Moral Disagreement, Self-Determination, and the Epistemic Death of Natural Law

The degree to which moral disagreement characterizes contemporary culture is well illustrated by the US Supreme Court decision in the *United States v. Windsor* (U.S. 570, 2013) case, decided on June 26, 2013, which struck down as unconstitutional one section of the 1996 Defense of Marriage Act (DOMA) that restricted the definition of marriage in federal law to a union between one man and one woman.

Writing for the court's majority, Justice Anthony Kennedy said that DOMA "seeks to injure" homosexual partners by denying them "due process and equal protection" under the law; he said that DOMA, passed by an overwhelming majority of both houses of the US Congress, expresses "a bare congressional desire to harm a politically unpopular group" and that the "law is motivated by an improper animus" toward members of that group. Justice Antonin Scalia disagreed. In his dissent, he said that "even setting aside traditional moral disapproval of same-sex marriage, . . . there are many perfectly valid . . . justifying rationales" for DOMA. He accused the Supreme Court's majority of "affirmatively concealing" these rationales from the reader giving the impression that "only those with hateful hearts" could have voted for DOMA, coloring DOMA supporters as "unhinged members of a wild-eyed lynch mob."[1]

The Universality of the "Natural Law"

Western ethical tradition defends the existence of a natural moral law. It understands that law to be universal in three respects: in its *application*, *knowability*, and *normativity*.

Phenomenon of Moral Disagreement

If the natural law is a law of reason, universal in scope and binding on all rational agents, then we would expect to find among these agents, if not universal agreement, then at least widespread agreement on its foundational precepts, agreement widespread enough that any fundamental disagreement would be an occasional and exceptional phenomenon. But we find that many intelligent and perceptive people disagree with what other intelligent and perceptive people take to be the particular precepts of the natural law, and some people even reject the conception of a natural law altogether. Moreover, philosophically skillful and well-educated defenders of the natural law who set forward their best arguments frequently fail to convince their equally philosophically skilled and informed opponents of the rational superiority of their arguments. Consequently, disagreements arise that seem to be intractable.

This gives rise to a dilemma: either the traditional idea of a naturally knowable moral law is mistaken, or we can account for widespread moral disagreement in some other way. This essay presumes—and so does not argue for—the correctness of the traditional idea. Its purpose is to *account* for moral disagreement in the past century, par-

1. Part IV; he continues: "The avowed purpose and practical effect of the law here in question are to impose a disadvantage, a separate status, and so a stigma upon all who enter into same-sex marriages made lawful by the unquestioned authority of the States." *United States v. Windsor*, 570 U.S. (2013). Scalia dissent at II, b. The court decision and Scalia dissent are available at the website of the US Supreme Court, accessed November 6, 2018, https://www.supremecourt.gov/opinions/12pdf/12-307_6j37.pdf.

ticularly the past six decades. It looks at the rise of moral disagreement from the domain of moral theory, specifically moral psychology. It examines the problem by looking at the reflexive—self-determining—effects of judgments and volitions on reason, will, and affect.

The Term "Moral Psychology" as Used in This Essay

The *Oxford English Dictionary* defines moral psychology as "the psychology of morality and human action."[2] This might lead one to believe that moral psychology includes reasoned psychological accounts of human motivations and actions, accounts of why people choose as they do, how morally relevant mind-sets instantiate in a community, and how those mind-sets become deep-seated cultural mores. One would be disappointed, though. Given the empirical turn in the social sciences in the last fifty years, most of the moral psychology done today is conceptualized as a subconcentration of experimental sciences such as cognitive neuroscience and evolutionary biology.[3]

Whatever the merits of that way of proceeding, my account does not follow it. It examines rather how emotions and thoughts determine—shape or cause—choices and other types of volition, and how those choices and volitions realize within us—bring into our characters—morally relevant self-determinations, self-determinations referred to by Wojtyła as the "intransitive" effects of free choice.[4] These self-determinations are predispositions—Wojtyła's "dynamisms"[5]—of mind, will, and emotion instantiated by practical

2. *Oxford English Dictionary*, 3rd ed., s.v. "moral psychology."

3. E. Christian Brugger, "Moral Psychology," in *New Catholic Encyclopedia Supplement 2012–13: Ethics and Philosophy*, vol. 3, ed. Robert L. Fastiggi (Detroit: Gale, 2013).

4. Karol Wojtyła, *The Acting Person*, trans. Andrzej Potocki (Dordrecht: D. Reidel, 1979), 149–150.

5. Wojtyła understandably focuses on dynamisms of the will; I broaden the discussion to the dynamisms that arise in our reason and emotion on account of willing. Also, he speaks more of dynamisms instantiated *by* the will than dynamisms *of* the will. We are speaking of similar realities. The will's dynamisms have causal tendencies, one of which is in will itself. So I speak about the orientations *of* will instantiated in the will by acts of the will.

judgments and free choices whose objects always include intelligible goods.[6] These dispositions orient us as actors to further judgments and choices like those that instantiated them. In this sense, the prior acts of intelligence and will are in a sense architectonic. Their directionality in relation to human goods impresses a self-determining rule or measure that remains unless and until it is rejected by contrary judgments and volitions. I say more about this below.

It is appropriate here to issue certain caveats. The following exercise is a foray into somewhat uncharted waters. I propose ideas by way of beginning a conversation in what might be referred to as "moral dynamics." I know I catalogued the essay above under "moral psychology." But what I am doing does not fall strictly within that discipline, at least not as it is practiced today. Moral dynamics may explain better what I am doing and carry less baggage: neither metaethics, nor fundamental moral philosophy, nor normative theory, nor phenomenology (nor cognitive neuroscience!), but rather an *explication of operationalized practical principles within acting persons.*

In what follows, I do not go much further than identifying reasonable correlations between cognitions, volitions, emotions, and cultural attitudes. I do not attempt to demonstrate the correlations by an appeal to empirical research. I obviously do not mean to say that populations unanimously exhibit all the characteristics I iden-

6. Wojtyła, *Acting Person*, speaks of the "ego" as the "principal object" of an action (150): actions not only cause changes in the world around the person, but also change the person (the ego) himself: "the engagement in freedom is objectified . . . in the person and not only in the action, which is the transitive effect" (151). But when he turns to the anthropological nature of the objectifications, of the dynamisms that arise in the ego as a result of action, he sheds little light on what is going on in the acting person; he speaks of "the reality of fulfillment in an action," but not of the nature of that fulfillment (152), and of "the ontological status of the personal fulfillment of the ego in the action" (153), but not in what this fulfillment consists. He speaks of "internal realities" and "objectifications" that take place in the self as a result of the "engagement in freedom" (151), but of the nature of the realities and objectifications he says little. My account is meant to shed light on the question of the nature of the intransitive effects of moral action.

tify. The degree to which the thought processes of any individual corresponds to the dynamics I note vary according to factors such as prior beliefs, values and commitments, moral authorities, mental health, environmental upbringing, biopsychology, and so on. Finally, I apologize in advance for the awkward neologism "psycho-moral." By it I simply mean that which pertains simultaneously to the domains of practical reasoning and choosing. Perhaps "moral" should be sufficient, but because I mean to draw attention to the psychic component, I have chosen to use the former.

The Practicality of Moral Reasoning

This essay presumes that the natural moral law exists and that its voice, to use a metaphor, is universally audible; that is, its contents or principles are intelligible or knowable to all.[7] Since the type of knowledge we have of its principles is practical, not for its own sake but for the sake of action, and since knowledge for the sake of action is anticipatory of future possibilities, not merely the possession of true information about already-existing realities, our basic affirmation of the propositional content of the principles of the natural law, by definition, is not the affirmation of speculative propositions but of practical propositions, not the affirmation of something that is the case, as, say, when we affirm the truth of Planck's Constant, but of what *can be done* or what it would be good to do or pursue. To use Aquinas's term, practical knowledge concerns what "is to be."[8] The practicality of ethical pursuits means that our practical knowledge is always correlated with an appetitive interest in the realization of possibilities toward which practical principles direct. That interest is a *natural psychic movement toward* the known goods that we believe can or might be realized through action on their behalf.

I agree with Ratzinger that the evidential character of the nat-

7. Among these intelligible contents of the natural law are included the precepts of the Decalogue.

8. *ST* I-II, q. 94, a. 2c

ural law has weakened considerably as a result of the cultural loss of Christian faith.[9] Another way to say this is: When reason stands before the principles of the natural moral law decoupled from the authority of religious belief, the force of the law's reasonableness and its power to command assent are weaker than when reason is supported by religious belief. This implies that the natural law's "voice," the voice of the *is to be* (which includes *ought to be*), is strengthened or weakened in relation to the prior value-beliefs one brings to the knowing of that law.

Why should one's religious beliefs influence the strength of the voice of the natural law? Both those with faith and those without it are attracted to human goods, such as friendship, health, knowledge, and harmony with God. The attraction is an intelligible awareness that realizing these things through action promises some type of unique benefit, some kind of human fulfillment. As a principle of ac-

9. In *Values in a Time of Upheaval* (San Francisco: Ignatius Press, 2006) [first published as *Werte in Zeiten des Umbruchs: Die Herausforderungen der Zukunft bestehen* (Rome: Libreria Editrice Vaticana, 2004)], Joseph Ratzinger argued that the doctrine of the natural law is disregarded today as sectarian (27). Reason, he famously stated in 2002, borrowing an expression from medieval theologians, seems to have a "wax nose" (*The Beauty and the Truth of Christ*, "Message to Communion and Liberation Meeting in Rimini," August 24–30, 2002); it can be "pointed in any direction, if one is clever enough." We need to see that faith and reason "purify and heal one another" (43), and that faith "makes [reason] return to itself" ("Current Situation of Faith and Theology," Address to the Congregation for the Doctrine of the Faith with the presidents of the Doctrinal Commissions of the Bishops' Conferences of Latin America, Guadalajara, Mexico, May 1996). This may not have been obvious in the seventeenth century, even to some Christians. But history bears it out. The transparent quality of common morality "retained its evidential character only for as long as the entire culture . . . bore the imprint of Christian tradition. . . . With the crumbling of the fundamental Christian consensus . . . all that remained was a naked reason that refused to learn from any historical reality but was willing to listen only to its own self [Reason] became blind" (Ratzinger, *Values in a Time of Upheaval*, 65). "We may surely say that this slender remnant of rational basic moral certainty [i.e., the thin surviving ethical consensus today] is not the product of reason alone but is based on a surviving remnant of insights from the Jewish-Christian tradition" (Ratzinger, *Values in a Time of Upheaval*, 66–67).

tion, the awareness first takes the form of an "is-to-be": we are aware of what *can* be done, of attractive possibilities. When possibilities are considered in relation to one another, in relation to the way the realization of one good or set of goods bears upon the realization of other goods, including their realization in other persons, we become aware of obligations—of an "ought-to-be." We become aware that we could will in ways that are not consistent with love and respect for all human goods. Both those with faith and those without it are aware that they can, but should not, make choices on grounds they believe to be unreasonable. This awareness derives from assent to the *per se nota* practical principle *malum vitandum* (i.e., "that which is contrary to human good is to be avoided").

For those without faith, this *ought* (*not*), as an intelligible entity, possesses at the very least the intrinsic attraction of its own reasonableness, its promise of moral integrity for the person deliberating, and the appeal of the goods that the person believes it (the ought) protects and promotes. For those with faith, the *ought* has added appeal. We are aware that its directiveness is somehow an expression of God's will, and so we are aware that the relationship of harmony that exists between ourselves and God is to some extent at stake in our response to it. This strengthens its power to command assent.

These epistemic factors support our knowing of the principles of the natural law. How, then, do we explain radical moral disagreement? By "radical" I mean more than disagreement among intellectuals at the level of theory. I mean fundamental differences of judgment within and between populations regarding the content of concrete moral norms as well as the failure of rational enquiry and debate to resolve the disagreements in favor of the principles of the natural law. At this level, disagreement did not arise in the West until after the Second World War (1939–45), and not widely until the 1960s. In trying to understand better "what happened," we need to turn to the widespread change in the status of moral authorities around that time.

Commitments and Moral Authorities

A commitment is a settled disposition of will—a self-determination—deliberately instantiated with respect to some intelligible or sensible good or goods (e.g., religion, marriage, beauty, fame, pleasure). As a *cognitive principle*, it disposes us toward future practical judgments consistent with the good or goods it singles out; as a *volitional principle*, it disposes us toward future choices consistent with the good(s); and as an *affective principle*, it disposes us to a range of emotions consistent with value perceptions regarding the condition of the good(s) singled out by the commitment. So, if those goods are being promoted, we ordinarily experience positive emotions; if they are being impeded, damaged, or destroyed, we experience negative emotions.

Our commitments are grounded in our assent to practical propositions specifying some state of affairs realizable through action—some way of being, some kind of doing, or some type of possessing—as choice-worthy. Said another way, our commitments are grounded in what we value. Although many things account for the strength of our commitments, chief among them is the liveliness of the hoped-for end we intend in making them—for example, the livelier Christians' hope for heaven, the stronger their commitment of faith.

But the strength also correlates to the strength with which we hold some source to be a moral authority. A moral authority is a source whose judgments, beliefs, and possibly actions provide a reason for thinking or acting in some way.[10] As authoritative, the authority invests certain moral judgments with persuasive force over what they (the judgments) would have if the source were not held to be an authority.

We invest sources with moral authority based on our judgments and beliefs. For example, small children believe their parents can mete out great rewards and punishments; adolescents believe inclu-

10. Germain Grisez, *Christian Moral Principles* (Chicago: Franciscan Herald Press, 1983), 275.

sion in a peer group has special relevance to their well-being; committed Catholics believe that the teaching Church speaks on behalf of Christ and that Christ is God.

It follows that if a source I take to be a moral authority supports some commitment of mine, all other things being equal, this strengthens my commitment (because I have additional reasons supporting it). If an authority opposes it, this weakens it, at least to some degree. If I have strong reasons other than the concurring judgment of an authority grounding my commitment, then the authority's judgments are of less consequence for the strength of my commitment. But if my independent reasons are weak, then the influence of an authority is likely to be more consequential. If my reasons are weak, and something causes me to negatively revaluate my authority, perhaps even to abandon one authority for another whose judgments are contrary to my prior authority's, this can cause me to reconsider my commitments.

We see how milestones in moral development will often involve all the cognitive and volitional principles mentioned above: beliefs, values, commitments, and authorities. For example, the adult child of an alcoholic father who comes to believe that her father no longer can hurt her, revalues her father's demands upon her, and consequently sets aside commitments related to those demands. Or the cradle Catholic who has dutifully followed his parents' faith until college asks himself during his freshman year, "Do I really believe this?," "Should I continue to live this way?"

Devaluation of Traditional Moral Authorities

Although there is no necessary correlation between our moral commitments and our revaluing of moral authorities, the more our commitments are legalistically grounded, the greater the correlation. Legalistic thinking sees the requirements of morality as principally the domain of rules imposed by authorities for purposes of remaining in harmony with the authority or a group represented by the authority. The sanction of authority and the benefits promised by conformity constitute the chief reasons for acting in accordance with commitments.

Consequently, the widespread revaluation of moral authorities in the West in the mid-twentieth century precipitated a crisis of moral commitment. Practically overnight, the major sources of moral authority—God, Scripture, the churches, societal customs/mores (i.e., tradition), and parents—fell under the knife of suspicion. I do not consider here the reasons for the revaluation, some of which, it seems to me, were sound and others that were spurious.[11] For our purposes, I need only note the indisputable fact of the revaluation . . . and gradual devaluation.

Ratzinger highlights the centrality of the loss of faith. I think it is more accurate to call it the devaluation of the moral authority of God.[12] We have already argued that our beliefs ground our moral authorities. Belief in a personal God who judges according to our deeds, and whose punishments and rewards are eternal, is a powerful psycho-moral principle strengthening our belief in and conformity to moral precepts that we associate with his will. If one ceases to believe in God, or comes to believe he is not a judge, or that his judgments are unrelated to what I do, the authoritative basis of our conformity to those norms diminishes. With the cooperation of theologians, especially moral theologians and Scripture scholars, doctors of Christian eschatology in the twentieth century were first doubted and then denied.

11. The revaluation stemmed partially from sound beliefs such as that traditionally accepted authorities should not be unreasonably shielded from criticism in those domains relevant to the exercise of their authority (the new "hermeneutics of suspicion"), and partially from fallacious beliefs such as the conclusion that because some traditional authorities are untrustworthy, they *all* should be jettisoned as moral authorities (recall the common bumper sticker that read, "Question Authority!").

12. It is possible that *living* faith never played a large role in securing moral consensus in traditional Europe. Nevertheless, strong notions of religious and political authority backed up with severe sanctions for disobedience, together with widespread legalism in the Christian moral life—acceptance of rule-based morality *because* the rules were sanctioned by accepted authorities—conspired to instill conformity to traditional moral principles.

Although people continued to say they believed in God, they ceased believing that he is a just judge; heaven was assured, and hell was a bogeyman they were happy to be done with. God remained an object of nominal belief, but he lost his moral authority. Consequently, the authority of Scripture and the churches also diminished. Moreover, for several reasons, the authority of parents and custom is ordinarily closely associated with religious authority: customs are often bound up with religious values, the parental generation is usually more religious than the filial generation, and the beliefs that move us to invest parents and mores with authority are often bound up with the religious beliefs and values of our community. So, parental authority and the authority of societal custom also diminished. In a generation, a paradigm shift from traditional moral authorities to nontraditional authorities, such as academics, musicians and celebrities, political elites, ideologies of liberation, and what has come to be called "youth culture," took place in Western culture.[13]

Just as an adolescent can feel a kind of satisfaction and invigoration in challenging the views of the parents for whom she feels contempt, many baby boomers felt invigorated by challenging the moral authority of churches and traditional mores, especially in the taboo domain of sexuality. Because of earlier legalism, reasons for supporting traditional moral norms, beyond an appeal to authority, were weak. Predictably, a revaluation of authorities corresponded to a reconsideration of moral commitments.

Reconsideration of the Norm against Contraception

Most vulnerable among these commitments was the norm against contraception. In the non-Catholic world, the exceptionless nature of that norm had been denied by religious authority in the first half of

13. My broad-brushed painting here, I know, ignores subtleties and overlooks other factors relevant to the "paradigm shift." For the sake of this exercise, I leave the account in this generalized form, which, however incomplete, is at least telling part of the story.

the twentieth century. In the secular world, the rising feminist movement during that same period vigorously championed the merits of birth control. Continued conformity among Catholics relied heavily upon their continued regard for Church authority. When Catholics began to devalue this authority, acceptance of the norm declined. Opponents presented their reasons for disregarding the norm with increasing force. Those who did not have strong counter-reasons to disregard the once-forbidden alternative and who no longer had strong reasons from authority to maintain their commitment began to deliberate, some for the first time, over the legitimacy of choosing contraceptive intercourse. They faced incompatible alternatives: on the one hand securing the benefits to be gained by disregarding the norm (mainly avoiding the difficulties involved in periodic abstinence or of having children) and on the other maintaining their commitment to the norm despite their weakening regard for the moral authority of the Church.

Scholars as diverse as Ratzinger[14] and MacIntyre[15] have noted

14. Ratzinger argues that the anti-metaphysical vacuum produced by the Kantian epistemological turn toward the subject was the womb in which utilitarian ethics was gestated. Secular rationality reduced the scope of practical reason to the realm of the empirical and technical, and consequently reduced its task to a calculation of the consequences of acts. See J. Ratzinger, "The Renewal of Moral Theology: Perspectives of Vatican II and *Veritatis Splendor*," *Communio* 32 (2005): 357–68, esp. 364; also see Gerald McKenny, who compares and contrasts MacIntyre and Ratzinger and the problem of moral disagreement, in "Moral Disagreement and the Limits of Reason," in *Intractable Disputes about the Natural Law: Alasdair MacIntyre and Critics*, ed. Lawrence Cunningham (South Bend, IN: University of Notre Dame Press, 2009), 195–226, esp. 215.

15. In October 2004, Cardinal Ratzinger, then prefect of the Congregation for the Doctrine of the Faith, wrote a letter to Fr. John Jenkins of the University of Notre Dame asking the university to reflect on the problem of the inability of men and woman today to find a "common denominator" for ethics. He invited Notre Dame to undertake a project aimed at addressing some of the complexities of the issue, both at the theoretical and practical levels. Alasdair MacIntyre was asked to contribute a lead essay reflecting on problems arising from the theoretical assertion of the universality of the natural moral law in relation to the practical fact of widespread intractable moral disagreement in the contemporary world. Eight scholars representing

the relevance of the modern turn toward utilitarian reasoning upon contemporary moral disagreement. That turn has given rise to a widespread denial of moral absolutes. As exceptionless, moral absolutes act as strong psycho-moral principles protecting the goods to which they refer. If I believe that some norm may never be violated, I cannot violate it without first overcoming the internal objection of my conscience. This includes disregarding emotional motivation built up over time in favor of conforming to the norm. By contrast, if I believe a norm is subject to exceptions, acquiescing to set it aside under this or that circumstance requires less of me. Whether its rejection was in the form of a conscience violation or an otherwise sincere judgment, history shows that the bare intelligibility of the exceptionless norm against contraception did not command the assent of many people when faced with strong opposition to the norm. Decoupled in people's minds from lively motives based upon authority, the evidential character of the norm collapsed.

Denying the norm entails affirming that the procreativity of intercourse (the procreative good) can licitly be willed against (even if only in marriage); in other words, it entails a denial of the inviolability of the procreative good of marriage. Those who chose contraceptive intercourse made two morally relevant choices: to perform some action they believed might bring into existence a new human

---

a range of disciplines (e.g., philosophy, theology, law, social science) were asked to reply to MacIntyre's essay; MacIntyre was then asked to respond to the eight replies. MacIntyre's two essays are "Intractable Moral Disagreements" and "From Answers to Questions: A Response to the Responses," in *Intractable Disputes about the Natural Law*, 1–52 and 313–51, respectively. Drawing on the Aristotelian-Thomistic tradition, MacIntyre attempts both to illustrate how adherence to conflicting practical premises derived respectively from the Aristotelian-Thomistic and the utilitarian tradition gives rise to apparently intractable moral disagreement and to rationally vindicate the former tradition vis-à-vis the latter; he argues that when faced by substantive criticisms of its basic methodology, utilitarianism is neither able to respond by drawing on resources internal to itself nor even adequately understand itself unless viewed through the lens of the Aristotelian-Thomistic tradition. Nevertheless, because of their principled assumptions, proponents of utilitarianism still may not be persuaded that their theory is fatally flawed.

being (they chose potentially fertile intercourse) and to perform some action they believed would prevent that new life from coming-to-be. Through making and carrying out the second choice, they realized within themselves—cognitively, as a rule for future action, volitionally, as a disposition of will in favor of that rule, and affectively (although more gradually), as the settled acceptance of themselves as particular kinds of people—a contraceptive self-determination. They caused in themselves a future-oriented disposition to believe and act in accord with the conditional directive: If I believe new human life is a threat to desired goods, I may will against its coming-to-be.[16]

Reconsideration of the Norm against Extramarital Sex

Because there is a logical relationship between marriage and children—marriage is unique in that it is the kind of community that is naturally fulfilled by the spouses' conceiving and rearing children—once you assent to and act upon the proposition that the procreativity of sexual intercourse may be willed against, the rational connection between sex and marriage weakens. Whatever other intelligibility it may possess, sex between complementary partners of sufficient age and health is a type of behavior through which one welcomes new life. And the good of marriage is intelligible in part precisely as a union of persons sufficiently stable in which to welcome new life and whose acts of bodily communion are *per se aptus* for the generating of new life. Aided by consequentialist reasoning and the winds of change beating against the ramparts set up by authority, the post-1960s generation predictably reconsidered and ultimately denied the exceptionless norm restricting sex to marriage.

16. I consider in more detail the nature of these self-determinations in E. C. Brugger, "Free Choice, Self-Determination and Contraceptive Acts," *Fellowship of Catholic Scholars Quarterly* 35, nos. 3/4 (Fall/Winter 2012): 24–29.

Reconsideration of the Norm against Killing

The denial was expressive partly of a resentment on the part of some women of the gestational consequences *for them* of sex. The new promiscuity made those consequences even graver, since an unwanted pregnancy for an unmarried woman promises considerable social hardship. What seemed radical for Margaret Sanger to say in the 1920s was common by the 1970s: "No woman can call herself free who does not own and control her body, . . . until she can choose consciously whether she will or will not be a mother."[17]

By the 1970s, at least four psycho-moral dynamics of modern character were in place: devaluing of traditional authorities, consequentialist beliefs, contra-life dispositions, and resentment toward the procreative consequences of sex. The next predictable step was the reconsideration of the exceptionless nature of the norm against intentionally killing the innocent.[18] Contraception is chosen to eliminate the problem of unwanted children. If contraceptives fail, one asks, "What are my options?," and one who does not believe that abortion is exceptionlessly wrong is likely to consider abortion a real alternative. The US Supreme Court taught with judiciousness in 1991 that "abortion is customarily chosen as an unplanned response to . . . the failure of conventional birth control."[19] The logical structure of the justifica-

17. Margaret Sanger, *Woman and the New Race* (New York: Brentanos, 1922), chap. 5, available at http://www.bartleby.com/1013/5.html.

18. *Griswold v. Conn.* (381 U.S. 479), which legalized the possession of contraceptives for married couples, was decided in 1965; *Eisenstadt v. Baird* (405 U.S. 438), which legalized possession for unmarried couples, was decided in 1972. Colorado passed the first liberal abortion law in the United States in 1967, New York in 1970. *Roe. v. Wade* (410 U.S. 113) and *Doe v. Bolton* (410 U.S. 179) were decided in 1973, the United Kingdom's Abortion Act passed in 1967, Australia's Victorian Menhennitt ruling was made in 1969, and the Levine ruling occurred in 1971.

19. *Planned Parenthood of Southeastern Pa. v. Casey* (91–744), 505 U.S. 833 (1992). Justice Kennedy states that those who wish to turn back the clock on *Roe v. Wade* "simply . . . refuse to face the fact that for two decades of economic and social developments,

tion for contraception shares several things in common with abortion. One contracepts to eliminate the problem of unwanted children; one fixes one's will against the intelligible good of human life, precisely by choosing to prevent its coming to be. When despite one's prophylactic efforts life nevertheless comes into existence, one's psycho-moral inclinations are already disposed against the new life. Assisted by consequentialist reasoning and abetted by specious arguments minimizing the moral status of the unborn, many began to support, and many more to tolerate, abortion, at least under certain circumstances.

The judgment that abortion is legitimate under such and such conditions is practical and so a directive for action. Those who come to that judgment may not have an abortion, but ordinarily they approve of others doing so when the conditions arise. The women who had abortions and the men and women who supported them introduced within their wills, and wider characters, a disposition against the good of unborn human life. Unless one has reasons in the future to reconsider and reject one's judgments and actions (in religious terms, unless one "repents"), those reasons endure as a measure for future judgments and actions.

What reasons could cause one to reconsider abortion? The reasons that constitute the basis of the practical rationality of the norm against killing; reasons related to the good of human life. But in approving abortion, people already have rejected those reasons precisely *as reasons* against their decision to approve it. Because will, as a rational appetite, is moved by reasons, the reasons, acting as volitional determinants, determine too the will with respect to future volitions. One's will remains characterized by an appetitive aliveness in relation to the goods that abortion promises to secure, and a dullness sets in toward the goods realizable through rejecting intentional killing.[20]

---

people have organized intimate relationships and made choices that define their views of themselves and their places in society, in reliance on the availability of abortion in the event that contraception should fail."

20. The psycho-moral logic continues to unfold with the issue of infanticide. I

A Flawed Analogy

Princeton philosopher Sarah McGrath laments the fact that in the face of substantial moral disagreement over the legitimacy of abortion, we cannot appeal to something analogous to an eye exam to determine whose moral vision is superior.[21] She suggests that the issue parallels the diversity of opinion on the question of which shade of green is "unique green." Unique green is that shade of green that is neither bluish nor yellowish. When asked to select the shade that is unique green, different subjects with normal color vision will select different shades. Just as in the case of our controversial moral views, she argues, opinions about which shade is unique green not only fail to be unanimous, but they are also substantially divided. Perhaps if there were relatively widespread agreement as to which shade is unique green, then the dissenting judgments of a few who possessed otherwise normal color vision could be dismissed. But the fact that the actual division of opinion is substantial suggests that human beings are not reliable detectors of the relevant property.[22]

For the analogy to work, practical reason's counterpart to "normal color vision" would have to characterize both defenders and opponents of abortion. The counterpart to normal color vision is *impartial moral reason*. That impartiality has at least three qualities. First, one's reason is proportionally sensitized to the goods at stake on all sides of the abortion debate, at least those related to women with problem pregnancies and their families, *and* those related to unborn children

---

was not surprised when the May 2013 edition of the prestigious international bioethics journal *Journal of Medical Ethics* was dedicated in full to a discussion of the legitimacy of "after-birth abortion"; see Alberto Giubilini and Francesca Minerva, "After-Birth Abortion: Why Should the Baby Live?," *Journal of Medical Ethics* 39, no. 5 (May 2013): 261–63.

21. Sarah McGrath, "Moral Disagreement and Moral Expertise," in *Oxford Studies in Metaethics*, vol. 3, ed. Shafer-Landau (Oxford: Oxford University Press, 2008), 87–107, example on 99.

22. McGrath, "Moral Disagreement and Moral Expertise," 99.

threatened with abortion.[23] Second, and correlative to the first, one's will is proportionally alive to the goods at stake on all sides of the issue. And finally, one's emotional powers of empathetic responsiveness extend proportionately to all the persons whose goods promise to be affected by choices for the available alternatives under consideration.

Are those who procure, approve the procuring, or otherwise affirm the legitimacy of procuring abortion operating from impartial moral reason? Although they may exhibit sensitivities, even extraordinarily strong ones, toward the plight of vulnerable women with problem pregnancies, they also invariably exhibit a wide and manifest blind spot in relation to the good of the life of the victims of abortion—one that disposes them to choices contrary to the good of unborn human life. That blind spot is explicable in terms of the rational desensitization and volitional and affective dulling toward the good of life that they produce in themselves when they first judge, whether through rationalization or sincere error, that abortion is sometimes legitimate.

McGrath's terminology suggests that human reason is analogous to an instrument designed to detect the presence of a particular substance, as a smoke or metal detector identifies and registers the properties of smoke or metal. The relevant property is moral rightness. She suggests that radical moral disagreement arises at least partly because human reason is not reliable at detecting that property; our moral detectivity is simply too weak.

To the extent that this implies that moral truths are factual properties of things, it badly misunderstands the nature of practical reason. To clarify the misunderstanding, we should start by discarding the ambiguous term "moral facts." A fact is a quality of something actual, something that already exists. To the extent that I am in ra-

23. I say "proportionally" because some of the goods at stake are more basic than others (e.g., the good of maintaining uninterrupted employment is instrumental, the good of life is basic). So, one's reason must be sensitized proportionately to the different types of good.

tional possession of it, it is a speculative truth. But a *moral* truth is not an already existing state of affairs rationally apprehended. It is my right reasoning that a contemplated volition is consistent with a will that remains open to the integral good of persons and communities. Moral truth is my understanding of an anticipated reality. Being a reliable detector for the "property" of moral truth, therefore, means precisely what I said above: being in possession of moral powers sufficiently sensitized to the plurality of goods at stake in complex situations. But one who is color-blind, no matter how intelligent, motivated, sincere and otherwise perceptive, is not a reliable navigator on a roadway whose signposts are color-coded.

The basis of practical rationality per se is the recognition of basic human goods. Saints and sinners alike recognize them and choose in light of their realization. But the basis of the practical rationality of the *norms* of the natural law is the integral interrelationship between human goods. To make correct judgments when faced with incompatible alternatives, each of which promises some benefit we are interested in and none of which promises all the benefits we are interested in, we need to be more than rational. We need to be practically reasonable, exemplified in the Christian tradition by the moral virtue of prudence: we need to possess the ready ability to *see* all the human goods affected by our contemplated courses of action and to assess *how* we should choose in light of what we see (including the option of refraining from choosing) so as to uphold at least minimum respect for all those goods.

Practical reasonableness relies upon at least four things: the rightful valuing of trustworthy moral authorities, the espousing of sound practical principles (at least not rationally assenting to unsound ones), a disposition of will free from significant determinations contrary to human goods, and emotions tutored to respond impartially to the goods of persons and communities. If any of these are eliminated, moral blind spots are likely to arise. If they arise in whole populations, cultural crisis ensues.

Conclusion

A perfect storm struck the West in the middle of the twentieth century. The widespread denial of the exceptionless nature of many of the most significant negative norms in the Western canon, the devaluation of traditional authorities, and the instantiation of contra-life self-determinations left whole populations unable to see what practical reasonableness requires with respect to many issues associated with sexuality and human life. People still see, are interested in, and know how to realize limited instantiations of human goods, often with extraordinary sophistication. But many are no longer capable of judging rightly what morality requires of them in situations of critical importance to their own well-being and the communities of which they are parts. This has given rise to a cultural condition where defenders of traditional morality and those of the new morality engage in moral discourse (if at all) as if in different languages. Although the language of the new morality follows a utilitarian idiom, the idiom for many is a rational guise, however unwittingly adopted, concealing emotivist commitments. The inability of the new morality's philosophical and theological defenders to see the rational flaws in their own arguments is not, *pace* McGrath, because human reason per se is not a reliable detector of "moral properties." It is because the reasoning, willing, and affectivity of many in contemporary culture have been shaped by self-determinations of their own making, determinations that have instantiated blinds spots into their moral faculties, rendering them effectively unable to see moral truths that otherwise are evident.

PART III

LIVING THE CATHOLIC TRADITION

Politics, Vocation, and Education

JOHN FINNIS

6 • THE TRADITION OF REASON AND JUSTICE

Traditions are creations of human thought, imagination, and action that persist or recur by being transmitted from person to person, eventually across succeeding generations of persons. Legal theory has rightly been interested for nearly a century in the type distinctions that Max Weber, in his vastly learned 1920s work on society and economy, drew between the "charismatic," the "traditional," and the "rational" in human affairs, especially in human exercises of authority and governance, and by his association of the "legal" with the rational. But the contrast between traditional and rational needed to be qualified. Though an unquestioning adherence to traditions that are themselves closed to questions does indeed contrast with rationality, Weber's American translator Edward Shils, himself a polymathic scholar, emphasized in his worthwhile and wide-ranging book *Tradition* (1981, paperback 2005) that many rational activities such as those of natural science are reliant upon traditions. Without the handing down and "transmission" that are the essence of tradition, neither the method of the natural sciences nor their huge accumulation of true results could be known or conveyed as information to those who can make use of it, whether in further "pure" science or in technologies and useful works and products of every kind, for human betterment. It is now part of the recent tradition in philosophy of science (Heisenberg, Polanyi, Popper) to emphasize these traditions at the heart of legitimate science.

It would be good to pursue Shils's reflections on the role, the merits, and the dangers of tradition and traditions—and on the need for traditions in many domains of human existence. But here I discuss something more important: the Tradition, what I have called in my title "the tradition of reason and justice." I want to add quite a lot to what I said in my address to the Thomas More Society in Melbourne in 1989, which appears now in volume 5 of my collected essays as "Faith, Morals, and Thomas More." In the middle of that I said:

> More wrote and wrote. He did so because to write for publication is to act in the public realm, to participate in the realm of common, ideally of universal discourse, about things which are in that realm as the faith of the Gospel supremely is. What is reasonable can integrate feelings [I had been quoting More's contemporary the Protestant reformer William Tyndale, denouncing Catholicism as only "an historical faith" rather than "a feeling faith" such as Tyndale wanted; and I had mentioned More's recent biographer Richard Marius's condescending criticism of More for writing so much against the ideas of men like Tyndale] if it is not dominated by feelings, by private experience, but expresses the insights and judgments which any reasonable being would make on the available evidence, including the evidence of witnesses. What the Catholic Church hands on in her faith and worship expresses the insights and judgments of a vast succession of reasonable human persons who received, tested, and handed on the whole tradition (including the Scriptures) in which the divine act of publicly accessible revelation is to be made effective until the end of human history.

In revisiting and expanding considerably on what I there called "the whole tradition," I can also say something about the ultimate foundations of the law, and of the moral truths on which any acceptable law is founded.

The Tradition is unique among traditions. It is not only explicitly conscious of its own status and content as, at once, both tradition and reason. It is also concerned to demonstrate, and retain, its full critical reasonableness: with acute awareness that there are alternative traditions, this tradition understands itself as valid for all human persons whether they have heard of it or not. The papal encyclical on this, *Fides et Ratio* (1998), has gaps in its identification and treatment of the Tradition, gaps that I want to fill in a bit. I do so without presupposing the principles of doctrine and theology. An encyclical is an act of handing on that strand of the Tradition that we may call the tradition of faith. It presupposes those doctrinal principles. It does so on the meta-presupposition that presupposing them—treating them as principles, *principia*, starting points—is fully reasonable. That meta-presupposition is what I address as an essential element in answering the question why and how there is a tradition that deserves to be called the Tradition—the tradition of reason (and therefore also of justice, and indeed of faith also).

Fides et Ratio 85.2 says:

> the great tradition . . . , beginning with the ancients, passes through the Fathers of the Church and the masters of Scholasticism and includes the fundamental achievements of modern and contemporary thought.

Fair enough. But who are these "ancients"? It would be easy to assume that they are the Greek philosophers, mathematicians, natural scientists, and historians of the fifth, fourth, and later centuries before Christ, outstanding thinkers of whose work the Church Fathers and scholastics, not to mention the Roman lawyers both pagan and Christian, would make ample use. That is the assumption on which modern educational curricula and encyclopedias of philosophy, science, and culture are largely shaped: the roots of the Tradition are Greek.

But that is wrong. Fundamental to the great tradition are theses about reality and morality that were consistently affirmed by the prophets of Israel, and thus by the Old Testament—that library whose whole literary construction is shaped by these prophets' teaching. Their main theses about reality and morality are radically superior to the corresponding positions of even the best Greek philosophers and are fundamental to the elements of today's thought that can and should be defended, explored, deployed, and handed on.

I discuss four of these theses under the labels Creation, freedom, justice (and humanity), and faith (as intelligent and rational acceptance of divine revelation). Each of the four theses (and there are others) was a rupture from both the past and the whole surrounding matrix of civilizations and cultures. Each of these theses would later be taken up and rendered into more reflexively philosophical form by thinkers who had developed and deepened those new, Jewish insights in or soon after becoming Christians—thinkers who saw how the established Greek philosophical tradition, with its schools and sects, could and should be transformed and radically improved by those same Jewish insights. The four theses are directly—or, in the case of the fourth, indirectly—fundamental to the rule of law as we know of it. And they are, therefore, fundamental to the philosophy or theory of law. And to our law. A society's laws, and its juridical and doctrinal understandings of law and of its own laws, are a kind of crystallization of the understandings and misunderstandings widespread in that society about reality in its deepest aspects, and about human goods and the principles of right and wrong choosing. And both the works of my teacher and former colleague H. L. A. Hart and the works of my former longtime colleague Ronald Dworkin—the two most influential English-speaking legal theorists of the last century—indicate sufficiently (though discreetly) that the thoughts of each of them about law (differing thoughts, of course) and about particular laws, doctrines, and projects of law reform (not much difference between them here!), were thoughts profoundly shaped by beliefs and attitudes about these four theses—all four of them—and about the entire Tradition that has conveyed those theses to us. Neither Hart nor Dworkin expounded those underlying beliefs and attitudes of theirs in their teaching or public writings (except, in the case of Dworkin, in his last year or so of life). But they were of decisive importance, I believe, for that teaching and writing.

And the theses at stake are indeed truths that none of us can afford to take for granted. They are truths that it is the special responsibility of a Catholic university to appropriate and reaffirm. At the end of this essay, I say a bit more about the circumstances in which that must be undertaken by such a university and, in one way or another, by any Catholic today and in the coming years.

Part I

So, the first thesis: Creation. The idea of Creation is now so central to the great tradition that it seems commonsense even to those of our contemporaries who reject it—for them, it's the alternative to be refuted, the only alternative to care about. Charles Darwin, in his 1876 autobiography (published seventeen years after the *Origin of Species*), speaks frankly of the

> extreme difficulty or rather impossibility of conceiving this immense and wonderful universe, including man with his capacity of looking far backwards and far into futurity, as the result of blind chance or necessity. When thus reflecting I feel compelled to look to a First Cause having an intelligent mind in some degree analogous to that of man.

The thesis he found so compelling—that reason warrants the rational judgment that everything in the immense and wonderful universe has a First Cause that is no part of but entirely transcends the universe, of which it is the First Cause by decision and activity of its intelligent mind—is one that notably surpasses the best in Plato's or Aristotle's philosophizing about the divine causality at work in the world. When articulated more explicitly than this terse remark by Darwin, it clearly involves the denial that there are any divine being or beings within the universe. It involves the radical distinguishing of the entirety of Nature from the divine nature, the de-divinizing of Nature and at the same time its de-absolutizing, revealing Nature's (the universe's) thoroughgoing contingency and its utter lack of any elements that might explain, account for, its existence as a totality of intelligible beings and interactions. This is the metaphysical reasoning and judgment articulated as a matter of commonsense (our commonsense) handed down—eventually to us (as to Darwin)—from Genesis 1, from Psalm 19 ("The heavens declare the glory of God"), from the precision attributed to the mother of the martyred seven brothers in 2 Maccabees 7:28 ("when you see the heavens, the earth, and all that is in it, you know that God made all this from nothing"), and again from the masterly summation of the Hebrew creation tradition in Rabbi Saul's letter, as Paul, to the Romans: "God's invisible attributes, his everlasting power and divinity, are made visible to reason by means of his works since the creation of the world" (Rom 1:20).

This new thesis in the Tradition liberated and motivated human thought for unrestricted inquiry into the intelligibilities of the entire natural world. That practical meaning of the thesis can be discerned in Aquinas's critique of certain monotheistic believers in creation and providence who, as Muslim professors (Mutakallimun), held that the transcendent power of the divine designer works its effects by divine decision moment by moment and independently of natural causalities (which are thus more apparent than real). St. Thomas's response to this is a reply also to those who imagine that the designer rationally envisaged by the Psalmist, St. Paul, and Darwin initiated everything merely by one tremendous initial creation of natural potentialities that since then have been merely left to their own operations and independent working out of their initial potentialities. No, says Aquinas to both sides in his consideration of divine providence, what we think of as effects of natural causes are precisely that—effects of natural causes, in chains or sequences of causation that can fruitfully be investigated by natural sciences; and at the same time, all these natural effects and causes are being caused, here and now as much as at the beginning of time, by the power of the intelligent designer. They are wholly effects of their natural causes and of the transcendent (beyond Nature) cause that explains both the creation of Nature from nothing and all the workings of Nature ever since. (Reflection on this "wholly . . . wholly"—on the thing or event in question being not partly attributable to Nature and partly to divine power, but rather in whole to natural causes and in whole to God—orients us to the true meaning of the word "transcendent.")

This elegant solution of opposing problematic positions is a permanent acquisition of human wisdom, securing the place and integrity of the natural sciences. We need only add two things. One, insofar as modern science, not least the macroevolutionary biology in which Darwin's role was strategic, discloses the emergence from time to time of genuinely new species, new kinds of organisms and organs and forms of life, the Thomist distinction between Creation and Providence may appropriately be softened to allow that Providence includes an ongoing if not continuous Creation. And, two, any such ongoing creation is doubtless by way of what we all easily call, since at least Crick and Watson's 1953 discovery of the structure and working of DNA, new information.

For today—by a remarkable, unintended, but real analogy with Aristotelian accounts of "form"—we understand the workings of organic life as workings directed, at the microlevel, by a series of intra- and intermolecular realities, activities, relationships, and patterns that natural scientists concur in finding most adequately describable in terms of *information*: messages and messengers, expressions, programs, sense and nonsense, transcription, reading, translation, copying, and so forth—as aspects of the working of a code with four or five "letters," the four nucleotide bases in DNA and the slightly different set of four bases in RNA, without which DNA cannot perform its essential functions. All these terms—"information," "code," "program," "messengers," and so forth—are being used by analogy with their focal or central-case usage in relation to our activities as intelligent beings communicating with other intelligent beings by intentional acts of meaning. So, I call the information described in modern natural sciences analogous information, to distinguish it from the central-case kind of information conveyed by, for example, scientists in conversations, research programs, reports, articles, and other communications with each other.

Among the empirical realities that persuade scientists of the need to use this analogy is the capacity of organisms to repair themselves when damaged, to work around, and respond ingeniously (and even proactively) to lesions, insults, diseases, and threats to their immunity, in ways impossible to machines (however complex) of the pre-information technology (IT) era (and imitated only partially and somewhat clumsily by the IT machines of today). That capacity, along with the capacity we call metabolism, to ingest and transform external materials into its own organism, and the capacity to reproduce itself by replication without loss to itself, together mark the great advance that the living makes over the nonbiological. But even the nonbiological world of molecules, atoms, and subatomic particles came to be understood, by a revolution in scientific thought in the early to mid-twentieth century, as essentially an activity according to pattern or dynamic structure—a revolution that has not been absorbed by those who think of the world as the movement in space of tiny particles of matter. The concept of matter cannot be eliminated, but whatever it stands for is entirely dominated by the patterns of activity that remain more or less stable while the matter within them comes and goes without that really mattering.

So much more could be said about all this! To give just an intimation of the natural realities themselves, let me say that each one of the 60 to 100 trillion cells constituting one's bodily makeup includes within it a unique genome that includes (along with thousands of millions of other components) 3 billion pairs of bases from the four DNA bases, arranged within each cell in a way partly unique to each of us but common to all the other cells in the same body, thus enabling one's coherent growth and organic functioning as the specifically human but uniquely individual person each human person is. But "a genome," like "a molecule" or "an atom" or "an electron," is to be thought of as essentially an ongoing activity focused by its pattern or (in a dynamic sense) structure. A cell exists as a whirlpool of molecular activity in which the component molecules and their components, each set unimaginably numerous, are being amended and replaced in a constant stream while retaining their lasting identity by virtue of the more or less constant pattern or structure, the (analogous) information that utterly unconsciously the cell "knows how" to read and apply in its activity. And the same goes at the level of the organism. So, every day of one's life, about 500 billion cells in one's makeup are destroyed and replaced by others functioning to substantially the same pattern. Not one of these cells can any laboratory or network of laboratories replicate, yet one's makeup, dominated as it is by its information both specifically human and peculiarly individual, "knows how to do it." The analogous knowledge is that without which the (analogous) information would not be information.

Our information-generating and -exchanging conversations, books, and lectures are utterly different from the chance selection of letters by an army of monkeys pressing computer keyboards (or two-symbol Morse Code transmitters). So, too, the operations of Nature. Like the deploying of instruments, breath, eyes, and muscles in the performing of a vast symphonic or operatic composition envisaged and settled by its composer, these operations of Nature—as I have been indicating—deploy atomic (physical and chemical), molecular (chemical, biochemical, and biological), and organic operations largely if not wholly describable, and commonly described, as involving transmission and utilization of information. They are operations as far removed from mere chance (or randomness) as they are from the purposes or causality of cosmic stellar divinities such as Plato and Aristotle (in differing ways) supposed are at work within and from within our universe. And our empirical modern natural science makes a radical breach or rupture with the idea of cyclical operations of an eternal cosmos, the idea dreamed of by Greek popular religion and postulated by sophisticated pre-Socratic atheistic atomists. Instead, our empirical science (as distinct from the philosophizing of some scientists) tells us, with abundant evidence, of a universe with a definite beginning—and beyond this (the empirical evidence leaves us to infer)—nothing, and neither time nor space. It tells us, with abundant evidence, that this universe is evolving from the evidently less information-rich to the increasingly amply information-rich. This evolution has had such a manifest directionality—including the directionality of acceleration in increase of (analogous) information—that after less than 14 billion years it saw the emergence of the stable species we call human beings. We and our human forebears are animals so remarkably evolved—whether gradually, in the decisive stages, or not, and whether in the chance-dominated ways proposed by neo-Darwinist empirical hypotheses, or not—that our brains and their processes can support spiritual operations, that is, the operations of intentional reflection on, and communication of, abstract and reflexive meanings. They can likewise support the insights needed to understand, and to choose to investigate, these evolved forms of life and being, and the whole history of these forms of life, and something of their more or less probable future.

There was thus a change in the structure of reality so transformative that it could be called a kind of rupture with the past of evolution of Nature and life. All along, the transcendent mind, will, and power have been causing, progressively as well as initially, the existence and content of that vast, expanding, and evolving accumulation and transmission of analogous information that we call Nature. With the emergence of human beings, and of human intelligence, will, and free action, the universe is at last in a position such that the transcendent Creator can choose and bring into effect the choice to initiate also a transmission of central-case information to members of this newly emerged species of being, humankind. Mind can speak to mind, spirit commune with spirit.

And beyond bare possibilities, there are historical facts. The Jewish people in fact reached a settled and superior understanding of the universe's origins and natural intelligibility centuries earlier than Greeks reached their own standard and inferior understanding. This accomplishment of the Jewish people seems to have been, in fact, an accomplishment both of natural reason (intelligence) reflecting on experienced realities and of the receptivity of that people's prophets and priests to divine communication (in any of the modes they came to call revelation). It was reflected and articulated with remarkable consistency and coherence throughout the body of developing and temporally stratified traditions and writings we call the Old Testament. This accomplishment or acquisition is a central element of the great tradition that has so shaped our common sense that no one can now take seriously the pagan conception of a partly divinized world. And those who spurn the Creation thesis, in favor or defense of their own atheism or pantheism, cannot conceal their truncation of rational inquiry, their ukase against some legitimate questions about the explanation of the existence and intelligibility of what we empirically experience and scientifically infer.

In modern times, those who thus declare a proper field of further enquiry "out of bounds," or who tacitly ignore it, often do so on the basis of an honestly (and vividly) felt consideration, the argument from evil. That is the argument that persuaded Darwin to set aside his own reasonable reflective inference from natural order to intelligent creation. But appealing though it can be to sentiment, it was and is a mistake. It mistakenly presumes that divine causality would be of a kind that could be quality-assessed by the standards we apply to natural causality, or to the causality whereby conclusions are explained by their premises, or to the causality whereby human actions are explained by their author's choices, or human crafts by their objectives—the standards we apply in those domains to assess something defective, monstrous, wrong, evil, or a failure. That God's causality is transcendent entails that the argument from evil against divine existence and creative providence fails. It fails not because it entails that the evils pointed to are only apparent, but because, on the standards appropriate to and known now only to the creative wisdom—a wisdom capable of conceiving and bringing about, from nothing, the ever more astounding intelligibilities of Nature's patterns of activity—the universe in which evils (or what by other standards are evils) are to be found (along with all that is intelligible to us as really good) may nonetheless be something good and in important respects better, more intelligently selected by its Creator, than a universe without those evils.

The Old Testament's consistent understanding of Creation and providence invites the philosophical developments and defenses that Christian thinkers subsequently provided for it and that are a central treasure in the patrimony we call the Tradition.

Part II

The Tradition has a second main component, a component contributed to it more vividly and fully by the Hebrew people than by the Greek: the thesis that we can, and from time to time do, make free choices. In other words, we have "free will." Here again it is not a matter simply of proof texts in which the Old Testament articulates this freedom—though such texts can easily be found—but also a matter of the whole narrative of personal and communal responsibility for choices made, of covenants freely entered into and broken and restored by renewed undertaking. Aquinas was not adding a simply New Testament teaching or philosophical thesis to Genesis's meaning when he said that man's being "made in the image of God" is a matter of man's having freedom of choice and mastery over his or her own acts.

For Genesis 1 affirms that man was made in God's image only after it has presented God as freely choosing to create the universe and freely selecting what components it will have—so as to be this universe rather than other possible good universes or no universe at all. And in the evolution of the Abrahamic and Mosaic revelation and the writings it inspired, Genesis 1 may well be later than the book of Deuteronomy, itself shaped by the teaching of some of the most important of the prophets of Israel. Deuteronomy encapsulates its apparently postexilic presentation/redaction of the Covenant between God and his people in the choice:

"See, I set before you on this day life and good, evil and death.... Therefore, choose life" (Dt 30:15, 19).

Against Hellenistic doctrines of fate, Ben Sirach, writing about 200 BC in the book we call Ecclesiasticus or Sirach, sums up the whole teaching of the Old Testament on human freedom:

> Do not say "It was God who made me sin." God does not cause what he hates ... When he created man in the beginning, he left him free to make his own decisions [or in the hands of his own counsel/deliberation]. If you wish you can keep the commandments, and it is in your power to remain faithful. He has set fire and water before you; you stretch out your hand to whichever

you prefer. Life and death are set before man; whichever a man prefers will be given him. (Sir 15:11, 15:14–17)

Like the Church Fathers from Justin Martyr and Irenaeus in the second and third centuries to John Damascene in the eighth, Aquinas teaches the radical freedom of the will, its capacity to prefer one option to an alternative such that nothing either outside or inside one's make-up explains one's preference save that act itself of choosing (preferring). For reasons one might call pedagogical, Aquinas minimizes—to the point of tacitly concealing—the extent to which this thesis marks a transformation of (if not rupture with) Aristotle, whose subtle and strenuous account of human deliberating and acting never affirms real and true free choices, but only a kind of freedom from external constraints: what Aristotle calls "choice" (*prohairesis*) is only of the one course of action that one's reason judges good; if one acts otherwise, as often happens, one does so not by unreasonable choice (says Aristotle) but by *akrasia*, subjection to one's inner desire(s) shaped up by one's past formation and dispositions. By this concealment, as in some other ways, the genius of Aquinas's synthesis of the great Tradition obscures from our view the extent to which the Tradition's Christian form has broken from Athens and preferred Jerusalem (while bringing over from Athens everything that helps articulate Jerusalem's own wisdom as not only revealed but also accessible to natural reason).

Here I offer just two summary sets of observations about the truth that (though not everything we do is freely chosen) we can make choices that are free in the strong, far-reaching sense I just defined. First, just as God's causality, though absolutely necessary to explain the existence and the astounding intelligibility and non-randomness of Nature, is so transcendent that it can and should be said to be wholly the cause of natural events that are wholly the effects of natural causes, so too God's causality must be the cause of acts of human free choice, acts that truly have no cause other than their making by the human person who makes them, and are wholly the responsibility of that person and not of Nature or of God.

As Aquinas explains in his general philosophical teaching about God's existence, nature, and action, one cannot predicate anything of God—existence, nature, action, causality, gender, or anything else—without a shift in meaning so drastic that it amounts to denying of God any of the usual and humanly central meanings of these terms and predicating them of him only to the extent and in the sense that is necessitated by the need to account for the existence, characteristics, and operations of Nature (including human willing and action).

Correspondingly, divine providence, as understood in the Tradition initiated and established in the Old Testament, is emphatically not the fate, or destiny, in which Greek thought, like that of other civilizations, still encloses and more or less smothers its intimations of human freedom. Providence is emphatically distinct from, and far truer to reality than, the cosmic determinism to which Ronald Dworkin has recently given voice. According to the second of his Einstein lectures in December 2011, there is such an uncountable multiplicity of entire universes (multiverses)—he postulates them "bubbling out of the landscape"—that the beauty and "magic" of "the universe" (including this set—imagined by him—of multiverses) consist above all in its inevitability. And so, at the climax of the argument, he cries out, "It's inevitable that I exist!" Such a denial of his own parents' freedom of choice, and equally of his own and yours and mine, is a profound and, I think, inexorable implication of atheistic or pantheistic denials of Creation, when they are clung to against the overwhelming evidence of the Creator's existence, causality, mind, and selection (in Creation) between possibilities.

Second, to speak of human free choices is also to speak of deliberations about the merits and demerits of the alternative options between which one must choose, and thus it is also to speak of conscience as one's intelligent reflecting on those merits, whether reflecting in advance and generally (in abstraction from particular circumstances) or concretely in particular circumstances, or reflecting retrospectively on what one could and should (or should not) have chosen. The sense of personal responsibility for one's own character and the reality of conscience are also realities known more clearly in the Jerusalem of the Old Testament (brought to its full development in the New Testament) than in the Athens of the philosophers. This clarity about freedom and responsibility is new in human history and a permanent pillar of the Tradition. The clarity is itself an aspect and resultant of the proclamations and teachings of the remarkable thinkers we call the prophets of Israel, the *nabi* or (as they understood themselves to be) spokesmen of God—especially their teachings about justice.

Part III

Thomas Aquinas begins his big treatise on justice by adopting the definition of justice promoted by Justinian's Digest (533 AD). There, in that ambitious work of discreetly integrating Roman law into the now fairly firmly Christian tradition, the definition appears, near the beginning of Book I, with an attribution to Ulpian, perhaps the most influential of Roman jurists: "justitia est constans et perpetua voluntas jus suum cuique tribuere"—"justice is the firm and lasting willingness to give to each his rights"—and the precepts of right, or *juris praecepta*, are to live honestly, to do no harm to others and to give to each what he is entitled to ("honeste vivere, alterum non laedere, suum cuique tribuere"). Modern scholars of Roman law like my Oxford colleague Tony Honoré are confident that this definition cannot rightly be ascribed to the great Ulpian, and they tend, moreover, to treat it as mere "humdrum endorsement of existing law," of existing (positive) legal rights. In Aquinas, the definition is much richer in significance and open to the widest horizons of human entitlement to respect; and Honoré himself accepts that the definition's unknown author is linked with the circle of that notable Christian intellectual, Origen. Honore argues from other passages, more authentically attributed to Ulpian, that he was "the pioneer of human rights," that is, of justice and equity for all. And to explain Ulpian's insights, Honoré cautiously points not only to Stoicism and the cosmopolitan and egalitarian policies of the late Antonine emperors around the turn of the second and third centuries AD, but also to the possibility that Ulpian was exposed to Christians through courtly circles and "will have welcomed the universalism and care for the weak that marked Christianity."

I would add that Ulpian was from Tyre, the great trading city not far north of Mt. Carmel, in a region long hostile to Israel but by the time of Jesus open for him and his disciples to visit and for people from the area to go to Galilee to hear him preach—as the Gospels record.

No need to speculate further here. What is certain is that the Jewish people, through from Moses and the prophets, and the priestly crafters of legislation inspired by them, manifested a far-reaching and novel understanding of the requirements of justice centuries earlier than Greece and its great philosophers. Read Exodus 21–23, Leviticus 19 and 25, and Amos and other prophets on the duties owed by all to the poor, widows, newborns, orphans, strangers, servants, and read—among much else—Deuteronomy 4's reflection that the precepts of the Law are themselves just, a matter of intelligence and wisdom. The far-reaching prophetic insistence on the duties of justice as implications of the rejection of idolatry—that is, as implications of recognizing the transcendence of the one Provident Creator—is an insistence developed somewhat further by the convert Rabbi Saul in his letter to the Romans, as an implication of that same recognition of the divine nature from God's works "from the creation of the world." To shut one's eyes to these works, to refuse to acknowledge, glorify, and thank the Creator, is such a failure of reason that passions take its directive place, resulting not only in orientation to and practice of obscene perversions but also in injustices of the many personal kinds that St. Paul there lists (Rom 1:29–31). For the injustices identified and excluded from conscientious deliberation by the Ten Commandments not only are identified in the revelation of God's will to Israel but also equally are in principle identifiable by—accessible to—the natural reason and conscience of anyone anywhere who is open to serving truth and justice: Romans 2:8–15.

The humanism of the prophets who preceded Paul was, at least in its emphasis, notably more political than his. The Hebrew prophets' humanism was more centered on the misdeeds, the chastisement, and the redemption of a whole people led astray in the first instance, though not only by the misdeeds of their political leaders. It was and is a humanism focused on the humanity of the exploited, vulnerable, despised, the humanism of a call for justice to each and all. It proposes even that all are lovable and, at least as neighbors or companions, to be loved as much as oneself: Leviticus 19:18. But in many of those we call the prophets, such as Amos, Hosea, Isaiah, and Micah, there is a further humanism and universality—the expectation or prophecy that eventually all nations will go up to Jerusalem to be taught by God his ways and walk in his justice, their disputes settled by him, so that the nations will live in peace with each other, each retaining its identity (even its own religion perhaps distinct from Israel's), while God restores to dignity and a proper place all lame and banished individuals: Micah 4:1–6, expanding on Isaiah 2:2–4.

The information conveyed in what we call the New Testament, about the unambiguously everlasting significance and destiny of each individual human person, one by one, completed and deepened the prophets' message of responsibility for justice. The thesis becomes Christ's and St. Paul's, St. Peter's and St. John's: we are to live lives fully respectful of the human goods each of us has been given as seed and "talents."

Part IV

My colleague Tony Honoré, whose scholarly monograph on Ulpian I have just drawn upon, was a close collaborator and coauthor with my doctoral supervisor H. L. A. Hart. In the chair of jurisprudence in Oxford, Hart was succeeded in 1969 by Ronald Dworkin, who in turn was succeeded in 2000 by John Gardner, who in 2014 published a book of essays on law in general, titled *Law as a Leap of Faith*. Let me dwell a little not on the book, nor on law in general, but on the phrase "leap of faith." In many minds, non-Christian and Christian (even

Catholic, now), the words "leap" and "faith" go together: between faith and reason, or indeed reasons, there is no bridge—so one must leap, if one chooses to, or stay with reason, if one chooses not to leap. Although that is certainly not the teaching of John Paul II's encyclical *Fides et Ratio*, I do not think the issue is fully confronted or clarified in that encyclical, partly because the document does not, so far as I can see, take time to clarify what the revealing is that constitutes, as divine revelation, the precise object of true faith. Indeed, while the encyclical cites various important teachings of the First Vatican Council about faith and revelation, it omits that council's teaching that faith is properly in no way a leap in the dark (*nequaquam sit motus animi caecus*: DS 3010) and that the Catholic faith is reasonable and attested by many objective signs making clear that its content is indeed revealed to us by the Creator, signs such as prophecies and miracles, and most importantly words and actions of Jesus of Nazareth (DS 3009). For having faith (as that council conceives it) is a matter of believing in the truth of propositions held out to us for a fully reasonable judgment, a judgment whereby one accepts them as true because one judges that the propositions have been affirmed, on the authority of God—no liar—by the various witnesses to the faith whose content is what God has communicated, some of these credit-worthy witnesses being prophets divinely inspired, some of them being writers divinely preserved from asserting error, some of them being witnesses to Jesus the Christ, and some of them the teachers of the community he founded (DS 3008, 3009, 3011).

Though expressed in the philosophical language of Aquinas and the idiom of the nineteenth century, all this conciliar thinking is no more than making more articulate what is partly articulated, and certainly manifested, in that teaching of the Hebrew prophets which finds its completion in Jesus and his specially articulate witnesses John, Peter, Paul, and the author of the letter to the Hebrews. By faith, these men did not mean merely some sort of chosen commitment or stance or attitude or dedication to forms of worship and speech about "our God." Still less did they mean the "deep basic attitude"—or "sense of the objective intrinsic significance of human life" and "sense of the magic of the universe," "basic convictions or commitments" that are basically "emotion" and "feeling"—which Ronald Dworkin spoke of in defining his "religion without a god," and claimed is what believers in God mean by "belief" or "faith." Rather, Jesus—and then John, Peter, Paul, and the others—meant an objective certitude about the truth, the truths (true propositions) that God is the Creator and is transcendent master of Creation and of its history, and loves and wills the good, individually, of the only creatures who, like him, can choose and, if they will, can bring about good and refuse to intend evil; and that he communicates those of his purposes that he chooses to communicate (reveal), to chosen men and women among his chosen and thereby informed people. Let that be the fourth of the four theses. It points to truths, some of which are known only by revelation and in that sense are known by the circumstances of their origin, but the truths of faith include also many important truths that are accessible also—the very same truths—to reason independently of revelation: notably, the other three theses and indeed all the truths of a sound morality.

Like Creation itself, with its hitherto ever increasing (and indeed accelerating) complexity of development-directing information, the prophetic tradition—from Abraham in the nineteenth century before Christ, Moses in the twelfth, Amos and Isaiah and others in the eighth, and so on down to the later parts of the book of Daniel in the second or first—was a tradition of extraordinary complexity, and this richness includes elements that, when they become isolated from the dynamic master directive-idea, result in monsters, cancers, and various other kinds of illness. The prophetic visions of a non-cyclical history proceeding with definite direction toward messianic transformation of this world have (by side effect) contributed, down to today, to severe illnesses of the social, the ecclesiastical, and the political order through myths of revolutionary transformation, third ages, inevitable progress, and the like. But at its heart, the tradition of the prophets in Israel was a tradition of love of, and submission to, nothing but truth. By its rational clarity and truthfulness about fundamental features of reality, it contributed greatly to the Tradition we know. At the historic climax of Israel's prophetic tradition in Jesus, and in John the Evangelist, Peter, Paul, and the other witnesses to Christ, the prophetic sequence was inserted into a lasting context and frame, more deeply informed about history's direction and more capable of containing the prophetic richness in a dynamically stable order and directive idea: the Church that is not simply this bearer of information but is also and primarily the new Israel and new Jerusalem, and indeed is the beginning of a new Creation, above all of and for human persons, the society-with-God that will not be completed within this world and its history.

The Hebrew prophets' critique of idols and polytheism, and of human sacrifice and human castes of every kind, was a rational, even rationalist critique. God's speaking to these prophets, by inspiration and the supernatural influence the Church calls grace, was not (when its manifestations are taken as a whole) an irruption imposing itself on passive and unprepared minds. Rather, it was more in the nature of a dialogue, in which the divine voice speaks to a questioning intelligence. Just as (as St. Paul saw) denial of Creation both promoted and was promoted by immersion in moral corruption, so the intelligence and rational good judgment of the prophets was healed from distraction, evasion, and the lies of self-deception and immoral cultures and—thus purified and sanctified—was able to receive intimations of the divine nature and purpose. True, those intimations, both in the manner in which they were conveyed and received and in their content, went beyond what natural reasoning from insights into experience is able, from its own resources alone, to affirm. But the insights articulated as these intimations were insights fulfilling and perfecting, not making a rupture with, intelligence and intelligent inquiry.

A monument of the prophetic tradition of Israel is the Gospel of John. Whether it is a writing of St. John son of Zebedee and brother of St. James, or of another John, disciple and close associate of Jesus (and apostle, though not of the Twelve), and whether written up toward the end of the first century or as I think (*pace* many scholars) much more likely, almost fully composed within twenty years of the Resurrection to which it credibly witnesses, this book in every chapter gives voice to the questionings of intelligent persons (including the author) who are determined not to be deceived—who want nothing but the truth, not myth. These persons are sober, realistic, responsible even when—or precisely when—dealing with the extreme "otherness" of a transcendent Creator's reaching into the natural order of creation to intimate the definite (though not immediate) future transformation of human existence by a rebirth into God's, a rebirth completed through and beyond death. Only in the empty tomb does this man—the beloved disciple—see enough to definitively convince him, finally, of the authenticity of the man from Nazareth who bore, and more than bearing, lived out, the message, the new information: John 20:8.

The first generations of Christians, like John in his Gospel's prologue (and like St. Paul in his address to the Athenians [Acts 17:22–31] and his letters, e.g., to the Romans) saw and in due course grasped the opportunity of completing the prophetic tradition's openness to the Greek traditions of dialectical enquiry that we call philosophical. I have been speaking about that openness in this chapter. I have been insisting that it is far more than an openness. Rather, it is an appropriation, by way of which, eventually, the now completed prophetic tradition of Israel was in a position to transform the foundational results of Plato's and Aristotle's reflective investigations, rejecting some fundamentals of their worldview while appropriating the sound parts of their dialectical methods and philosophical vocabulary (words crystallizing insights). For the truths of creation, freedom, and true justice and honesty of life are indeed transformations. From a perspective that remained hostile to the first thesis, if not also to the other three—say, the perspective of Celsus in the late second century or of Fichte, Marx, and Nietzsche (not to mention countless other metaphysicians in the nineteenth and twentieth centuries)—the appropriation of these theses by the Christian continuation of the

Hebrew tradition seemed more a rupture with reason itself than a continuation or even transformation of the Hellenistic intellectual tradition of philosophy. But what is rupture—or, rather, transformation and continuity—is to be judged only from the perspective of that tradition which most adequately understands and articulates the truth about the issues in question, the tradition that has judged truly.

How does one determine which that tradition is? It must be a tradition that teaches without reservation or equivocation that there is truth and error, in relation to nature and logic and forms of choice and action, and teaches that truth is to be earnestly sought and all error conscientiously avoided. It must, accordingly, be a tradition that establishes institutions in which, in a world of ever increasing complexity and information, truth can be patiently winnowed from error, and the winnowing and its fruits passed on, as both methods and results, to new generations. It must be a tradition that has an adequate account of rival traditions and of the points at which they remained ignorant of, or failed to understand, or refused to accept, the truths central to the central Tradition. No tradition can be accepted that fails to acknowledge the truths of Creation, freedom, and moral responsibility for justice.

And if a tradition is to be recognized as the Tradition, it must be a tradition into which there is a way—a way lying open to natural reason on the basis of experience (in the broadest sense of experience that includes rationally warranted acceptance of credible human testimony). For, as Aquinas, one of the supreme exponents of the Tradition, states and repeats, the truths that we call truths of faith are such that they can (and should) be defended and expounded not only to people who assume the truth of the books of the Old Testament, or to people who assume the truth of the New Testament, but also to people who do not assume or accept the truth of either but are open to being persuaded to accept that truth—persuaded simply from a starting point in natural reason ("simply," in the sense that the reasoning proceeds entirely without any reliance at all on revelation or the historical events that count as evidence of revelation). This natural reason—reason unaided by revelation—is informed by experience of life in family and society, and can be enhanced by learning in mathematics and the natural sciences and history and, on the basis of all these, by the highly reflexive natural reason we call philosophy. The Gospel must be acceptable as true not only to those who have had little of such learning but also to those who have much. And it is. Parts of it are both (1) knowable directly and wholly by natural reason and (2) affirmed also in the sources of divine revelation; the other parts of it are (3) not accessible directly by natural reason, but (4) only by way of those sources of divine revelation, sources that, nonetheless, can and should be judged credible by the criteria of careful, open-minded natural reason ("open-minded" because willing to proceed on the basis that natural reason's judgments do not amount to a closed system of propositions but are open to new further evidence and information). Those criteria of credibility include the coherence and cumulative richness of the content of what is proposed as revealed, and the openness of that propositional content to the advances of the knowledge accessible directly to natural reason.

To repeat: a tradition cannot be worthy of one's choice to commit one's trust to it if it asserts, or intimates, that we have no freedom to choose, and therefore no moral responsibility in acting or declining to act, and in thinking honestly and reasonably rather than by wish fulfillment and self-deception. A tradition cannot be worthy of trust if it denies that knowledge of truth is truly a good, and that error and illusion or delusion is really an evil to be fled from. Nor can a tradition be worthy of trust if it denies or ignores the truth that, because this and the other basic human goods are good for other persons as they are for oneself, one has responsibilities of justice out of rational love and respect for that good (those goods) in others as in oneself—responsibilities to everyone, though not equally to everyone alike.

Part V

I have been articulating a rational judgment that the prophets of Israel, and the theologians of Judah who elaborated their insights in narratives and psalms and other works of what we call the Old Testament were neither deluded nor deceptive when they judged themselves to be conveyers of information from God. The judgment I have articulated is one made by considering their insights, affirmations, and works as a whole. When so considered, the rational clarity and soundness of their teaching, superior in soundness on fundamentals to even the best of the Greek philosophers—along with its constancy and coherence across many centuries and many prophets, and its iteration and reiteration in the face of bitter opposition from the surrounding culture and cultures—are important among the features that make that judgment one that is not merely rational but both responsible and reasonable. The judgment's reliability in turn enhances, and is strongly enhanced by, the still more momentous judgment that Jesus of Nazareth—in one aspect of his reality the greatest of all prophets—neither deludes nor was deluded when he affirmed his divine authority to disclose and enact the salvific information that both announces and opens the way into the new form of creation called the kingdom of God.

That disclosure, the Gospel, includes the information that it brings to a close the sequence of the prophets, and we should expect no new public revelation. The apostolic age closed with the death of the last witnesses to Christ's words and deeds.

The value of his deeds as warranting his words should be assessed with due attention to (among other things) Creation—for of all miracles, the establishment and sustaining of Nature by Creation ex nihilo is somehow the most wondrous, astonishing in its disclosure of divine capacity for utter mastery and purposefulness. Such power and purpose not only made indubitably feasible Christ's signs and miracles but equally can make feasible the unimaginable transformation of Nature in the new creation promised for the race of bodily creatures that God made also intelligent and spiritual.

Since the close of the apostolic age, the information in revelation is handed down (*traditur*), transmitted, in the two forms of tradition known as Holy Scripture and (now in a narrow sense) Tradition. These are mutually interrelated in the way lucidly enough expressed in the Second Vatican Council's Dogmatic Constitution on Divine Revelation, *Dei Verbum*. They develop through the centuries in the form of those expositions, clarifications, disambiguations, and deepening appropriation of Scripture and tradition as a whole, expositions that we call doctrine when they are made authoritatively by the Church founded by Jesus. The propositional content of all this, and its rational defensibility, is clarified by sound philosophy assisting sound theology, theology that takes as its principles and pillars the doctrines of the Church founded by Christ to initiate and build up the Kingdom, the new Creation. Both the interpretation of Scripture and the formulation and interpretation of doctrine proceed by a method similar to the method proper for assessing—antecedently to theology as such—the credibility of revelation: of considering, so far as possible, the whole. This is a matter of assessing each part in the light, so far as possible, of all the other parts, while recognizing the greater significance (for the overall assessment) of those parts that both enable the other parts to take on their full sense (coherent with the others) and most securely warrant the truth of the whole. (I am referring to the greater significance of the words and deeds of Jesus of Nazareth as described in Gospels justifiably understood as intending to tell the truth about him, and about his words and deeds as they actually took place in the history of Galilee, Samaria, and Judea between 27 and 30 AD.) And this assessing can all count as part of, indeed central to, the Tradition of reason and justice because it is responsive to one of the defining features of the Tradition: that it both opens itself to, and provides the intellectual resources for, a rigorous testing of the warrant for every judgment it holds out for acceptance as true.

The Tradition does not teach at all that the virtue of faith *need* be acquired or held by way of judgments made after consideration of evidence about the matters I have been indicating. On the contrary, true faith can be passed on and acquired by simple trust in persons and their simple profession of faith. But it does teach that grace perfects—completes—nature, and that the grace and virtue of faith can fittingly be the appropriate extension (into commitment, and orientation of life) of a judgment reached after deploying all the resources of natural, critical intelligence and reason, and made without leap, indeed without stretch.

Part VI

The grievous rupture from the Tradition that we call the Reformation had as one of its longer-term consequences the emergence of a counter-Tradition, developed as a response—in no way inevitable—to the long prepared but suddenly rapid advances of the natural sciences in the early seventeenth century. Philosophers like Hobbes, followed more or less closely by many successors such as (to mention only English speakers) Locke, Hume, and Bentham, drew from the new successes of the natural sciences a series of unsound conclusions about the nature and proper methods of practical reason, ethics, and political theory, and thus also about philosophy in general and legal theory in particular. By the 1950s, many philosophers were declaring or assuming that political philosophy and ethics are dead, are beyond philosophy, and are incapable of getting beyond ideology or reportage of meanings. In partial resistance to this view, H. L. A. Hart set himself to revive the branch of political philosophy we call legal theory or jurisprudence by tracking some of the self-understanding of a reasonable practical reason. But his Humeian skepticism about ethics made mistaken most of what he wrote about morality in his master book *The Concept of Law*, and made (at best) radically incomplete his tracking of practical reason. His successor Ronald Dworkin identified some of Hart's basic mistakes about social morality (as Hart in the end conceded) and went on to produce an account of legal reasoning in which both the appropriate significance of moral principles and the necessity for assessment of the legal system as a whole are affirmed with some justification and success.

But Ronald Dworkin's own account of morality remained undeveloped (despite some enhancements in his last five years). Deeply committed to a "liberty" of self-will that denied to law and government (and their electors) any proper and effective concern with the truth about human goods, his vigorous defense of the notion of objective morality never engaged with substantive foundational issues, that is, with first principles of practical reason, their content as directing us to human goods as intrinsic aspects of human flourishing, and their implications for principles of justice and right choice and action. Only this lack of engagement can account for the ease with which Dworkin subscribed to the conventions current in his milieu in promoting first euthanasia (under the misleading name of assisting suicide) despite its grievous implications for all (and first for the poor and vulnerable), and later also same-sex unions and their institutionalization as "marriage," despite the grievous implications of this for the children to be generated precisely for a life without a mother or without a father, and despite also the wider consequences of so radically obscuring and defacing the meaning of a commitment so central to human well-being and to the sustainability of peoples and their states.

Reflecting on the theoretical work of these two outstanding senior colleagues of mine, I conclude that it was constrained and undermined by mistaken denials built into the highly conventional tradition that I am calling the modern counter-Tradition. To these scholars, I believe, the main voices of the Tradition remained distant and effectively silent, muffled and, where audible at all, presumed to be unsound. That distance or inaudibility has some causes in weaknesses—undeniable but I believe avoidable and surmountable—in the Tradition's past responses to the counter-Tradition. Still, the deep and real grounds of my eminent colleagues' resistance are surely the theses themselves, in the first instance the theses of Creation and freedom, truths that challenge us, by their implications, to grasp and affirm what Marx and Nietzsche (to mention only two) found intolerable: that we have a nature that is not self-made, and that we ought to advance beyond natural reason's findings to the reasonable submission of faith, the reasonable acceptance of the new information made available to all by a revelation that natural reason, accurately deployed, invites (and even requires) us to accept on the credible testimony of its witnesses and in fulfillment of reason's own intimations and anticipations (otherwise unfulfilled). These are all truths that, when carefully acknowledged and accepted, open the way to the detailed intellectual work of practical theory in all its forms, and to the work of lawmaking for a community that is civil, sustainable, and worthy of our allegiance. All such work will be also a contribution to fulfilling a responsibility we have, in gratitude, and for truth's sake—the responsibility of handing on the Tradition, as the University of Notre Dame Australia was established to do.

Part VII

To succeed in carrying out that responsibility over the coming century, so that at century's end they will still be handing on the Tradition, Catholic universities and their professors and students, but also Catholic bishops and their clergy and laypeople, like you and me, will have needed outstanding courage, rooted in clarity about Creation by the uncreated spirit we call God, about the freedom of created spiritual animals we call human persons, about the equality of all human persons as sons and daughters of God, notwithstanding the large and often relevant inequalities (e.g., of aptitude and of culture) among them, and about the invitation to participate in the new Creation revealed, first gradually and then definitively, to and by the Church as the seed and first seedling of that new harvest of divine purpose. Courage will be needed because—for complex, tangled reasons (causes)—the counter-Tradition, of which Hart and Dworkin were most civilized representatives and promoters, has gained and continues to gain a cultural and political ascendancy, precisely as a tradition, a tradition given also, increasingly, legal form and force over the Tradition. In the name of, and (since this is no mere matter of insincere tactics) for the sake of, goals identified as diversity, neutrality, and equality (interpretative forms of peace and justice), the counter-Tradition now actively suppresses the articulation and communication—the public and private handing on, transmission—of the Tradition. The counter-Tradition denounces essential elements of the Tradition as offensive to persons in their self-direction, autonomy, self-esteem, self-fulfillment, gender (self-) identification, and other stances that like all these are conceived (admitted) to be motivated by emotions but guided toward satisfactions by reason in emotions' service. It denounces as bigotry, patriarchalism, or mere conservatism or traditionalism (and with even more pejorative labels) many propositions and forms of commitment, action, and abstention that the Tradition has rightly judged to be essential to justice (across whole lifetimes and generations) for children and for women (and men), and essential to the many-faceted common good of created beings with the nature—the basic forms of flourishing—that we truly have and can intelligently discover both by reason and revelation. And these denunciations are increasingly given legal effect not only by the abrogation of the old laws protective of a public morality in line with the Tradition, but also by the imposition of prohibitions (and commands!) to give effect to a new public morality—and human right—of nondiscrimination.

Across my nearly half century as a university teacher, the counter-Tradition's political and legislative causes to which Hart and Dworkin gave their support have had advancing, partly gradual, partly accelerating success, not yet altogether complete or uninterrupted, but with bright prospects of success in the "final" stage—legalized and subsidized euthanasia.

Early in my teaching (and learning) years, I heard those notable Catholic philosophers Elizabeth Anscombe and Peter Geach discussing English society's "advance" toward that goal, and the prospect that only Catholic hospitals and institutions would remain as safe havens. But the counter-Tradition, with its quasi-philosophical but at bottom unphilosophical presuppositions, beliefs, and attitudes, has subsequently reached into institutions, even centers, of the Tradition. Safe havens have become hard to find and keep. Retaining, reconstructing, and revivifying the judgments and institutions of the Tradition in the face of the now emerging legal and cultural order will be most demanding work. We should do it on the basis that we have better information than the secular world and our peers in it, better information about the nature of reality, its direction, and the future really available for men, women, and children—the future we have learned what we need to know about it from the one who, as we commemorate today, Corpus Christi, was willing to lay down his life for his friends to communicate that truth, first by witnessing to it and then by handing it on as the core of the Tradition—worthwhile work to do and to hand on.

MARK KINGWELL

7 • FUGITIVE DEMOCRACY

A Gift in Time

The motive power of democracy is love.

Henri Bergson

When we are all guilty—that will be democracy.

Albert Camus

Humour is the very essence of a democratic society.

Number 2 in *The Prisoner*

Prologue: Democracy's Gift

Which is it, then: love, guilt, or humor? Let me begin with a simple-sounding but vexing question. What exactly is the essence, or motive power, of democracy, anyway?

Most philosophical answers to the question would not reference any of love, guilt, or humor—and perhaps so much the worse for them. They *would*, however, likely include reference to *forms or schemes of justification*, such as popular elections, representative assemblies, and plebiscites; or to *notions of philosophical legitimacy* that might be thought to underwrite and motivate the forms and schemes, that is, to ideas of individual equality and value that make the *demos* the proper locus of political power. This is rule by the people, in short, both as a matter of procedure and in reference to the essential source of legitimacy. The simplest articulation of this combined standard notion of democracy might be the popular slogan "Nothing about us without us"—itself a rhyming transliteration of the more euphonic Latin version: *Nihil de nobis, sine nobis*. Which is to say, no policy or regulation that affects a person should be decided in the absence of that person's consent, in some form or other, usually via elected representation or polled and summed interests.

I do not dwell here on the many pathologies that attend the working out of this noble ideal of political will.[1] Nor do I linger on the various kinds of hostility to the democratic impulse that haunt all politics. Summarizing his reactionary position, the Catholic philosopher Joseph de Maistre, then ambassador to Russia, is supposed to have remarked to Czar Alexander I that "The principle of popular sovereignty is so dangerous that even if it were true, we would have to conceal it."[2] The remark was typical; as Terry Eagleton puts it, Maistre "maintained that public order depended in the end on a single figure: the public executioner. . . . Since he held that human beings were evil, aggressive, self-destructive, savagely irrational creatures in need of being terrified into craven submission by an absolute sovereignty, the public executioner played no mean role in his political imagination."[3] Two centuries later, the young Thomas Mann would opine: "As far as democracy in Germany is concerned, I believe completely in its realization: that is precisely what makes me

1. The seeds of the present study may be found in Mark Kingwell, "The End of *The End of Democracy*," *Descant* 42, no. 4 (Winter 2012): 204–17; adapted as "Incivility, Zombies, and Democracy's End," the Introduction to Idem, *Unruly Voices. Essays on Democracy, Civility, and the Human Imagination* (Emeryville, ON: Biblioasis, 2012), 11–26.

2. Maistre's proximate target was Rousseau, particularly the latter's ideas of natural freedom, emancipation, and the general will, as set out in *Du contrat social ou Principes du droit politique* [The social contract, or principles of political right] (1762). Maistre's considered objections to popular sovereignty can be found in *Against Rousseau: On the State of Nature and On the Sovereignty of the People* (Montreal: McGill-Queen's University Press, 1996).

3. Terry Eagleton, *Culture and the Death of God* (New Haven, CT: Yale University Press, 2014), 25–26.

pessimistic."[4] There are historical variants of the sentiment that are too numerous, and too depressing, to list, but the problem is not one that belongs only to the pre-democratic past.[5]

I am concerned, instead, to put into question an often overlooked assumption in this standard view of democracy, namely, that its presumed acts of justification take place in a timeless space of advice and consent, a place without a determinate past and a specific future—or set of specific possible futures—governing its inner logic. At an extreme, this assumption accounts for the curiously ahistorical tone of much democratic theory, which tends to enter into its discussions at a level of abstraction, and with dubious assumptions of homogeneity among citizens, divorced from awareness of particular social facts and narratives. These facts and narratives typically concern, to take just the most obvious: (1) cultural, regional, religious, and other identities; (2) the state of technology, including its uneven distribution within the target population; and (3) the intergenerational differences that produce tensions in all populations.[6]

Overly abstract democratic theory can thus easily leave itself open to the charge, levelled at thinkers at least since Locke, that the subjects of the state are comprehensively male, middle aged, prosperous, articulate, and above all driven by forms of self-interest. Such individuals cannot help at least flirting with the toxic endgame of competitive identity vividly described by Thomas Merton:

> I have what you have not. I am what you are not. I have taken what you have failed to take, and I have seized what you could never get. Therefore you suffer and I am happy, you are despised and I am praised, you die and I

4. Thomas Mann, *Reflections of a Nonpolitical Man* (New York: Frederick Ungar, 1983), 354. [First published in 1918 as *Betrachtungen eines Unpolitischen.*]

5. See, e.g., Jacques Rancière, *La haine de la démocratie* [Hatred of democracy], trans. Steve Corcoran (New York: Verso, 2006). I discuss some of Rancière's ideas in "Throwing Dice: Luck of the Draw and the Democratic Ideal," *PhaenEx* 7, no. 1 (Spring/Summer 2012): 66–100; reprinted in Kingwell, *Unruly Voices*, 103–30.

6. A good critique of this general tendency may be found in John O'Neill, *The Missing Child in Liberal Theory: Towards a Covenant Theory of Family, Community, Welfare, and the Civic State* (Toronto: University of Toronto Press, 1994).

live; you are nothing and I am something, and I am all the more something because you are nothing. And thus I spend my life admiring the distance between you and me.[7]

That condemning portrait of individualism is at one critical extreme, to be sure! A more proximate and common danger of the assumptions of ahistoricity and self-interest is the generation of "democratic" results that are driven exclusively, or almost so, by the summing of short-term individual interests. This in turn can generate an aggravated version of the familiar "tragedy of the commons."[8]

In the simple versions of the tragedy—collective action problems such as races to the bottom or collective self-defeat—we observe that the general pursuit of (rational) individual interests can lead to outcomes that are bad for everyone, as when the common pasture is destroyed by overuse. Such outcomes demonstrate, at a minimum, that collective interest is logically distinct from the aggregation of individual interests.[9] When a temporal dimension is added to the outcome metrics, the self-defeats may become actively unjust: depriving future generations of goods that we may ourselves enjoy short of self-defeat. One thinks here of environmental health, natural resources, and other likewise nonrenewable goods. Exploitation of these goods can, as a matter of time itself, produce zero-sum games that nevertheless appear, if viewed only synchronically, legitimate.

My concern in this chapter, then, is to consider the temporal dimension of democracy, particularly its relation to the idea of tradi-

7. Thomas Merton, *New Seeds of Contemplation* (New York: New Directions Press, 1961), 48.

8. For the canonical statement of the problem, see Garrett Hardin, "The Tragedy of the Commons," *Science* 162 (1968): 1243–48.

9. There is a voluminous literature on the topic of collective action problems, but an especially clear overview, in the context of urban planning, can be found in Henk Voogd, "Social Dilemmas and the Communicative Planning Paradox," *Town Planning Review* 72, no. 1 (January 2001): 77–95. See also Mark Kingwell, " 'Fuck You' and Other Salutations: Incivility as a Collective Action Problem," in *Civility in Politics and Education*, ed. D. Mower and W. Robison (New York: Routledge, 2012), 44–61; reprinted in Kingwell, *Unruly Voices*, 149–68.

tion. But I do not address the familiar liberal conception of tradition, which seeks to frame justification of a basic social structure amid a plurality of possible conceptions of the good, including ones that identify themselves explicitly as traditions.[10] I am interested, instead, in asking whether democracy itself should be understood as a tradition. The motive question is not What is democracy? It is, rather, What is the relationship of democracy to time?

In what follows, I analyze the notion of *fugitive democracy* as the true meaning of the democratic ideal, once appropriately temporalized.[11] This attempt at temporalization of the democratic entails a critical engagement with the concepts of *tradition* and *progress*. And so, to that end, I suggest that the substance of democratic relations must go beyond politics, punctuating normal sequences of events with kairotic ruptures. These ruptures in turn work to realize an imperative of ongoing trusteeship—a kind of gift economy—at the heart of democracy. What I mean by gift economy will emerge more clearly in the succeeding sections, but let me say something about it as part of these prefatory remarks.

A gift is something freely given, that is, proffered without expectation of profit or return. It is the opposite, even the negation, of a transaction.[12] Our cultural gift-giving practices have devolved such that this basic distinction may no longer be so obvious. We give gifts at Christmastime, for example, with a sense that we will also receive them. Lists are made and checked off as the relevant goods are matched with their recipients. Some families and businesses—also schools and voluntary associations—striving to limit the economic burden of comprehensive transactional gifts, adopt schemes such as

10. See, e.g., Will Kymlicka, *Liberalism, Community, and Culture* (Oxford: Oxford University Press, 1989 and 1991).

11. A seminal work here is Sheldon S. Wolin, "Fugitive Democracy," *Constellations* 1, no. 1 (1994): 11–25; see also Wolin, *Democracy Inc.: Managed Democracy and the Specter of Inverted Totalitarianism* (Princeton, NJ: Princeton University Press, 2008).

12. Here I follow the analysis of Lewis Hyde in *The Gift: Imagination and the Erotic Life of Property* (New York: Vintage, 1979).

"Secret Santa." Here a jumble of names is sorted by an unseen hand, and each person purchases a gift for just one other, and receives one in turn, possibly from someone other than the recipient of the first gift. In practice, such rather feeble attempts to restore a gift economy in the thoroughly capitalized atmosphere of Christmas tend to backfire: gifters contact their recipients to gauge desires, in turn creating a kind of indirect, or by proxy, shopping network barely distinguishable from simple transaction.[13]

Now I would not want to deny that there may well be much good fellow feeling in these exchanges. But they are not gifts in the pure sense. They do not defy and even undermine the presumptive logic of transaction, which is what a genuine gift does. For the genuine gift creates a scale of value that cannot be reduced to cost or benefit: it operates beneath, or behind, the dominant patterns of tit-for-tat exchange. And I want to say, any conception of political life that does not take account of the enduring value of gift economies in human affairs—Hobbes, for example—has made a baseline conceptual error about the subjects of its own theory. Humans are not fully human in the absence of some kind of free bestowal of their goods. A political theory of total transactional reduction is a philosophical nonstarter.

When it comes to the subject before us, this is my central claim: democracy is itself a gift. Too often, the idea of giving democracy has meant some form of cultural and political imperialism. We can think, here, of the Vietnam-era image of a bomb-spewing B-52 with the slogan, "If you don't come to democracy, democracy will come to you." Or the cynical reporter in Billy Wilder's 1948 film *A Foreign Affair*, which concerns American visitors (and love affairs) in occupied

13. In a variant sometimes known as Thieving Secret Santa, participants contribute wrapped gifts and then take turns either opening a gift and keeping it or "stealing" an already opened but abandoned gift. This game is also known as a white elephant gift exchange, Yankee Swap, Dirty Santa, Devil's Santa, Nasty Christmas, Snatchy Christmas Rat, Chinese Christmas, or the Grinch game—all names that suggest that while the game preserves a more genuine gifting culture in being anti-transactional, it is also considered competitive, if playfully so.

Berlin during the Second World War: "If you give a hungry man a loaf of bread, that's democracy," the character muses as his plane approaches the starved city's barely functioning airport. "If you leave the wrapper on, that's imperialism." (Significantly, the Berlin Airlift of 1948–49—a rolling operation begun around the time that Wilder's film was released—is considered by many to be a rare act of genuine giving in foreign affairs: food, personnel, and medical supplies provided without any consideration of recompense.)

The *gift of democracy* should rather be considered in terms of the phrase's double genitive "of." I mean the phrase's use of that same grammatically unstable "of" that creates ambiguity in phrases such as the *death of honor*. In such cases, the path of adjectival modification can flow in both directions: the phrase "death of honor" can mean both an honorable death *or* the demise of honor itself. When we utter the phrase "gift of democracy," then, let us preserve the ambiguity rather than attempt to resolve it. Thus the meaning of democracy's gift is *both* the benefits that democracy bestows upon us *and* our own acts of democratic bestowal.

At the conclusion of this chapter, I try to answer the question concerning *to whom* the gift of democracy is given, and what kind of democracy that gift might be. To begin the journey toward those conclusions—itself a kind of narrative of received benefits and forwarded trust—I turn now to some enabling thoughts about justice, time and authority, and tradition.

Justice

The notion of democracy's gift may seem to raise immediately the cognate issue of intergenerational justice. The most widely accepted version of justice to future generations is found in John Rawls's magisterial *A Theory of Justice* (1971).[14] The basic orientation of his discus

14. See John Rawls, *A Theory of Justice* (Cambridge, MA: Belknap Press, 1971 and 1999), esp. section 44; idem, *Political Liberalism* (New York: Columbia University Press, 1993), 274; idem, *Justice as Fairness: A Restatement* (Cambridge, MA: Belknap Press, 2001), esp. sections 49.2 and 49.3.

sion is twofold. First, in the original position, where his hypothetical social contractors don't know who, in particular, they are—including to which generation they belong—a unanimous decision will be made for the fair synchronic, as well as diachronic, distribution of goods and services. In the event, Rawls argues that this distribution will follow his two principles of justice, namely, that there will be (1) equal access to life options and (2) a "difference" mechanism that will guarantee that the least well-off will derive some benefit from any allowable social inequality. Second, the general claim that the site of justice is the "basic structure of society," to use Rawls's widely adopted phrase, seems to take sufficient account of persons both living and to come who will exist under that basic structure.

Rawls therefore argues that the original-position contractors agree on a *savings principle*, which is "subject to the further condition that they must want all previous generations to have followed it." He goes on: "Thus the correct principle is that which the members of any generation (and so all generations) would adopt as the one their generation is to follow and as the principle they would want preceding generations to have followed (and later generations to follow), no matter how far back (or forward) in time."[15] This conclusion is known as *just savings*, and while there can be no sense in which it is binding on factual previous generations, the principle is part of just basic social structure because it is what the (present) contractors would have wanted from their forebears *had they been them*, and thus it is what they will (at present) bind themselves to, for the sake of those to come. The principle of just savings is therefore thought to be binding on all previous and future generations.

Like much of Rawls's theory of justice, the argument is both ingenious and somehow disappointing. The disappointment is not just of the standard academic variety, whereby flaws in the argument might be discussed—though there has been plenty of that.[16] I mean also

15. Rawls, *Political Liberalism*, 274; *Justice as Fairness*, 160.

16. I won't attempt to cite the body of criticism here. A telling early response was

the feeling that this conclusion, while possibly valid, seems without traction on our concrete inheritances from the past and our fraught decisions about the future. Nor does its sufficientarian logic ground a more comprehensive *trusteeship* conception of justice: the argument that we have not just a minimalist duty to leave some version of Locke's "enough and as good" to future people, but a responsibility to shift our basic position away from consumption (even curbed consumption) of goods and toward care of shared resources. I suggest that the notion of a tradition is a more viable way to plot a viable connection between the basic democratic principle (those who are affected must decide) and justice (there must be a valid distribution of resources, goods, opportunities, and potentials).

In his lively and clever book of popular Christian apologetics, *Orthodoxy* (1908), G. K. Chesterton had already addressed the issue of intergenerational injustice, using the trademark style of witty paradox. One result of this approach is that *Orthodoxy*, like Chesterton's *Heretics* (1905) before it, can be read with pleasure by believers and unbelievers alike.[17] But his arguments are not idle or facetious, and his attacks on willful comprehensive skepticism (a fashionable disease) and rampant materialism (a form of mania) are still worth attending to. He also, perhaps unexpectedly in a book on Christian belief, has much to say about democracy.

In the fourth chapter, "The Ethics of Elfland," Chesterton offers this general statement: "the democratic faith is this: that the most terribly important things must be left to ordinary men themselves—

Kenneth J. Arrow, "Rawls's Principle of Just Saving," *Swedish Journal of Economics* 75, no. 4 (December 1973): 323–35; cf. the later concerns expressed in Thomas Schramme, "Is Rawlsian Justice Bad for the Environment?," *Analyse & Kritik* 28 (2006): 146–57.

17. Chesterton was an indefatigable controversialist—his own age's Christopher Hitchens, perhaps—and he cannot resist jibes at contemporaries. My (unfair) favorite: "Surely one might pay for extraordinary joy in ordinary morals. Oscar Wilde said that sunsets were not valued because we could not pay for sunsets. But Oscar Wilde was wrong; we can pay for sunsets. We can pay for them by not being Oscar Wilde." G. K. Chesterton, *Orthodoxy* (Peabody, MA: Hendrickson, 2006), 53. [Originally published in 1905.] All further quotations are taken from this edition.

the mating of the sexes, the rearing of the young, the laws of the state. This is democracy" (43). (One presumes "men" might, even for him, eventually become "men and women," especially if mating and child rearing are so terribly important.) He goes on immediately, in a crucial passage:

> But there is one thing that I have never from my youth up been able to understand. I have never been able to understand where people got the idea that democracy was in some way opposed to tradition. It is obvious that tradition is only democracy extended through time. It is trusting to a consensus of common human voices, rather than to some isolated or arbitrary record. (43)

Then, in a now-famous dilation on the point, Chesterton puts the matter in the following bold terms:

> Tradition may be defined as an extension of the franchise. Tradition means giving votes to the most obscure of all classes, our ancestors. It is the democracy of the dead. Tradition refuses to submit to the small and arrogant oligarchy of those who merely happen to be walking about. All democrats object to men being disqualified by the accident of birth; tradition objects to their being disqualified by the accident of death. . . . I, at any rate, cannot separate the two ideas of democracy and tradition; it seems evident to me that they are the same idea. (43)

These are bold claims expressed in memorable language. No wonder both *democracy of the dead* and *small and arrogant oligarchy of those who merely happen to be walking about* have passed into the lexicons of many.

There is much to quarrel with in Chesterton's resulting discussion of social issues. He is too forgiving of the dangers posed by doctrine (96), too sanguine about the mechanism of democratic franchise (116), and too dismissive of the idea of social change (30–31). It might be thought that Chesterton emerges in this book as the answer to Kierkegaard's lamenting question: Among the Christians, is there a Christian? Yes, at least one, but he may also be the only one! Chesterton's humility and optimism are winning, but his notion of tradition is not sufficient on its face: it willfully ignores the evidence of traditions in practice, their tendencies to ossify, corrupt, and even oppress, not just on the basis of bare power or deception but also *in the name of tradition itself.*

And so, despite some concluding protestations that Christian orthodoxy is "the only *logical* guardian of liberty, innovation and advance" (137), his presumptive conception of democratic tradition is too backward looking. Guided by the idea of orthodoxy—meaning, whether Christian or otherwise, inherited ideas of right reason—such a tradition cannot take full account of the temporal dimensions of democracy. Yes, the interests of the dead, expressed in what they have left us, must be part of the democratic conversation—including the conversation about democracy itself. Without an unwavering orientation in the other direction of the vector, however, we are likely to lose hold of our own duties to those who—notably, unlike the dead—have no way of expressing interests except via the exercise of our own imaginations.

It seems to me, then, that one crucial aspect of this imagination—the same imagination that allows each of us as individuals to entertain a sense of self—must be a critical examination of the very idea of time. I have been speaking, consistent with both Rawls the political philosopher and Chesterton the Christian apologist, as if time is itself uniformly distributed, typically along a more or less straight line. But we know from our own temporal existences, in which we (among other things) live out memories over and over, and attempt to construct narratives of identity by recursively imposing present knowledge on past events, that time is neither uniform nor linear. I turn now to a brief discussion of two concepts of time—there may well be others!—that help us deepen our understanding of tradition, tradition as democracy, and democracy as tradition.

Two Concepts of Time, Two Concepts of Authority

In his brisk history of secular political consciousness and the public sphere, *Modern Social Imaginaries*, Charles Taylor remarks in passing how different concepts of time, or time-consciousness, are necessary for the emergent modern political order. "The eighteenth-century public sphere thus represents an instance of a new kind: a metatopical common space and common agency without an action-transcendent constitution, an agency grounded purely in its own common actions."[18] This "metatopical common space" was, crucially, continuous and evenly distributed across its participants; that is why it could become the basis for what we now recognize as democratic civil society. Despite this continuity and equality, however, it was not considered to have originated ex nihilo: there are founding myths and moments that are considered to create the possibilities of public space. But these moments of origin, Taylor argues, "are displaced onto a higher plane, into a heroic time, an *illud tempus* which is not seen as qualitatively on a level with what we do today." And so, "the founding action is not like our action, not just an earlier similar act whose precipitate structures ours. It is not just earlier, but in another kind of time, an exemplary time."[19]

The distinction Taylor suggests here has many forebears. One clear way of capturing its impact hinges on the fact that Greek has two words that both translate as "time": *chronos* and *kairos*. Chronological time is the time of measurement and portioning, the time that passes. In its modern manifestation, the history of chronological time is nicely traced by both Taylor and other, more radical thinkers such as Guy Debord in *Society of the Spectacle* (1967). This conception of time is crucial to the emergence of a shared public sphere—but also to the emergence of a work world in which time can be subject to transaction. This is especially true in the special set of social relations that Debord calls "the spectacle," in which everything and everyone is a commodity. This is secular time, in the sense that it is "of the age": the space of everydayness, work, and exchange.

The visible sign of this time, as Lewis Mumford among others has

18. Charles Taylor, *Modern Social Imaginaries* (Durham, NC: Duke University Press, 2004), 96.

19. Taylor, *Modern Social Imaginaries*, 97.

noted, is of course the clock. The mechanism of keeping good time, once the holy grail of sailors looking to measure longitude, is here revealed as the enabling condition of capitalist labor relations. "The popularization of time-keeping," Mumford notes, "which followed the production of the cheap standardized watch, first in Geneva, was essential to a well-articulated system of transportation and production."[20] The clock keeps time by making its units identical and measured; it appears first as a shared community property in (as it might be) the town hall or church tower, matching the more ancient tolling of bells to a visual representation of time passing. Later, as technology advances, the mechanism of *chronos* time is bionically conjoined to the human frame in the form of the pocket watch and, eventually, the wristwatch. When I fasten on a wristwatch, in other words, I am signaling to myself and others my contract with the telling of time, expressing an agreement in some sense with the proposition that time is money. The same integration of technology and biology is essential to the logic of time-and-motion studies in factory production, as exemplified by the "scientific oversight" model of Frederick Winslow Taylor. "The enormous saving of time," Taylor writes in *The Principles of Scientific Management* (1911), "and therefore increase in the output which it is possible to effect through eliminating unnecessary motions and substituting fast for slow and inefficient motions for the men working in any of our trades can be fully realized only . . . from a thorough motion and time study, made by a competent man."[21]

We can summarize the qualities of secular, *chronos* time this way: it is (1) every day, (2) profane, (3) homogeneous, (4) linear, (5) hori-

20. Lewis Mumford, *Technics and Civilization* (Chicago: University of Chicago Press, 2010), 17.

21. F. W. Taylor, *The Principles of Scientific Management*, in *The Early Sociology of Management and Organizations*, vol. 1, *Scientific Management* (New York: Routledge, 2005), 129. Cf. Rem Koolhaas, *Delirious New York: A Retroactive Manifesto for Manhattan* (New York: Monacelli, 1974), which relates Taylor's time-motion ideas to the spectacular rise of first-generation skyscrapers in Manhattan, especially the Empire State Building; I expand on this latter point in *Nearest Thing to Heaven: The Empire State Building and American Dreams* (New Haven, CT: Yale University Press, 2006).

zontal, and (6) egalitarian. We constantly encounter this time, measuring it and meeting its demands by being on time, matching our movements and achievements to its punctums, saving time and spending time, each of us equally available to time, and having it available to us. Debord closely associates this time with the emergence of labor mechanisms and the bourgeois conception of society, taking time away from the more natural cyclical rhythms of seasonal agriculture and, before it, hunting-gathering to create a time world in which production is potentially constant. Workers may now punch in to the line 24/7, as we would say today, making the relation to the time clock explicit. Consistent with orthodox Marxist critique, Debord argues that this process is inseparable from the emergence of class, and so class conflict.

In a crucial middle section of *Society of the Spectacle*, "Time and History," Debord notes how time itself becomes a form of social distinction and conflict during this triumph of *chronos* time:

> The social appropriation of time, the production of man by human labour, develops within a society divided into classes. The power which constituted itself above the penury of the society of cyclical time, the class which organizes the social labour and appropriates the limited surplus value, simultaneously appropriates the *temporal surplus value* of its organization of social time: it possesses for itself alone the irreversible time of the living. The wealth that can be concentrated in the realm of power and materially used up in sumptuous feasts is also used up as a squandering of *historical time at the surface of society.*[22]

Once measured and parceled out, subjected to transaction in the form of paid labor, time immediately becomes a commodity with the potential, like any commodity, to support an upper tier, luxury version of itself. Free time, leisure time, ample time, time off—these all immediately beckon as goods at the margins of a world ruled by time-as-labor and labor-as-time.

It is not necessary to detail here how the commodification of time

22. Guy Debord, *Society of the Spectacle* (Detroit, MI: Black & Red, 1983), sec. V:126. [Originally published as *La societé du spectacle*, 1967.]

creates the familiar pathologies of demented leisure characteristic of late capitalism: the living-for-the-weekend enthrallment that, with every reference to "hump day" or "TGIF," partly emphasizes the unshakable dominance of the work week.[23] Too often concealed is the persistence and bravery of those workers who demanded the regulated ten-hour, and eventually eight-hour, workday, and still later the two-day weekend.[24] Of more immediate interest, though, is the fact that those battles about time already accepted the premise of what time was. Both Taylor and Debord note that this secular, *chronos* time of labor and production-consumption achieves—one might even say *must* achieve—global reach. It is part of what Heidegger calls "the age of the world picture," the picture in which everything, including ourselves and our temporality, are in principle available for disposal: the comprehensive *standing reserve* or *enframing* (*Ge-stell*) of technology whereby everything, including human desire and possibility, is made fungible in the name of use.[25]

Debord joins other Marxist critics such as E. P. Thompson in noting the effects of this time: "With the development of capitalism, irreversible time is *unified on a world scale*. Universal history becomes a reality because the entire world is gathered under the development of this time. . . . What appears the world over as *the same day* is the time of economic production cut up into equal abstract fragments. Unified irreversible time is the time of the *world market* and, as a corollary, of the world spectacle."[26]

Thompson: "Indeed, a general diffusion of clocks and watches is

23. But see Mark Kingwell, "The Work Idea: Wage Slavery, Bullshit, and the Good Infinite," in *The Economy as Cultural System: Theory, Capitalism, Crisis*, ed. Todd Dufresne and Clara Sacchetti (New York: Bloomsbury, 2013), 127–40; reprinted in Kingwell, *Unruly Voices*, 181–96, and as the introduction to Kingwell and Joshua Glenn, *The Wage Slave's Glossary* (Emeryville, ON: Biblioasis, 2011).

24. Witold Rybczynski's *Waiting for the Weekend* (New York: Viking, 1991) tells a gripping version of this story, set against the Babylonian origin of the seven-day week itself.

25. Martin Heidegger, "The Age of the World Picture," in *The Question Concerning Technology and Other Essays*, trans. William Lovitt (New York: Harper & Row, 1977).

26. Debord, *Society of the Spectacle*, sec. V:145.

occurring (as one would expect) at the exact moment when the industrial revolution demanded a great synchronization of labour." Thus a new ethos of punctuality and efficiency is born: "In all these ways—by the division of labour; the supervision of labour; fines; bells and clocks; money incentives; preaching and schooling; the suppression of fairs and sports—new labour habits were formed and a new time discipline was imposed."[27]

Compare Charles Taylor: "A purely secular time-understanding allows us to imagine society horizontally, untouched by any 'high points,' where the ordinary sequence of events touches higher time, and therefore without recognizing any privileged persons or agencies, such as priests and kings, who stand and mediate at such alleged points. This radical horizontality is precisely what is implied in the direct-access society, where each member is 'immediate to the whole.'"[28]

Now, Taylor may be thought too sanguine about this larger temporal development in modernity, even though he does allow that there are persistent local verticalities even in the comprehensively horizontal world of the secular: uneven access to goods, disjointed proximity to glamour or celebrity, corruptions of power. But Debord's sense of the dominance of spectacle in a society in which cyclical time has been lost, while accurate enough, may seem to invite a kind of nostalgia or romanticism about the time-out-of-time. One may accept the value of Debordian Situationism's tactics of *dérive* and *détournement*—drifting and repurposing through the byways of the spectacle-dominated city, rather than resisting in some pre-doomed alternative organization—but still detect an odor of charming failure in the analysis. One of the aims of this chapter is to restore vitality to the Situationist project without inviting any new moments of romance; more on this in the final section.

27. E. P. Thompson, "Time, Work-Discipline, and Industrial Capitalism," *Past & Present* 38 (1967): 69, 90.

28. Taylor, *Principles of Scientific Management*, 157.

The larger point about both the benefits and the costs of secular time is politically significant. Even as it invited commodification and disposal, the achievement of egalitarian secular time was a necessary condition for the emergence of popular sovereignty in full force. Without a sense of immediate access to a nonhierarchical present, however attenuated or subject to doubt, there can be no conviction that we, the people, are the creators of our social order, nor that, to use Taylor's words, popular elections—not bloodlines, transcendental access, or historical precedent—are "the only source of legitimate power." He goes on: "But what has to take place for this change to come off is a transformed social imaginary, in which the idea of foundation is taken out of the mythical early time and seen as something that people can do today. In other words, it becomes something that can be brought about by collective action in contemporary, purely secular time."[29]

This cannot be done purely through action at the level of secular time, however. Not only will a *narrative of origin* continue to prove necessary to the development of democratic society, but it will also be necessary to keep open the ever-present possibility of an *eruption of justificatory argument* concerning legitimacy. This kind of argument is distinct from the day-to-day business of collective action, still more from policy making and the regulatory business-as-usual of politics.

The narrative of origin is familiarly sketched in the various versions of contractarian thought experiment that come down to us in the liberal tradition: Hobbes's state of nature, Locke's presocial order, even Rawls's original position (though the last does not indulge in a dubious appeal to history or human nature that undermines our respect for the early modern examples). Notably, Rousseau, who sounded such a strong keynote in *The Social Contract* about man being born free but living everywhere in chains, would chide Hobbes for not stripping away enough of the accretions of social contagion in his conception of natural man. The humans for whom presocial ex-

29. Taylor, *Principles of Scientific Management*, 110.

istence was "solitary, poor, nasty, brutish, and short" were, Rousseau argued, already highly socialized beings trained to pursue their own competitive self-interest. This criticism, though well aimed, does not, however, thereby lend more credence to Rousseau's alternative, which invites the parallel objection that it is a species of special pleading. Rawls's atemporal version of a justificatory scheme, with the original position framed as a thought experiment that one might undertake at any time, draws fire concerning what, precisely, must be excluded by the veil of ignorance to generate a unanimous outcome. The political narrative of origin will always be controversial.

The eruption of justificatory argument, because it is grounded in actual rather than imagined history, seems more promising. Such an eruption might be discerned in historical narratives of democratic process, such as Bruce Ackerman's magisterial account of the American republic, in which the founding plays the originary role, including sometimes heated appeals to the founders' intentions, but open to returns to originary discourse at times of crisis: the Reconstruction after the Civil War, the New Deal in the wake of the Depression. Ackerman argues that the truly democratic republic, no matter how atavistic its self-narrative, can never foreclose on the option of returning to the democratic drawing board.[30] To be sure, founders' intent remains itself a disputed property, both in everyday judicial argument and in returns to constitutional first principles. More darkly, the same return to originary framing can be glimpsed in Carl Schmitt's notion of the *exception*, which is decided upon by the sovereign, and in Walter Benjamin's rejoinder about the *violence* in all acts of political establishment.

The contrastive term for secular time gives us an insight about what this complicated narrative of origin and legitimation might look like: the tradition that is distinctively democratic. That is, we are now in a position to characterize the useful diacritical opposite of *chro-*

30. Bruce Ackerman, *We the People*, vol. 1, *Foundations* (Cambridge, MA: Belknap Press, 1991), and vol. 2, *Transformations* (Cambridge, MA: Belknap Press, 2000).

nos time, namely, *kairos* or transcendental time. It is (1) mysterious, (2) divine, (3) eternal, (4) infinite, (5) vertical, and (6) hierarchical. In many cases, this kind of time—the time of divine intervention or communion with the eternal realm—is familiar as part of an anti-democratic social order, in which privileged access, or anyway claims thereto, keeps a steeply hierarchical class division firmly in place, ostensibly as part of a Great Chain of Being or Divine Universal Scheme. The forerunner here might be, of course, the Platonic Theory of the Forms, with realms of knowledge and reality arranged in rigid order. The upward ascent of the self-freed slave of Plato's Cave, struggling through blindness and pain toward the sun's light, is an ascent to eternity as well as reality—for they are the same.

But these towering religio-philosophical edifices have their less grandiose analogues even in our own world. I mean, for example, the sense of time beyond time that still marks genuine leisure, play, and idleness, the *skholé* of Aristotle even now to be found in our aimless games and blissful moments of "flow," or the true holiday, where the usual tyranny of work and use-value is suspended in the name of carnival or sabbath.[31] The common desire for what the Germans call *Freizeit*—time free of obligation—is united with the transcendence of time available to almost any North American urban dweller in a baseball game, say, where time is told only in outs and innings, in a pastime that is played in what is usually called a park. (The cognate game of cricket arguably offers even more in the way of time out of time!) In his paean to baseball, Milton scholar and commissioner of baseball A. Bartlett Giamatti references *Paradise Lost* (IV, 434–35) in an expression of Aristotelian leisure, which he calls "the ideal to which our play aspires." From the poem: *Free leave so large to all things else, and choice / Unlimited of manifold delights.* "But in fact, the serpent is already there," Giamatti notes, "and our sports do not simulate, therefore, a

31. See Mark Kingwell, "Idling toward Heaven: The Last Defence You Will Ever Need," *Queen's Quarterly* 115, no. 4 (Winter 2008): 569–85, and the introduction to Kingwell and Joshua Glenn, *The Idler's Glossary* (Emeryville, ON: Biblioasis, 2008).

constant state. Rather, between days of work, sports or games only repeat and repeat our efforts to go back, back to a freedom we cannot recall, save as a moment of play in some garden now lost."[32]

I suggest below that these and other *ludic episodes* to be found within everyday existence are portals to the gift of democracy, for they remind us of the resistance to transactional reduction that grounds the most valuable features of our common life. The question for present purposes must be this: Is there a sense of *kairos* or transcendent time that can exist as a proximate option for a democratic tradition? To advance the argument that there is, once more lodged squarely in the idea of democracy's gift, I now sketch another useful distinction, between two kinds of social authority.

We can associate two kinds of claim, both indispensable to democratic thought, with the two notions of time I have here contrasted. As Taylor notes, the linear secular time of the modern world-picture is a necessary condition of a political world in which *everyone* feels capable of meaningful action. We are at once decentered and enabled. The voice of authority that addresses itself to secular time is that of a wisdom tradition. The claims of such a tradition are typically (1) conservative, (2) continuous, and (3) linked to the past. This is the species of authority we associate with scriptural reference, for example, or embodied rituals passed from generation to generation.

The "wisdom" in question need not always be of world-shaking profundity. The traditions of games such as cricket or baseball, with their "laws" and prescribed behaviors, a spirit of continuity that good players and fans come to respect and honor, demonstrate this kind of authority. The claim is not "It shall be done this way because it has always been done this way," but rather "It shall be done this way because we acknowledge the accumulated fitness and rightness of doing it this way." Origins are not lost in time, but they are recognized as essential to our current projects, whatever they might be. The wis-

32. A. Bartlett Giamatti, *Take Time for Paradise: Americans and Their Games* (New York: Summit Books, 1989), 44.

dom tradition of democracy is acted out in, for example, the various iterations of the Westminster model of parliamentary democracy, the rule of common law, and even such detailed inheritances as the writ of *habeas corpus* and the chancery court. We may debate these details, as when we seek to reform unbalanced first-past-the-post elections, say, but we will do so in the terms set out by the tradition.

This voice of authority, though it ought to be respected, cannot close off even more radical ruptures in the fabric of social life. The authority of *prophetic intervention* must likewise be recognized, a kind of eruption of new energy that rends the time of everyday life and exposes a harsh light of higher responsibility. This voice, then, is (1) radical, (2) discontinuous, and (3) linked to the future. The prophetic voice need not be utopian, however; it may be hortatory or even scolding of our complacency and laziness. It is the voice that condemns the money changers in the temple and called out the Pharisees for their hypocrisy. It is, as Terry Eagleton notes with some relish, "the sour unreasonableness of a document that admonishes us to yield up our lives for the sake of strangers that is most striking, not its diffusion of sweetness and light. There is nothing moderate or middle-of-the road about the scandalous extremity of its demands, as a theologian like Kierkegaard was aware."[33] In a non-Christian context, we might detect this voice in the lately mocked but actually stirring *soixante-huitard* and Situationist slogan: "Be reasonable: demand the impossible." It is the voice that demands that we occupy Wall Street.

The common ground of these two voices is language, the shared discursive space of democratic politics. Human history, Hegel said, was carried in language, transmitted from one epoch to the next in history and philosophy. This is the sense of discursive immersion that Heidegger refers to when he says, provocatively, that language speaks us not the other way around. Language is the house of Being. Heidegger was no democrat, as we unfortunately have cause to know; even so, his infamous *Rektoratsrede* on "Die Selbstbehauptung

33. Eagleton, *Culture and the Death of God*, 136.

der Deutschen Universität" (1933) is itself, necessarily, a discursive intervention that we can even now examine and criticize. Democracy never sleeps when language is present. And while we listen to the voice of authority and their claims to both the horizontal and vertical temporalities of shared social space, we can never abandon the individual responsibility that is the condition of granting legitimacy—a responsibility, as both tradition and prophecy would agree, can never be bought or sold. *Nihil de nobis, sine nobis*, indeed.

Living Traditions?

Let us now, with these thoughts in mind, turn to the question of tradition. "A real tradition is not the relic of the past that is irretrievably gone," Igor Stravinsky argued; "it is a living force that animates and informs the present."[34] Stravinsky was thinking specifically of music, of course. What is a tradition in the political sense? Can we speak meaningfully of a *real tradition of democracy*, or is the very idea mired in confusion? I dwell here on a vivid example of the problem, one drawn from fiction but nevertheless rooted in real social movements and events. Evelyn Waugh offers some typically effective mockery of the notion of tradition in a minor part of his second novel, *Vile Bodies* (1930), which is also seriously concerned with the question of culture and its demise—about which more in a moment.

First, the mockery. The male protagonist, Adam Fenwick-Symes, is attempting to earn a living as a newspaper gossip columnist known as Mr. Chatterbox. Working under a "black list" injunction that certain society people, suing his proprietor's newspaper, shall not be mentioned in the column, Adam resorts to invented subjects. Among these is the dashing Captain Angus Stuart-Kerr, who, unlike most big-game hunters, "was an expert and indefatigable dancer." But, as with several other characters, including a sculptor whose work is so

34. Igor Stravinsky, *The Poetics of Music in the Form of Six Lessons*, Charles Eliot Norton Lectures 1939–40 (Cambridge, MA: Harvard University Press, 1947 and 1993), chap. 3. [Originally published as *Poétique Musicale*, 1942.]

in-demand it cannot be purchased and a fashionable couple quickly claimed as everyone's best friends, Adam's invented Scotsman is all too real. A rival gossip sheet begins to mention the deeds of the captain: spotted at a point-to-point meeting, he is known as the hardest rider in the Hebrides.

Adam decides to put a stop to this appropriation and so writes this in his next column:

Some people [he wrote] are under the impression that Captain Angus Stuart-Kerr, whom I mentioned on this page a short time ago, is a keen rider. Perhaps they are confusing him with Alastair Kerr-Stuart, of Inverauchty, a very distant cousin. Captain Stuart-Kerr never rides, and for a very interesting reason. There is an old Gaelic rhyme repeated among his clansmen which says in rough translation "the Laird rides well on two legs." Tradition has it that when the head of the house mounts a horse, the clan will be dispersed.

To this bit of foolery, the narrator adds a footnote, also worth quoting in full:

This story, slightly expanded, found its way later into a volume of Highland Legends called *Tales from the Mist*, which has been approved to be read in elementary schools. This shows the difference between what is called a "living" as opposed to a "dead" folk tradition.

Tales from the mist indeed!

Without wanting to blunt the edge of Waugh's irony, let us note that the episode nicely exploded the use of a living/dead distinction—one that, at the beginning of the current essay, seemed still to retain some power. That is, if a "living" tradition is one in which a fabricated story, plausible only because sufficiently silly prima facie, could be taken up and folded into the "lore" of a culture, then perhaps one's tradition is better off dead. The Scots, in this rather elaborate joke, are no better or worse than middle-class personages who seek proximity to glamour by reading the gossip pages in the first place. The limits of invention are also shown in the novel: when Adam attempts to influence male fashion, he first succeeds (black suede shoes for formal wear) and then fails (bottle-green bowler hats for town—a fiction that only one sad aging beau attempts to emulate, by badly dying his existing headgear).

Waugh has a more serious point to make here than just poking fun at those who grasp after culture. *Vile Bodies*, like *A Handful of Dust* (1934) and especially *Brideshead Revisited* (1945), sounds a young fogey's lament for the disappearing country-house culture of Edwardian England. The suggestion is that the devastation of the First World War must be seen to include a way of life that is quintessentially English, replaced by a harsh modernity of industrialization and democratization. Tony Last, in *A Handful of Dust*, is seen as the last of a breed—and ends his days the casual prisoner of a Dickens-loving madman. The estate of Brideshead and the Anglo-Catholic Marchmain family symbolize, in Waugh's greatest novel, the generational and cultural tensions of the slide into another world war.

These tensions become the essential springwork of Waugh's fictional and moral vision. A large section of the conclusion to *Vile Bodies* offers an unabashed, almost sentimental celebration of the aristocratic order, complete with exchange of gifts and good wishes between the social orders and caroling waifs given punch by a faithful servant. The background fact—that Adam is there with the daughter of the house, Nina Blount, pretending to be her husband—is remarked only by the neighboring rector, who has previously decided that Adam is mad. Nina's father, Colonel Blount, is in effect suborned to adultery under his own ancestral roof.

Already another war is coming. (Recall that this novel was published in 1930.) Adam will end up on the front lines, carrying a pocket-sized "Huxdane-Halley bomb (for the dissemination of leprosy germs)"—an especially nasty but very Waughvian detail. The shadowy Father Rothschild is the sole character in *Vile Bodies* who seems to sense this impending conflict. He is also the voice of moral judgment about the generational demise of traditional culture represented by the Bright Young People who are the book's ostensible heroes. In fact, Waugh's attitude is complex.

In a discussion of the younger generation, the Rt. Hon. Walter

Outrage, MP, then briefly prime minister (he alternates the position with dizzying swiftness with a certain Lord Throbbing), complains thus: "I don't understand them, and I don't want to. They had a chance after the war that no generation has ever had. There was a whole civilization to be saved and remade—and all they seem to do is to play the fool." Fr. Rothschild is less damning: "Don't you think," he says, "that perhaps it is all in some way historical? I don't think people ever *want* to lose their faith either in religion or in anything else. I know very few young people, but it seems to me that they are all possessed with an almost fatal hunger for permanence. . . . And this word 'bogus' they all use. . . . They won't make the best of a bad job nowadays." Rothschild goes on to suggest that the motto both of his Church and of the older English generation might be something like "If a thing's worth doing at all, it's worth doing well," whereas the Young People say, "If a thing's not worth doing well, it's not worth doing at all." He concludes that this inversion "makes everything very difficult for them."

Another party to the discussion, which may be considered the center of Waugh's novel, Lord Metroland, is less sympathetic. "Anyhow," he complains, "I don't see how all that explains why my stepson should drink like a fish and go about everywhere with a negress." Fr. Rothschild acknowledges the problem: "I think they're connected, you know," he says, taking his leave for further behind-the-scenes business of state. "But it's all very difficult." Indeed.

The link between the recurrent slang term "bogus," flagged by the Jesuit, and the various inventions and deceptions throughout the novel seems significant to me. In the usage, a thing is bogus if it is boring, or tiresome, or done by someone else with too-serious intent, or simply unpleasant. Like more contemporary versions—"lame" would be one recent favorite—the judgment is vague and all purpose, but no less effective for that. And it is clear that any association with truth or authenticity is long broken: bogus decidedly does not mean fake or insincere. Quite the reverse, since these traits are among the amusing non-bogus features of the comedy—which is admittedly quite black. Two rather harmless young characters, one a penurious nobleman and the other a carefree flirt and party girl, die suddenly during the action, the first by suicide and the second through madness. Waugh is already, preconversion, familiar with the wages of sin, including the uncomfortable knowledge that sometimes those sins go unpunished even as others die.

We may seem to come a fair distance from the question of tradition, but I suggest in fact not, especially since this twisting of "fake" and "bogus" nicely captures the central problem of tradition, namely, how to carry something on in a manner we regard as authentic—even as, perhaps, our ideals of authenticity themselves are ever put in question and found unreliable. It may be that the very concept of authenticity, not just its various iterations, is found to be incoherent. Or it may be that the once-valid reasons for doing or cherishing something are no longer present, leaving a carapace of ritual obedience reflexively justified as tradition. (A character in Richard Powell's novel *The Philadelphian* [1956], musing on social convention in that most status-conscious of American cities: "We do something for a reason, and then the reason vanishes, but we keep on doing it because by that time it's a tradition."[35])

In such cases of defunct reason or conceptual emptiness, I suggest we have at least three options: (1) an aggressive "traditionalist" retrenchment, (2) a desperate rootlessness, and (3) what we might call the Nietzschean option, the *sprezzatura* of cool celebration. Here, to use Eagleton's words, "one's beliefs are more like one's manservants, to be hired and fired as the fancy takes you, than like one's bodily organs"; or, varying the metaphor, "as costumes one can don or doff at will . . . as with kilts and cravats, it is aesthetic considerations which govern the donning and doffing."[36] (Kilts again!)

35. Mrs. John Marshall (Carol) Wharton, the wife of an aging, respectable lawyer, says these words to her husband's young colleague, with whom she is contemplating a love affair. Richard Powell, *The Philadelphian* (New York: Charles Scribner's Sons, 1956), 218. The novel was later adapted as the film *The Young Philadelphians* (1959, directed by Vincent Sherman), starring Paul Newman.

36. Eagleton, *Culture and the Death of God*, 193. He adds: "The left-wing historian

Eagleton regards this last option as "cavalier" and seems to deride its "modernism" in favor of a principled postmodernism—and yet it is the latter conception that is most often attacked by the stalwarts of option 1. I prefer to call option 3 *fugitive*, in the sense that its energy comes from the combined freedom and responsibility of self-invention. But our acts of self-invention are never entirely aesthetic (in the pejorative sense detectable in Eagleton's characterization), nor are they without grounding in concrete practical realities of shared social life. That is, our circumstances allow for a range of options in framing our life narratives, but the range is not without limit: it is, as Bernard Williams put it, not a real option for *me* to live *my* life as a samurai warrior, still less (one might add) as a Klingon battle commander—though I may well act out these aspects of my desire-world in fantasy, online games, cosplay, and the like. We can say, after Mill, that these are "experiments in living." By their very nature, they stand opposed to reductive claims of tradition, especially those that are revealed as bogus, such as some parts of Scottish clan identity, and those that are actively harmful, such as the ethnic nationalism and bloodline dominance to be seen in Hutu-Tutsi hatred, religious intolerance of homosexuality, or Nazism.[37] Tradition becomes ideology—typically with violent results.

The gifts of option 3 are not just individual; experiments in living

---

A. J. P. Taylor once informed an Oxford Fellowship election committee that he had extreme political views, but held them moderately." This suggests the valid question of whether moderate political views, held extremely, might offer a better course.

37. The standard attack on spurious Highland clan identity is Hugh Trevor-Rope, "The Invention of Tradition: The Highland tradition of Scotland," in *The Invention of Tradition*, ed. Eric Hobsbawm and Terence Ranger (Cambridge: Cambridge University Press, 1983). But, as critics have noted, the distinction between "invented" and "initiated" traditions, particularly in the case of nation-states (a concern of this volume), can be difficult to hold without committing its own kind of special pleading. A better approach to the trappings of nationalism is, arguably, the one taken by Roland Barthes in his *Mythologies*, trans. Annette Lavers (London: Paladin, 1973) [originally published in 1957], which examines specific bits of cultural effluvia—steak frites, the Citröen motorcar, a *Paris Match* magazine cover—to reveal their ideology-driven fabrication.

create a milieu in which further, and sometimes more radical, experimentation is possible. This milieu, in its transtemporal existence, is what I mean by the democratic tradition. It is an imperfect standard, but let us say for the nonce that there is a valid possible distinction between *open* traditions and *closed* ones. The democratic tradition, by virtue of its structural combination of conservation (the present as a gift of the past, the future as a gift of the present) and innovation (we must each invent ourselves as we go on) strikes the correct balance to achieve openness. There is, to be sure, a democratic version of what Harold Bloom called "the anxiety of influence" operative here. How, indeed, could there not be? The freedom to self-invent is, as noted, importantly conjoined with responsibility. Every successful experiment is a bequest to future democratic generations; every failure is a cost that they will be made to bear.

The closest nonpolitical analogy to the open, anxious, free, responsible, conservative, and innovative features of this tradition is, it seems to me, the tradition(s) of scholarship. There may be closely held standards of responsibility here, as in science, where the by-word is "creative destruction" of results in the form of testing and reiteration. But even in less strictly policed regions of scholarship, we find constraints and standards that compel practitioners to go on in a certain way. And that way is forward looking—wanting to generate new results, new interventions, new interpretations—even as it is guided and governed by a vast inheritance. This, then, is a transtemporal discursive community, whose members are in an endless conversation about what is right, good, or simply interesting. Some ideas will reign for a time, only to be rejected, perhaps even reviled, later. Once dismissed, results may come into new favor. The only overarching rules of the process is that everyone who possesses the wherewithal to contribute to the conversations acquires, just in virtues of that wherewithal, the authority to do so.

In the democratic tradition, there is one clear difference: no credentials are demanded for inspection at the threshold of the discursive arena. You do not need a PhD to be a full member. There is no means test except the basic existential one; just being here is enough.

Fugitive Democracy

Too many accounts of tradition, positive and negative alike, rely on contrastive force, so that tradition is defended (or condemned) as against modernity, progress, change, or some similar forward facing value. I hope I have shown in the previous sections that the notion of a democratic tradition, if there is any valid version thereof, cannot be defended in this manner. For one thing, no account of democracy could rely on an unchallenged notion of such anti-traditional values.

Progress, for example, has been the cover and clothes of the worst depredations against human spirit and freedom, not least in its aspirations to an ideal state. Walter Benjamin is suitably chastening in his "Theses on the Philosophy of History" (1940):

> A Klee painting named Angelus Novus shows an angel looking as though he is about to move away from something he is fixedly contemplating. His eyes are staring, his mouth is open, his wings are spread. This is how one pictures the angel of history. Its face is turned towards the past. Where we see a chain of events, he sees one single catastrophe which keeps piling wreckage upon wreckage and hurls it in front of his feet. A storm irresistibly propels him into the future, to which his back is turned while the pile of debris before him grows skyward. This storm is what we call progress.[38]

Benjamin's image here is reflected in the small Paul Klee work Angelus Novus (1920), which Benjamin carried with him in his flight from France to Spain as the Nazi forces entered Paris. The words above were written in January of that year; fearing repatriation to Nazi Germany, Benjamin committed suicide in September in Portbou, Spain.

One needn't be such an obvious world-historical victim to see the force of Benjamin's argument, which indicts the logic of materialism

38. Walter Benjamin, "Über den Begriff der Geschichte" [Theses on the philosophy of history], in *Illuminations: Essays and Reflections*, ed. Hannah Arendt, trans. Harry Zohn (New York: Shocken, 1968).

and never-ending social change as a nightmare of instrumental rationality. One might think, here, of another famous artwork, Francisco de Goya's etching *El sueño de la razón produce monstruos* (1797–99). This image is Plate 43 of the eighty etchings that comprise Goya's satirical album *Los Caprichos* (*Caprices*).[39] It shows a sleeping male figure, his head slumped upon a work desk scattered with drawing instruments, beset by a rising flock of bat-like flying creatures, some that resemble owls, as a large cat, reminiscent of a sphinx, looks on. The title is usually translated as "the sleep of reason produces monsters," and the full epigraph reads this way: "Fantasy abandoned by reason produces impossible monsters: united with her, she is the mother of the arts and the origin of their marvels." This gloss suggests a benign Apollonian-Dionysian union, in controlled art, of constraining reason and rampant imagination, which would otherwise spin itself off into nightmarish vision.

But another interpretation offers itself, turning on the linguistic ambiguity that has the Spanish word *sueño*, meaning both "sleep" and "dream." Suppose that reason, rather than a helpful curb, is itself a generator of monstrous visions when it is allowed to run unfettered in human life. The original meaning captures Goya's *ars poetica*, perhaps, and executes a kind of self-satire in a series of works that mock pretension and excess in contemporary Spanish society. The inverted interpretation sounds, in addition, a subtle warning for the age about to unfold, in which reason will gather into its hands the reins of everything, including social order—and the results will be mon-

39. In a curious and controversial inversion of the standard anxiety-of-influence aesthetic tradition, the British artists Jake and Dinos Chapman purchased several prints from Goya's *Los Caprichos* series and then drew on them. According to Dinos Chapman, these acts of defacement did not constitute vandalism because the altered works *rose in value*. "You can't vandalize something by making it more expensive," he said. In 2005, the Chapman Brothers' "revised and improved" versions of Los Caprichos were selling for $26,000 each in the White Cube Gallery in London. For an account of vandalism, value, and renewed gift economies in discarded or rescued art, see Ben Lerner, "Damage Control: The Modern Art World's Tyranny of Price," *Harper's Magazine*, December 2013, 43–49.

sters that fly into the darkness from our dreaming, world-dominating minds.

Well, perhaps that is itself a flight of fancy. For a more grounded version of the point, compare Chesterton on the question of anti-traditional manias for change. "It is true that a man (a silly man) might make change itself his object or ideal," he notes. "But as an ideal change itself becomes unchangeable. If the change-worshiper wishes to estimate his own progress, he must be sternly loyal to the ideal of change; he must not begin to flirt gaily with the ideal of monotony. Progress itself cannot progress. . . . Change is the hardest and narrowest groove that a man can get into."[40] One could add the basic logical point that there can be no such thing as change unless and until there is something that is *not* changing. Change is a contrastive force. Consider that the paradox of Theseus's ship does not make us pause to question the idea of identity over time in the absence of some notion, or at least the *desire* for the notion, of the one and only ship that belongs to Theseus.

Even worse than a mindless devotion to change for its own sake is the peculiar stasis observable in "presentism," the perverse instantaneity in which everything seems to happen now and seems to demand a response even earlier.[41] The same social media that allowed for near-instant connection to coordinate resistance in Tahrir Square can effect, in New York or London, a radical disconnection and a generalized feeling of ephemerality. This shrinking of time is a blight on the democratic body, even a sort of *zombie virus* in which we consume our own consciousness at a pace just beyond our ability to process the world.[42] This never-ending preoccupation with the tyranny of the now,

40. Chesterton, *Orthodoxy*, 31.

41. For a brisk journalistic account of the details, see Douglas Rushkoff, *Present Shock: When Everything Happens Now* (New York: Penguin, 2013). It must be said that this book, while valuable as a diagnostic, suffers from a measure of discursive breathlessness, leaping from topic to topic with the speed of the very virus it wants to analyze.

42. I explore the trope of zombies in democratic life in Mark Kingwell, "Frank's Motel: Horizontal and Vertical in the Big Other," in *The Ends of History: Questioning the*

which can be neither completed nor overcome, renders individuals incapable of framing long-term interests of their own, let alone attending to the trusteeship responsibilities we the living bear to those who are still to come. It has been the case, historically, that democracies have defined themselves diacritically against tyrannies, the freedom from oppression of arbitrary rule.[43] We should see that a tyrant of one's own devising, internalized as a dominant part of one's self, is just as harmful to genuine freedom as one whose force is enacted from without.

Worse still, a self lived under the tyranny of the now is not capable of taking proper stock of its own history. Sheldon Wolin, an avowed "progressive" thinker, argues that one key factor in the emergence of "managed democracy" and its attendant threat of "inverted," or soft, totalitarianism is the speed of social change:

> Today, thanks to the highly organized pursuit of technological innovation and the culture it encourages, change is more rapid, more encompassing, more welcomed than ever before—which means that institutions, values, and expectations share with technology a limited shelf life. We are experiencing the triumph of contemporaneity and of its accomplice, forgetting or collective amnesia. Stated somewhat differently, in early modern times change displaced traditions; today change succeeds change.[44]

A casualty of that shift is the idea that "progress" might have the power to realize our desires for social justice. Early champions of progress "believed that while change might result in the disappearance or destruction of established beliefs, customs, and interests, the vast majority of these deserved to go because they mostly served the Few while keeping the Many in ignorance, poverty, and sickness."[45]

Stakes of Historical Reason, ed. Joshua Nichols and Amy Swiffen (New York: Routledge, 2013), 103–26.

43. E.g., in the Declaration of the Rights of Man and of the Citizen (Paris, June 24, 1793), we find these words offered in defense of the French Revolution: "in order that all citizens . . . may never permit themselves to be oppressed and degraded by tyranny." The same language is present in Robespierre's (rejected) Declaration of Rights (April 24, 1793), though it does not appear in the (accepted) 1789 declaration.

44. Wolin, *Democracy Inc.*, xviii.

45. Wolin, *Democracy Inc.*, xix.

The logic of this dialectic has since vanished, however, because there is nothing for the forces of "progress" to push off against. Meanwhile, our sense of time has become compressed and distorted; the outcome of such time is "the tyranny of efficiency" in the subversion of democracy's demand "that time be defined by the requirements for deliberation, discussion, reconciliation of opposing viewpoints, all of which suddenly seem 'time-consuming.'"[16] This, we might say, is the final, but alas self-consuming, victory of *chronos* time.

Nor does the damage end there. This condition of relentless change-upon-change leads, in turn, to a neglect of anything that stands in relation to that self as a public trust or a common good. Social change without direction, instead of leading to desired general goods, merely raises the specter of empty narcissism. "With postmodernism," Terry Eagleton argues, rather recklessly using a blanket label,

> history is reduced for the most part to commodified cultural heritage, an ever-present repertoire of inherited styles and a "presentist" approach to the past.... History is too brutely given for a culture which delights in an endless array of options. It is an unwelcome reminder that our freedom in the present is constrained by the irreparable fatality we know as the past.[47]

Under these conditions, postmodern thought is revealed as "depthless, anti-tragic, non-linear, anti-numinous, non-foundational and anti-universalist, suspicious of absolutes and averse to interiority."[48] Quite a catalogue of vices! We should, of course, be careful to distinguish our reactions to this denunciation from a thinker whose hostility toward postmodern thought is sometimes more vivid than reasoned. In concluding this chapter, I suggest *pace* Eagleton that one can—indeed must—retain the suspicion toward universalism and

46. Wolin, *Democracy Inc.*, 233. Wolin is particularly worried by the combination of such antidemocratic instantaneity with a misguided reverence for the past in the form of "originalism" concerning "Framers' Intent" and the US Constitution.

47. Eagleton, *Culture and the Death of God*, 188.

48. Eagleton, *Culture and the Death of God*, 188; see also idem, *The Illusions of Postmodernism* (London: Blackwell, 1996).

foundationalism, a variform version of Lyotard's "incredulity towards metanarratives," without sacrificing interiority, tragedy, and a sense of history.

And yet society is changing so fast that sometimes the tug toward both presentism and the bad forms of postmodern restlessness seems irresistible. In previous democratic moments, social change was itself a motor of political aspiration, not stasis. As Zygmunt Bauman has argued, "The considerable speeding up of social change" was seen by reformers as a necessary condition for the creation of "historical consciousness." And this consciousness was in turn "duly reflected in the . . . novel sense of history as an endless chain of irreversible changes, with which the concept of progress—a development which brings change for the better—was not slow to join forces." The resulting notion of constant progressive change, or perfectibility, "paved the way for utopia."[49] We have seen that this utopian impulse has its considerable downside risks, even assuming that such a thing as "constant progressive change" was possible—as Chesterton, for one, denies.

The answer is not, however, a decline into anti-utopianism, whether of the Fabian sort or, worse, the disengagement and cynicism that characterizes too much of the electorates in Western democracies, especially among young people who recently experienced income levels lower than their parents and record levels of under- and unemployment, even when highly educated.[50] Is there, perhaps, a form of anti-anti-utopianism that can keep alive the very idea of democratic aspiration without courting the dangers rightly associated with ideal outcomes? This is the crux of the concept of fugitive

49. Zygmunt Bauman, *Socialism: The Active Utopia* (London: George Allen & Unwin, 1976), 18–19.

50. Some alarming statistics concerning defection from electoral politics among young Canadians—dubbed Spectators—were reported by Michael Valpy, "The Young Will Inherit a Future They See as a Sham," *Toronto Star*, December 8, 2013; Valpy in turn drew on an analysis by David Herle, "The Spectators," *Policy Options*, November 2012, 19–20. News reports suggest a similar situation, if not worse, in other developed "democratic" nations.

democracy. In our initial analysis, the fugitive quality of democracy seems like a disadvantage, an escaped prisoner on the run. This, Sheldon Wolin suggests, is itself the legacy of a long-held but erroneous identification of democracy, and the political more generally, with a form of electoral politics and centralized government. "Institutionalization marks the attenuation of democracy," Wolin notes:

> leaders begin to appear; hierarchies develop; experts of one kind or another cluster around the centers of decision; order, procedure, and precedent displace a more spontaneous politics: in retrospect the latter appears as disorganized, inefficient. Democracy thus seems destined to be a moment rather than a form. Throughout the history of political thought virtually all writers emphasize the unstable and temporary character of democracy.[51]

This initial analysis prompts two urgent questions for democrats: Why is it that democracy is reduced, even devitalized by form? Why is its presence occasional and fugitive?

In a way, the answers are obvious. Such institutionalizations of the political are further evidence, if any was needed, of Robert Michels's "iron law of oligarchy," which decrees that the emergence of an oligarchy, or non-circulating elite, is an unavoidable consequence of the "tactical and technical necessities" of democratic politics, especially in systems of electoral representation.[52] Michels: "It is organization which gives birth to the dominion of the elected over the electors, of the mandataries over the mandators, of the delegates over the delegators. Who says organization, says oligarchy." Nor, argued Michels, is this a chance development in some cases rather than others. "Historical evolution mocks all the prophylactic measures that have been adopted for the prevention of oligarchy," he said, and the stated purpose of democratic movements—namely, to *eliminate* elites—cannot but generate them through the very attempts at elimination.

51. Wolin, "Fugitive Democracy," 19. In support of the last claim, Wolin cites Plato, *Republic* VIII: 557e–558a, and *Laws* III: 693d.

52. Robert Michels, *Political Parties: A Sociological Study of the Oligarchical Tendencies of Modern Democracy*, trans. Eden Paul and Cedar Paul (New York: Free Press, 1915). [Originally published in 1911.]

Like Oedipus, their every move away from social elite formation creates the tragic outcome of creating a political elite—which becomes itself social. This rule by an elite in the name of the *demos* is oligarchy; worse, joining the iron law with Chesterton's oligarchy of the living might be seen to raise the problem to a second power. (Michels was true to his conclusions: in his native Germany, he was a vocal socialist; he later emigrated to Italy and joined the socialist wing of Mussolini's fascist party.)

Put in less structural terms, we can say that the devolution to organized, hence corruptible, politics is just the inevitable development of a socialized citizenry, all of whom view themselves as either aspiring to or shadowing the trappings of bourgeois material comfort. Georg Lukács put it in the following terms, which reflect also on the changing nature of time and space under late capitalist conditions: "Bourgeois society carried out the process of socializing society. Capitalism destroyed both the spatio-temporal barriers between different lands and territories and also the legal partitions between the different 'estates,'" Lukács concludes: "Man becomes, in the true sense of the word, a social being. Society becomes the reality for man."[53] In toxic versions, this combination of aspiration and shadowing congeals into a comprehensive ideological myth—the American Dream, perhaps.[54] In Wolin's own measured words, "The democratization of 'advanced industrial democracies' comes down to this: the labor, wealth and psyches of the citizenry are simultaneously defended and exploited, protected and extracted, nurtured and fleeced, rewarded and commanded, flattered and threatened."[55]

One could be far more incendiary than this and denounce the managerial capture of democracy in more rousing language. But

53. Georg Lukács, "What Is Orthodox Marxism?," in *History and Class Consciousness: Studies in Marxist Dialectics*, trans. Rodney Livingstone (Cambridge: Massachusetts Institute of Technology Press, 1972), 19.

54. I explore the reach of this version of ideological conditioning in my "The American Gigantic," in *Unruly Voices*, 41–56.

55. Wolin, "Fugitive Democracy," 16.

such cries tend to dissolve quickly, or else devolve into a cynicism that edges always toward apathy. A better course is to work constantly to free democracy of its institutional shackles and return citizenship to the center of political life—even if only for rupturous moments at a time. Thus does the fugitive transform from prisoner on the run into a guerrilla warrior in the democratic cause. "Democracy is not about where the political is located but how it is experienced," Wolin notes.[56] And later: "Democracy needs to be reconceived as something other than a form of government: as a mode of being which is conditioned by bitter experience, doomed to succeed only temporarily, but is a recurrent possibility as long as the memory of the political survives."[57]

I note the *temporality* embedded in this revitalized notion of fugitive democracy ("the memory of the political," "recurrent possibility") and likewise its invocation of *authority* ("conditioned by bitter experience" and "doomed," but nevertheless doomed "to succeed"). This, I suggest, is precisely the living tradition of democracy. Though its orientation to future possibilities marks it as akin to some recent politico-theological conceptions of democracy, such as Derrida's "democracy to come" or Agamben's "coming community," it is rooted in the deep soil of inherited social life and concrete obligation to those both before and after us.[58] Unlike them, it does not ask for a vague "infinite responsibility" toward those who are yet to come, but it *does* enjoin a real infinite, namely, the infinite demand to renew and revitalize democratic legitimacy, here and now.

We might think, in this connection, of Gilles Deleuze's notion of *repetition*: that infinite miracle of singularity, the uniqueness that lies beyond law, equivalency, and transaction but that can be encoun-

56. Wolin, "Fugitive Democracy," 18.

57. Wolin, "Fugitive Democracy," 23.

58. See Jacques Derrida, *Rogues: Two Essays on Reason*, trans. Michael Naas and Pascale-Anne Brault (Stanford, CA: Stanford University Press, 2003), and Giorgio Agamben, *The Coming Community*, trans. Michael Hardt (Minneapolis: University of Minnesota Press, 1993).

tered again and again. "Repetition as a conduct and as a point of view concerns non-exchangeable and non-substitutable singularities," Deleuze says. "If exchange is the criterion of generality, theft and gift are those of repetition."[59] That is: only that which can be stolen can also be given, and vice versa. "Repetition belongs to humour and irony," Deleuze continues, "it is by nature transgression or exception, always revealing a singularity opposed to the particularities subsumed under laws, a universal opposed to the generalities which give rise to laws."[60] Repetition is festival, excess, rupture. In its democratic possibility, it is where you and I are citizens together, returning to our shared locus of trust, equal not in the sense of being exchangeable but precisely in respect of our infinite difference.

The possibility of repeating the democratic demand is the gift bequeathed to us by our forebears. The making of it, in the service of our own needs but also in trust to those who will come after us, is the gift we bequeath to them. That is, democracy is a gift that we must give to ourselves—so much is obvious—but it is also a gift of insight, that we the people are far more than an electorate, a voting bloc, a population. It is, then—to offer another double to match the double genitive of my opening section—a gift in time: one that is both received and given across *and* that must be given without delay if its benefits are not to be squandered in cynicism or complacency, frozen into institutional attenuation, stolen by the moneyed interest, or otherwise wasted.

59. Gilles Deleuze, *Difference and Repetition*, trans. Paul Patton (New York: Columbia University Press, 1994), 1.

60. Deleuze, *Difference and Repetition*, 5.

SISTER MARY PRUDENCE ALLEN, RSM

8 • PERSONAL IDENTITY

Does the Religious Vow of Obedience Impede or Assist Our Development?

Introduction

Religious life, from its beginning in the West, incorporated some kind of obedience in the context of the formation of members in its various communities. Up to the fourteenth century, the Augustinians, Benedictines, and later mendicant orders such as Franciscans and Dominicans elaborated specific ways that obedience was practiced within the framework of their unique charisms. From the Protestant Reformation and the Roman Catechism following the Council of Trent (1566) up to the Second Vatican Council (1962–65), a woman was often required to make a promise of obedience to her husband in the marriage rite. Today, in the rite of ordination of a priest, a man makes a promise to obey the bishop and his successors. Thus formal structures relating to the practice of obedience in the Church relate to the three paradigm vocations: religious consecration, sacramental marriage of laymen and laywomen, and priestly ordination.

Following the Second Vatican Council, there have been many critiques of the tradition of vowed obedience in religious life. Some claim that obedience impedes the maturing of a person by (1) defending a hierarchical structure of relations that stifles personal growth in those on the bottom of a hierarchy; (2) treating an adult more like a child, which keeps a person in a childish state; and (3) when sex and gender identity are added to the mix, by an institutionalized patriarchal sexism through which males perpetuate power over females.

Counterarguments have addressed these critiques to the effect that (1) obediential reality is both hierarchical and egalitarian; (2) obediential human reality is developmental, analogical, and rooted in free will; and (3) obediential interpersonal reality is a collaborative and complementary service through mutual submission out of love for Christ. These critiques draw upon Neo-Thomist and personalist foundations that integrate principles from philosophy, psychology, and theology. To answer the question posed in the title of this paper—Does the religious vow of obedience impede or assist our development?—I consider specific critiques and counterarguments from the perspective of a Catholic philosophy of the human person and interpersonal relations. This approach includes the individual person's operations of intellect, will, senses, and passions as well as the dynamics of interpersonal acts. For a person in authority, obedience is about things to be done; for the one obeying, it is about the motive and action being done; and for the community, it is about formation forever deepening integrity of response.

Hierarchical and Egalitarian Structures of Relations

Critics of the traditional vow of obedience often argue that hierarchal and egalitarian communities are mutually exclusive. Joan Chittister, OSB, in a lecture titled "Remember the Vision: Embracing the Dream," stated that a religious community should be "democratic—not hierarchical."[1] This set of exclusive alternatives is a common feature in discussions of religious obedience. Yet reality itself is both hierarchical and egalitarian in many respects. Just consider the hierarchical structure of the human body, beginning with its hydrogen

1. Joan Chittister, OSB, Keynote address, Meeting of the Leadership Council of Women Religious (April 19, 2006), 4.

atoms, organized into fluids, which in turn are organized by systems (e.g., cardiovascular) and by the intellect and will in the central form or soul of the living organic person. The Neo-Thomist Bernard Lonergan, SJ, refers to these hierarchical levels in the nature of a human being as the nested conjugate forms organized by a central form.[2] Each level follows its own laws that a higher level organizes into a higher set of laws. When the entire organism—a woman or a man—is considered, both have equal dignity and worth at the same time as they contain a hierarchical internal structure. Thus a community to which they may belong may be both egalitarian and hierarchical depending on its internal dynamism and structure.

Often persons who argue for the false alternatives of hierarchy versus equality often insert presupposition of a dualistic hierarchy. For example, Ellen M. Leonard, in "Contemporary Theologies of the Vows," describes the shift in worldview, from " 'the one-sided certainty of a mechanistic, dualistic world view [that] no longer holds' . . . [to] a holistic vision, and hierarchy is replaced by a community of equals."[3] Leonard's characterization of mechanistic dualism is clearly Cartesian. Diarmuid O'Murchu, MSC, gives another critique of dualism when he describes *"A dualistic mode of governance.* Taken literally, . . . this is very much an arrangement of the governing ones vs. those who are governed, the active vs. the passive, the powerful vs. the disempowered."[4] His concept of dualism seems drawn from nineteenth-century stereotypes common to master/slave models of obedience.

2. See Bernard Lonergan, "Human Development," in *Insight: A Study of Human Understanding* (Ontario: University of Toronto, 1992). In his words: "Organic, psychic, and intellectual development are not three independent process. They are interlocked with the intellectual providing a higher integration of the psychic. Each level involves its own laws" (494).

3. Ellen M. Leonard, CSJ, "Contemporary Theologies of the Vows," *Review for Religious* (September–October 2002): 511–21, here 513, referring to Barbara Fiend, SNDdeN, *Refocusing the Vision: Religious Life into the Future* (New York: Crossroad, 2001), 39.

4. Diarmuid O'Murchu, MSC, *Consecrated Religious Life: The Changing Paradigms* (Philippines: Claretian, 2006), 227.

In response to these critiques, it is helpful first to consider briefly some of the ways that the vow of obedience was lived in different religious traditions. Although the traditions of St. Basil the Great (329–79) and St. John Cassian (360–435) tended to emphasize a master/slave model for religious obedience, chapter 7 of St. Augustine's (354–30) *Rule* begins with the following words: "You should obey your prior as you would a father, with respect for his office, lest you offend God who is in him."[5] Two aspects of this innovation of St. Augustine are important: (1) obedience is directed primarily to God, and (2) it should be asked for and responded to in a familial relation of love.[6]

Sr. Agatha Mary, interpreter of Augustine's Rule, adds that viewing one's religious superior as a father is not meant by Augustine to be interpreted as a reduction of the one obeying to an infantile state, "what Augustine is talking about in his Rule is consistently a relationship between adults."[7] The key to Augustine's approach is his great emphasis on freedom of will as well as the loving filial relationship of the one ruling and the one obeying. "Obedience must be yoked to freedom, and freedom is only possible if obedience is motivated by love and respect."[8]

Augustine's Rule provided the foundation for many subsequent rules of religious life, for example, the Dominicans and the Religious Sisters of Mercy, among others. Ven. Catherine McAuley, foundress of the Religious Sisters of Mercy in Dublin, Ireland, in her *Familiar Instructions*, states that the practice of the virtue of the vow of obedience "is the great bond of union in the religious life, and makes all have

5. Agatha Mary, SPB, *The Rule of Saint Augustine: An Essay in Understanding* (Villanova, PA: Augustinian Press, 1991), chap. 7, 287. Another translation of the same rule reads: "You should obey superiors as fathers or mothers with the respect due them so as not to offend God in their persons." Adolar Sumkeller, OSA, *Augustine's Rule: A Commentary*, trans. Matthew J. O'Connell (Villanova, PA: Augustinian Press, 1987).

6. See Sr. Agatha Mary, *Rule of St. Augustine*: "To obey is to do more than fulfill a command; it is to accommodate oneself to another person—not only to his words but to the underlying currents of his thought" (288).

7. Sr. Agatha Mary, *Rule of St. Augustine*, 292.

8. Sr. Agatha Mary, *Rule of St. Augustine*, 294.

but one will, one heart and one soul in God."[9] The nineteenth-century original Rule and Constitutions of the Religious Sisters of Mercy states that the Sisters "are to obey the Mother Superior, as having authority from God, rather through love than servile fear."[10] In practice, Venerable Mother Catherine often used humor in the context of obedience, by composing limericks and requesting things such as (Irish) dancing for evening recreation to keep warm in a convent with little heat. The ability to laugh at oneself and together made the acts of obedience lighthearted and joyful, thereby fostering union in charity.

The 1965 promulgation of documents from the Second Vatican Council, *Perfectae Caritatis*, On the Renewal of Religious Life, directly faced the question of whether the vow of obedience helps or impedes the flourishing of personality: "They [religious] should use both the forces of their intellect and will and the gifts of nature and grace to execute the commands and fulfill the duties entrusted to them. In this way religious obedience, far from lessening the dignity of the human person, by extending the freedom of the sons of God, leads it to maturity."[11] The admonition of religious to exercise their intellect and will with their gifts of nature and grace introduces the important challenge for the dynamic interaction of faith and reason. Pope John Paul II elaborated in depth the importance of learning how this is done in his encyclical *Fides et Ratio*. "Faith and reason are like two wings on which the human spirit rises to the contemplation of truth; and God has placed in the human heart a desire to know the truth—in a word, to know himself—so that, by knowing and loving God, men and women may also come to the fullness of truth about themselves."[12]

9. Rev. Mother McAuley, *Familiar Instructions* (St. Louis, MO: Vincentian Press, 1927), chap. 7, 39.

10. Mary C. Sullivan, *Catherine McAuley and the Tradition of Mercy* (Notre Dame, IN: University of Notre Dame Press, 1995), 313.

11. Vatican II Council, *Perfectae Caritatis: The Decree on the Adaptation and Renewal of Religious Life* (Rome: Vatican, 1965), no. 14.

12. John Paul II, *Encyclical Letter Fides et Ratio: On the Relationship between Faith and Reason* (Boston: Pauline Books and Media, 1998), 7.

St. Pope John Paul II provided an example of the way that intellect and will work together from the perspective of philosophical anthropology. He describes the "annunciation dialogue" in which Mary hears the words of the angel, then she asks a question about how what he says can happen, and after he answers her question, she exercises her will in saying, "Let it be done to me as you have said." Thus she demonstrates her obedience to God's will for her by a spiritually mature dialogue and then by a full and free act of her will. John Paul II describes this "annunciation dialogue" as "clearly *interpersonal in character*"[13] in which "Mary exercises her free will and thus fully shares with her personal and feminine 'I' in the event of the Incarnation."[14]

Just as the personal act of obedience of Mary, Mother of God effected not just her good but the good of many in the world, the ability to respond to a requested act of obedience does not just benefit the individual sister; it also benefits the community to which she belongs. In *Religious and Human Promotion*, the Sacred Congregation for Religious widened the dimensions of the radiation of the vows from the flourishing of the individual sister to the flourishing of the community itself:

> *Experts in communion*, religious are, therefore called to be an ecclesial community in the Church and in the world, witnesses and architects of the *plan for unity* which is the crowning point of human history in God's design.
>
> Above all, by the profession of the evangelical counsels, which frees one from what might be an obstacle to the fervor of charity, religious are communally a prophetic sign of intimate union with God, who is loved above all things.[15]

To conclude this first section, the critique of proposed exclusive alternatives, either a hierarchical structure or an egalitarian structure for obedience can be considered as a fallacy of false alternatives. The equal dignity of each person in a community, created in the im-

13. John Paul II, *Mulieris Dignitatem*, no. 5.

14. John Paul II, *Mulieris Dignitatem*, no. 4.

15. Sacred Congregation for Religious and Secular Institutes, *Religious and Human Promotion* (Boston: St. Paul's, 1978), no. 24.

age of God with intellect and will, is not per se lost in a hierarchical living out of the vow of obedience. The structure of a religious community can be both egalitarian and hierarchical.

Obedience Makes Childish or Mature Adults

The criticism that many men or women remained in a "childish" state through their practice of the vow of obedience has often been made. This term specifies that (1) they do not take responsibility for their own decisions; (2) they remain dependent on another person for directing their lives; and (3) they cannot even think for themselves.

Patricia Wittberg, SC, in "Community and Obedience: Musing on Two Ambiguities," observed: "We have known of personal and psychological destructiveness of intentional communities for a long time. But—and this is far less obvious—the total subordination of the individual was also bad for the community, which could not really be healthy when it was composed of psychologically stunted and covertly resentful members. Some congregations are only now discovering how much their community weakened itself during the pre-Vatican era by overdominating individual sisters."[16] Here, Wittberg attributes the cause of the reduction to a childlike state to a dominating religious superior and not to obedience itself.

Sandra Schneiders, IHM, approaches the problem in a chapter on obedience from *New Wineskins* from the other point of view, namely, the subject who obeys: "The weaker a person's religious experience the more dependent she or he is on human mediation of the divine will. In other words, the tendency of the mediators to substitute themselves for God by equating their own will with the divine will meets the need of the semi-religious individual to know the divine will with a kind of mechanical certitude. The resulting unhappy marriage is what we should call legalism but often call obedience."[17]

16. Patricia Wittberg, SC, "Community and Obedience: Musing on Two Ambiguities," *Review for Religious* (September–October 2006): 526–35, here 527–28.

17. Sandra Schneiders, IHM, *New Wineskins: Re-Imagining Religious Life Today* (New York: Paulist Press, 1986), 145–46.

Schneiders goes on to describe how the weaker sister externalizes her decision-making authority in other persons, laws, or customs. She summarizes: "In other words, 'blind obedience' is magic, not faith. The simple equation without remainder of the will of the finite mediator with the will of the Infinite mediated is idolatry, not obedience."[18] Then, Schneiders recommends what "should perhaps be called 'religiously motivated cooperation,' rather than obedience, for, in reality, it is obedience only because it is part of our obedience to God which embraces every aspect of our lives."[19]

While there is no question that some religious remain immature in their practice of the vow of obedience, Sandra Schneiders seems to reject the vow itself because of the poor practice of the vow. She seems at times to accept the "grace of the office" that follows the line of authority from the constitutions, general councils, and gifts of the Holy Spirit for legitimately constituted general and local superiors. In her words, "We do have good reason to expect to find the will of God expressed to us in the privileged loci of mediation which are integral to our vocation. But we cannot turn this expectation into a requirement that God guarantee every act of authority or compensate us for the latter's mistakes by suspending our responsibility for the evil or error involved in our 'obedience.'"[20]

In 1215, at the Fourth Lateran Council, the Magisterium took a balanced approach to protect both those who have authority and those who serve through obedience: "For just as we wish the rights of superiors to be upheld so we do not wish to support wrongs done to subjects."[21] The most recent *Code of Canon Law* (canon 601) adds

18. Schneiders, *New Wineskins*, 148.

19. Schneiders, *New Wineskins*, 148. Unfortunately, the third and final volume of Sandra Schneiders's *Trilogy on Religious Life in a New Millennium*: *Buying the Field: Catholic Religious Life in Mission to the World* (New York: Paulist Press, 2013), which extensively considers the vows of poverty and of obedience, was not available when I prepared this essay.

20. Schneiders, *New Wineskins*, 148.

21. Norman P. Tanner, SJ, ed., *Decrees of the Ecumenical Councils*, 2 vols. (Washington, DC: Georgetown University Press, 1990), 241.

an important specification: "The evangelical counsel of obedience, undertaken in a spirit of faith and love in the following of Christ obedient unto death, requires the submission of the will to legitimate superiors, who stand in the place of God, *when they command according to the proper constitutions*."[22] This final qualification holds a key to guide the practice of the vow of obedience in communities with different charisms. For example, in our constitutions of the Religious Sisters of Mercy of Alma, Michigan, a section on the vow of obedience refers to canon 601 and states: "The decision of the superior must be obeyed except when a command is manifestly contrary to the laws of God or these Constitutions or involves a certain and serious evil."[23]

In her study of religious obedience, Sandra Schneiders often draws a false dichotomy between law and life, which instead of seeing that law protects and guides life argues that law itself is associated with the deadening of life. In one example, "The striking uniformity of everything considered 'essential' to religious life testified eloquently to the priority of law over life."[24]

Diarmuid O'Murchu, MSC, develops a similar line of thought around the concept of "the obedient adult":

> The old culture of blind obedience seems to be in vogue once more, with the oppression and unhealthy phobias it inevitably invites.
>
> For Religious women and men in this painful situation, we have a prophetic duty to honor the adult in ourselves, in each other, and in the leadership of the Church to which we belong. In this context our obedience is for life and not for death.[25]

O'Murchu proposes a new paradigm model of collaborative discernment in community with adult interdependence.

It is tempting to respond to these criticisms of the deadening effect of the vow of obedience on some individuals by offering counter-

22. John P. Deal et al., eds., *New Commentary on the Code of Canon Law* (Mahwah, NJ: Paulist Press, 2000), canon 601, p. 766.

23. Constitutions of the Religious Sisters of Mercy Alma, Michigan (1991), no. 29.

24. Schneiders, *New Wineskins*, 153.

25. O'Murchu, *Consecrated Religious Life*, 76.

examples of men and women who have flourished within traditional religious life through their practice of the vows of obedience. Consider, for example, St. Anselm and St. Hildegard of Bingen, who both flourished as Benedictine monks in traditional monastic structures of obedience in the eleventh and twelfth centuries.[26] But examples of success or failure of individual religious women or men can seem to cancel one another out. The question of whether the tradition of vowed religious obedience impedes or helps our development needs to focus on general principles and not on individual examples.

Instead, it is a better argument to consider the principles of how obedience can be lived. Jesus's authority is actually in doing the Will of the Father. In our emotional logic, we think that being obedient gives us no authority. But in God, in the realm of the spiritual life, especially of a religious, being obedient gives one freedom. Even in the Christian life, being obedient provides assurance that we are fulfilling the Will of God. An obediential response assures us not only that we are doing the right thing, but also that there will be sufficient grace to accomplish God's Will.[27]

The monastic Rule of St. Benedict (480–547) offered several steps in the progressive formation of the obedience of his monks' obedience toward a goal of radiant self-giving in which glory is given to God by one's life in community.[28] The three traditional vows in the Benedictine order are: stability, conversion, and obedience. Follow-

26. See Sr. Prudence Allen, *The Concept of Woman: The Aristotelian Revolution: 759 BC–1250 AD* (Grand Rapids, MI: Eerdmans, 1997), 262–70 and 293–314.

27. With gratitude to Mother Mary Quentin Sheridan, RSM, Superior General Emerita, for this insight and other help in writing this essay.

28. Leonard J. Doyle, trans., *St. Benedict's Rule for Monasteries* (Collegeville, MN: St. John's Abbey, Liturgical Press, 1948): "Listen, my son, to your master's precepts, and incline the ear of your heart. Receive willingly and carry out effectively your loving father's advice, that by the labor of obedience you may return to Him from whom you had departed by the sloth of disobedience. / To you, therefore, my words are now addressed, whoever you may be, who are renouncing your own will to do battle under the Lord Christ, the true King, and are taking up the strong, bright weapons of obedience" (Prologue, 1).

ing a list of seventy-two "instruments of good works," the rule introduces a chapter on obedience. The virtue of obedience is linked to the first four degrees of humility through a progressive unfolding and deepening in the formation of the monk.[29]

It may surprise contemporary religious who argue that obedience means "collective listening" to God to learn that St. Benedict stated that the Abbot should "call together the whole community and state the matter (any important business) to be acted upon."[30] The rule states further that "the reason . . . all should be called for counsel is that the Lord often reveals to the younger what is best."[31] The hierarchical structure of the monastic community is permeated by respect for the equal dignity of each and every monk, even the youngest in religion.

Moving from the monastic model to the mendicant Dominican model, two examples of persons flourishing within a different sort of hierarchical model of obedience include the thirteenth-century St. Thomas Aquinas (1224–74) and the fourteenth-century St. Catherine of Siena (1347–80). In the *Summa Theologiae*, Thomas argued that the vow of obedience was the chief vow because through it the religious offers to God his own will, in a kind of holocaust of total offering. A greater offering than just of his external goods through the vow of poverty or his body through the vow of chastity, the purpose of submitting one's will through the vow of obedience was to remove obstacles to charity.[32]

Thomas considers how persons should exercise their intellect and the will by seeking to understand a precept of the superior's will and promptly attempting to fulfill it. Obedience is a moral virtue and part of justice that "observes the mean between excess and deficiency."[33]

29. See *St. Benedict's Rule*, chap. 5:18–19 and chap. 6:20.

30. *St. Benedict's Rule*, chaps. 3, 12.

31. *St. Benedict's Rule*, chaps. 3, 13.

32. Thomas Aquinas, *Summa Theologiae*, 5 vols., trans. Fathers of the English Dominican Province (Westminster, MD: Christian Classics: 1981), vol. 4, *ST* II-II, q. 186, aa. 7–8.

33. *ST* II-II, q. 104, a. 2.

Aquinas also considers the relation of obedience to the passions. Lombardo describes it: "In sum, virtue does not eradicate passion but produces ordinate passions, that is, passions actively oriented toward human flourishing."[34] We can learn this virtue from the example of Jesus Christ, who showed us in the Garden of Gethsemane that it is permissible for us to want something with our human passions that God does not will and to bring our will in line with God's will.[35]

Central to Thomas's analysis of the passions is his view that a human person flourishes when his or her passions are permeated by reason. Lombardo amplifies: "the proper functioning of the passions according to their own structure is integral to human flourishing. Consequently, the moral evaluation of specific instances of a particular passion turns on whether that passion is functioning according to its own inner structure. Since the passions in their inner structure are directed towards our flourishing, and since moral goodness consists precisely in that flourishing, moral goodness is the default orientation of generic passion, even though generic passion is not itself morally good."[36] From the perspective of philosophical anthropology

34. Nicholas E. Lombardo, OP, *The Logic of Desire: Aquinas on Emotion* (Washington, DC: Catholic University of America Press, 2011), 106.

35. Lombardo, *Logic of Desire*, 222–23nn75–79: "Aquinas holds that Christ assumed ordinary human affectivity for our instruction. This emerges especially in his threefold explanation of why Christ prayed in Gethsemane in the way that he did: 'First, he wanted to show that he had assumed a true human nature, with all its natural affections. Second, he wanted to show that it is permissible for a man to want something on the level of natural affection that God does not will. Third, he wanted to show that man should submit his own affection to the divine will.' Christ shows us what virtuous affectivity looks like, and therefore what it looks like to be truly human, so that we can imitate him, both by striving for virtue and by accepting as fully compatible with virtue—and even necessary for virtue—those aspects of human affectivity that otherwise might seem like moral imperfections. In this way, Christ's human affectivity helps bring about our salvation. Aquinas maintains that his passion provides a particularly salvific example of virtuous affectivity." Lombardo refers the reader back to the following sources in the above paragraph. See Peter Lombard, *Sententiae* III 15.1; *ST* III, q. 14, a. 1; *ST* III, q. 21, a. 2; *ST* III, q. 46, aa. 3–6, in his notes.

36. Lombardo, *Logic of Desire*, 112.

and the dynamic interrelation of reason and faith, Thomas Aquinas's analysis of how a person ought to practice obedience is helpful to religious formation.

The Third Order Dominican St. Catherine of Siena reveals, in an outstanding collection of personal letters to her confessor, friends, and directees, how she personally flourished through her own practice of obedience and even further how she passionately called others to obedience according to the forms of their vocations. In sum, (1) she used many rich analogies about obedience, such as "cracking one's head of pride on a low doorway";[37] (2) she articulated that obedience is the responsibility of a person's own self-governance and that one strengthens the will by the act of killing self-will;[38] and (3) she claimed that obedience is owed not only to God but also to the Church.[39]

St. Catherine interweaves the themes of self-mastery and imitation of Christ throughout her letters. In a letter to some male novices of Augustine (Canon 1376), she writes the following advice:

> Never ever be afraid of anything—neither apprehension about not being able to persevere, nor the prospect that bearing up under obedience and the rule may be painful, nor anything that might happen. Keep your will good and holy, for your will is master of this wall, and with the pick-axe of free choice can maintain or demolish it as it chooses . . . For there is no one who can take away your mastery unless you so choose, and this is something ([God]) has given to everyone.[40]

The key to flourishing under obedience as described by St. Catherine above involves repeated acts of persons choosing to obey, such

37. Suzanne Noffke, OP, trans., *The Letters of Catherine of Siena*, 2 vols. (Tempe: Arizona Center for Medieval and Renaissance Studies, 2000), 1:52, 2:24, 2:41–42, and 2:121. For an elaboration of St. Catherine's ability to draw spiritual analogies, see Sister Prudence Allen, RSM, *The Concept of Woman*, vo. 2, *The Early Humanist Reformation, 1250–1500* (Grand Rapids, MI: Eerdmans, 2002), 380–98.

38. *Letters of Catherine*, 1:7n8, 1:50, 1:178, 2:128nn22–23, 2:516, and 2:642.

39. *Letters of Catherine*, 1:210, 1:215. See also 1:243.

40. *Letters of Catherine*, 2:128nn22–23.

as in in her wonderful phrase "your will is master of this wall," which can either be built or taken down by the "pick-axe of free choice."

Catherine's recognition that no one can take away one's own self-governance anticipates the central theme in Karol Wojtyła's *The Acting Person*. The human person is both the subject who acts and the object of his or her actions. In Wojtyła's words, "Every actual act of self-determination makes real the subjectiveness of self-governance and self-possession; in each of these interpersonal structural relations there is given to the person as the subject—he who governs and possesses—the person as the object—as he who is governed and possessed."[41]

Karol Wojtyła further develops this line of thought: "An important point to note in this connection is that it lies in the nature of the experience of 'I will,' in the nature of the will itself, that it never consists in something that only happens in man; on the contrary, it always occurs as an instance of 'acting,' indeed, is the very core of every acting. It is the person as such that is then 'active.'"[42] Following his analysis, we can see better why the inauthentic pattern of conformism, or just going along but not directly choosing to act, impedes a person's flourishing.

To complete this section on whether obedience helps or hinders a person's flourishing, it is important to consider the guidelines for authentic participation in community offered by Karol Wojtyła in *The Acting Person* and the guidelines for the formation of religious during his pontificate as Pope John Paul II. Karol Wojtyła described particular authentic ways and inauthentic attitudes for participating in communities in his section on "Intersubjectivity by Participation." All have relevance for how a person lives a vow of obedience in religious life.

Authentic participation involves "solidarity" through which a person accepts the goal of the community and works actively to par-

41. Karol Wojtyła, *The Acting Person* (Dordrecht: D. Reidel, 1979), 108.

42. Wojtyła, *Acting Person*, 110.

ticipate in its realization for the common good of each person in that community including one's own self. This attitude of solidarity would imply that a religious accepted the goals stated in the constitutions for the virtue of the vow of obedience as lived by his or her community and sincerely wanted to work toward their realization. Authentic participation is also willing to risk opposition when it serves as a constructive way to build the common good more effectively. Here, the key would be the way that an attitude of opposition would be expressed; it anticipates the third attitude for authentic participation as involving a capacity for dialogue that brings to light what is right and true and eliminates partial views.[43] In *Vita Consecrata,* John Paul II applied this third authentic attitude directly to religious life:

> The experience of recent years widely confirms that "*dialogue is the new name of charity*" especially within the Church. Dialogue helps us to see the true implications of problems and allows them to be addressed with greater hope of success. *The consecrated life,* by the very fact that it promotes the value of fraternal life, provides a privileged experience of dialogue.[44]

The two inauthentic attitudes Wojtyła calls "noninvolvement" and "servile conformism." The last mentioned has relevance for our previous discussion of obedience in religious life. "Thus conformism consists primarily in an attitude of compliance or resignation, in a specific form of passivity that makes the man-person to be but the subject of *what happens* instead of being the *actor* or *agent* responsible for building his own attitudes and his own commitment in the community."[45] This inauthentic attitude of conformism rests primarily on the person who decides to just go along and pretend. Wojtyła argues that conformism harms both the individual and the community:

43. Wojtyła, *Acting Person,* 283–87.

44. John Paul II, *Vita Consecrata,* Post Synodal Apostolic Exhortation on the Consecrated Life and Its Mission in the Church and the World, March 25, 1996, no. 74. Emphasis added.

45. Wojtyła, *Acting Person,* 289.

> A mere semblance of participation, a superficial compliance with others, which lacks conviction and authentic engagement, is substituted for real participation. Thus the specifically human ability of shaping creatively his community is dwarfed, annihilated, or perverted. This state of things cannot but have a negative effect on the common good whose dynamism springs from true personal participation.[46]

Wojtyła summarizes the negative effects further:

> Situations of prevailing conformism can never be accepted as satisfactory; for when people adapt themselves to the demands of the community only superficially and when they do so only to gain some immediate advantages or to avoid trouble, the person as well as the community incur irremediable losses.[47]

In a 2008 magisterial document titled *The Service of Authority and Obedience*, guidelines were offered to help all religious approach the practice of obedience or of exercising authority in formation or governing a religious institute as a real service to the Church in building a vibrant community. This document is well aware of the needs for a realistic understanding of the dignity of the human person and of contemporary challenges.

In conclusion, an answer to the critics who claim that the very practice of a traditional vow of obedience should be rejected because it keeps persons in a childlike state is that the motive and practice of the vow are developmental and analogical depending on the charism and practices within a particular community. The free will of the person submitting to acts of obedience may be exercised so that the person becomes more, not less, free. So, the motive of the person obeying and his or her self-governance in dying and rising in Christ are the key to mature flourishing.

46. Wojtyła, *Acting Person*, 290.
47. Wojtyła, *Acting Person*, 290.

Obedience as Males Perpetuating Their Power over Females or as Mutual Service

Obedience as embedded in a Church characterized as "patriarchal and sexist" has often been criticized in recent times. Sandra Schneiders introduces her three-volume work on religious life with the following reflection: "Feminism, a worldwide movement for the emancipation and participation of women, has deeply penetrated women's Religious Life. Feminism . . . is a public commitment to an active praxis of subversion of patriarchy, liberation of women and other oppressed groups, and reconstruction of family, society, and Church as communities of equals. . . . Do religious take their direction from a patriarchal ecclesiastical organization or from an emancipatory liberation movement?"[48]

As she develops her criticism, the topic of vocations surfaces: "Historically women have been excluded by dominant males from participation in virtually every sphere of society and every arena of action that involved power, decision making, status, or influence. Whatever the reasons given publicly, the real reason for women's exclusion has been gender. Perhaps the most egregious and painful such experience has been their exclusion from ordained ministry, with its attendant symbolism and reality of sacramental inferiority and dependence."[49] In her second volume, this theme continues with obvious bitterness: "The inappropriateness, to say nothing of the sheer affront, of having to introduce an outsider to preside at the most intimate community gatherings became increasingly evident. And for women it was exacerbated by the necessity of the outsider being male. The symbolic subordination and enforced sacramental dependence were galling to increasing numbers."[50]

48. Sandra Schneiders, *Religious Life in a New Millennium*, vol. 1, *Finding the Treasure* (New York: Paulist, 2000), xxvi.

49. Schneiders, *Finding the Treasure*, 68.

50. Sandra Schneiders, *Religious Life in a New Millennium*, vol. 2, *Selling All* New York. 2001), 389.

Diarmuid O'Murchu echoes the approach of Schneiders, albeit from a male perspective:

> Patriarchy is a loosely defined concept to denote the rule of governance, characterized by dominance and control, pioneered and facilitated primarily by men . . . One of the disturbing features of patriarchal governance is the underhand manner in which people are indoctrinated. They are encouraged not to think for themselves and, therefore, they tend to become increasingly dependent on the wisdom of the governing group. This easily breeds a culture of codependency in which people find it hard—nor indeed, are they encouraged—to behave like adults invoking their adult wisdom.[51]

He encourages women religious to follow a new path, "Women Religious are called to be different. They need to cast off the stereotype of the humble, obedient woman, whose loyalty is too easily identified with passive fidelity."[52] He encourages the new "Women's Redemptive Rage," which as "justice making" moves beyond the Church into a new spirituality in the world.[53] He argues that in this new consciousness "the vows take on a very different meaning," and "in this new paradigmatic view of Religious Life is the expansion of the contextual horizon of the Church to that of the World, as viewed from the perspective of the Kingdom of God."[54]

In the history of the Church, there have been different periods within which members of one of the three paradigm vocations were considered superior to the others. At first, especially from early medieval ages through the Abbesses and Abbots, religious life governed both the laity and priests who lived in proximity to the monastery. Later, when the universities were established to form diocesan and mendicant priests, and the center of education shifted away from monasteries, the members of the clerical state and magisterium began to achieve a greater importance in governing the laity and the many emerging religious institutes throughout the world. Follow-

51. O'Murchu, *Consecrated Religious Life*, 38 and 41–42.

52. O'Murchu, *Consecrated Religious Life*, 117.

53. O'Murchu, *Consecrated Religious Life*, 110*ff*.

54. O'Murchu, *Consecrated Religious Life*, 170.

ing the Second Vatican Council's call for universal holiness and the development of the laity as leaders of the new evangelization in the world, politics, and public life, the laity have now assumed a leadership in the Church through political and intellectual powers of persuasion.

The historical imbalances among the three paradigm vocations of religious life, ordained priesthood, and laity never realized the integral complementarity of mutual service calling all women and men into communal relations in "likeness of the Holy Trinity." Hans Urs von Balthasar had the vision of a dynamic complementarity of vocations in his book on *The Christian State of Life*.[55] Pope John Paul sought to call members of all vocations into relations of equality and mutual service to one another out of love for Christ and in "likeness of the Holy Trinity." To consider this call to mutual service, I turn briefly to John Paul II's analysis of obedience in sacramental marriage. We discover here a developmental approach toward the new evangelization of marriage that can then be applied back to the interpersonal relations of members from different vocations in the Church.

In a remarkable book written in 1914, the Anglican physician and liturgical scholar John Wickham Legg (1843–1921) provided evidence that for over four hundred years in over a hundred Anglican and Roman Catholic dioceses in Europe, marriage rites included either the direct promise by a woman to obey her husband or the advising of the wife and husband by the minister performing the marriage rite, which included the wife's duty to be obedient or subservient to her husband.[56] The earliest records indicate that from the ninth through thirteenth centuries, celebration of Roman Catholic marriage only requested mutual consent of the man and woman. Each diocese could

55. Hans Urs von Balthasar, *The Christian State of Life* (San Francisco: Ignatius Press, 1983).

56. J. Wickham Legg, *On the Retention of the Word Obey in the Marriage Service of the Book of Common Prayer* (London: Wells Gardner, Darton, 1915), http://anglicanhistory.org/women/jwlegg1915.pdf. The text was a liturgical consultation addressed to the Bishop of Oxford and written before the first of August 1914.

establish its own rites.[57] In the fourteenth and fifteenth centuries, an exhortation to the bride began to use the Latin phrase *obedire et servire*.[58]

A question arises in my mind about why a change from mutual consent to obedience and service was asked of the woman only. In addition to the obligation to serve through having children, there may be a further hypothesis worth considering. One factor may be that in the thirteenth century, in the development of the new universities in Paris, the freshly translated works of Aristotle became required reading of all students in the Faculty of Arts; the curriculum at Paris became the model for all the other universities in England and Europe for the next three hundred years.[59] In this way, all the men who went on to study theology, medicine, or law were influenced by Aristotle's theory that the virtue of women, because of a defect in her nature, was to obey, and of a man to rule.[60]

In the *Politics*, Aristotle elaborated his position by understanding obedience and ruling as differentiated by function, which in turn was derived from the nature that is proper to a particular kind of human being. Again in the *Politics*, Aristotle states: "Although the parts of the soul are present in all of them, they are present in different de-

57. Legg, *On the Retention of the Word Obey*. Two such examples of mutual consent are Nicholas I. Roman Pontiff (858–67) and a bishop of Salisbury, England (1217) (19).

58. According to Legg, *On the Retention of the Word Obey*, the Latin phrase *obedire et servire* was translated in English as "to be boneyre and buxsum in bedde and at borde" until the late seventeenth century, when the meaning of "buxum" no longer implied humble obedience (28).

59. See Sr. Prudence Allen, *The Concept of Woman: The Aristotelian Revolution (750 BC–1250 AD)* (Grand Rapids, MI: Eerdmans, 1997), "The Institutionalization of Aristotle," 413–43.

60. Aristotle, *Politics*, 1254b 16–25: "Hence the ruler ought to have moral virtue in perfection, for his function, taken absolutely, demands a master, artificer, and rational principle as such an artificer; the subjects, on the other hand, require only the measure of virtue which is proper to each of them. Clearly, then, moral virtue belongs to all of them, but the temperance of a man and of a woman, or the courage and justice of a man and of a woman, are not, as Socrates maintained, the same; the courage of a man is shown in commanding, of a woman obeying."

grees. But the slave has no deliberative faculty at all; the woman has, but it is without authority, and the child has, but it is immature."[61] With some slight exceptions, slaves, women, and children are obliged to obey free men because of defects in their nature and limitations of subsequent functions. Obedience of a woman to her husband was for Aristotle due to a natural imperfection in her nature resulting from her conception, within which her mother resisted the perfect reception of the human soul power (form) provided by the father.[62]

Yet Aristotle did allow that a woman could be delegated areas in a household to rule, or she might inherit rule because of wealth. Describing the rule of husband over wife as "constitutional" rather than royal, he concluded: "For although there may be exceptions to the order of nature, the male is by nature more fitted for command than the female."[63]

Returning to the question of the marriage vows of a woman, in 1534–47, the Reformation in England began.[64] As soon as other various reforms emerged, in every case the actual form of the marriage rite was changed from mutual consent to include a different vow for the wife than for the husband. This is found in the 1529 Rite of the Zurich Form of Marriage, in the 1536–46 Calvinist Reformation, in an Exhortation for the 1541 Marriage Service of Martin Luther ("obedience as wife's duty'), in the 1549 Rite of the First Book of Edward VI ("to love, cherish, and to obey"), in the 1551 Rite of the Second Book of Edward VI, and in the 1559 Book of Common Prayer (Anglican) ("Wilt thou obey hym and servie him?").[65] A second factor favoring the re-

61. Aristotle, *Politics*, 1260a 10–15.

62. See Sr. Prudence Allen, *Concept of Woman*, chap. 1, "Precursors to Aristotle," 53–81, and chap. 2, "Aristotle," 83–126.

63. Aristotle, *Politics*, 1259a35–1259b9.

64. See Hilaire Belloc, *How the Reformation Happened* (Rockford, IL: Tan Books, 1975).

65. Legg, *On the Retention of the Word Obey*, 33–51. The actual rite of matrimony asks the man, "Wilt thou love her, comforte her, honour and kepe her, in sickenesm and in healthe?" and asks the woman, "Wilt thou obey hym and servie him, love, honour, and kepe him, in sycknes and in health?" See *The 1559 Book of Common Prayer: Marriage,*

quirement of obedience on the part of the woman only may have been the emphasis in the Reform on a literal interpretation of Scripture. In this context, passages from Ephesians 5 and 1 Peter 3 were interpreted as definitive proof through revelation that women were to obey men.

It did not take long for the Roman Catholic Church to follow this pattern and to introduce the concept of a wife's obedience, even though the Council of Trent (1545–63) did not change the mutual consent and the *Sacramentale* of St. Charles Borromeo used the same vows for both husband and wife.[66] But the 1566 Roman Catechism asked for by the Council of Trent to be used by priests as their catechetical handbook not only introduced the recognition that marriage in the Church was a Sacrament but also, when signed by Paul V, contained exhortations to the wife "to obey her husband," to be "subject to their husbands," to be in "subjection," and with "a willing and obsequious obedience."[67]

From this time forward, obedience for the wife only was integrated in the actual marriage rites or exhortations offered by the priest or minister in both Catholic and Protestant services for four hundred years.[68] This form perpetuated itself until the Second Vatican Council, when in 1963, the Constitution on the Sacred Liturgy *Sacrosanctum Concilium* (promulgated by Pope Paul VI) stated in no. 77: "The mar-

---

accessed May 7, 2013, http://justus.anglican.org/resources/bcp/1559/Marriage_1559.htm, 1–8, here 2. In the exhortation following, Ephesians 5 and 1 Peter 3 are used to justify "Ye women, submit yourselfes unto youre owne housbandes as unto the Lord; for the housbande is the wyves headde, even as Christe is the headde of the Church" and "Saincte Peter also doeth instructe you very godly, thus saiynge, Let wyves be subject to their owne housbandes" (7).

66. Legg, *On the Retention of the Word Obey*, 66.

67. Legg, *On the Retention of the Word Obey*, 234. Rev. J. Donovan, trans., *The Catechism of the Council of Trent (of Pope Pius V)* (Baltimore: Lucas Brothers, 1829). This was the first worldwide catechism directed toward all priests and tied to Scripture passages, especially on the relation between Christ and the Church as analogous for the relation between husband and wife through authority of the revelation according to Paul in Ephesians 5.

68. See the appendix for a chronological list of dioceses and the words associated with obedience throughout Europe.

riage rite now found in the Roman Ritual is to be revised and enriched in such a way that the grace of the sacrament is more clearly signified and the duties of the spouses are taught." In the new rite promulgated in 1969, obedience for the woman was simply dropped from the Roman Catholic marriage rites. The promises were identical for wife and for husband.[69] The Scripture passages used previously to justify the wife's obedience alone were listed as possible, not required, readings for the couple to choose. This began an important phase of the new evangelization of the Sacrament of Marriage.

In 1988, Blessed John Paul specifically requested of Roman Catholics to understand what he called "the Gospel innovation," namely, that the passage in Ephesians 5:21 is asking for husbands and wives to carry out a "mutual subjection out of reference for Christ."[70] In this same section 24 of the document, the Holy Father elaborates specifically: "However, whereas in the relationship between Christ and the Church the subjection is only on the part of the Church, in the relationship between husband and wife the 'subjection' is not one-sided but mutual." Arguing that this is something "new" as an innovation of the Gospel, he stated further that Jesus Christ initiated this innovation himself:

> The "innovation" of Christ is a fact: it constitutes the unambiguous content of the evangelical message and is the result of the Redemption. However, the awareness that in marriage there is mutual "subjection of the spouses out of reverence for Christ," and not just that of the wife to the husband, must gradually establish itself in hearts, consciences, behavior and customs. This is a call which from that time onwards does not cease to challenge succeeding generations; it is a call which people have to accept every anew.[71]

69. See Archbishop Annibale Bugnini, "The Rite of Marriage," *L'Osservatore Romano*, April 17, 1969. After mutual consent, each one may say, "I, N. Take you, N, as my lawful wife (husband), and I promise you fidelity in riches and in poverty, in sickness and in health, in loving you and honoring you for all the days of my life" (7).

70. John Paul II, Apostolic Letter *Mulieris Dignitatem on the Dignity and Vocation of Women* (Boston: St. Paul Books & Media, 1988), no. 24.

71. John Paul II, *Mulieris Dignitatem*, no. 24.

Just to be sure that everyone understands that the previous tradition of woman's subjection alone is no longer to be practiced, the Holy Father described in his Apostolic Letter that the mutual submission of spouses to one another out of love for Christ as a challenge of the call to lives redeemed from original sin: "*But the challenge presented by the 'ethos' of the Redemption* is clear and definitive. All the reasons in favor of the 'subjection' of woman to man in marriage must be understood in the sense of a 'mutual subjection' of both 'out of reverence for Christ.'"[72]

The new evangelization of religious life and of the practice of mutual submission in the dynamic self-gift of members of each vocation to others in the Church is in likeness of the Holy Trinity. This analogous participation in the Holy Trinity is the reality of the *communio* that each of us is called to according to the charism of our particular vocation.

Pope John Paul II provided a direct application to our original question in this section of the relation of obedience to the three paradigm vocations in the Church. So far, we have mostly written from the perspective of philosophy of the human person, examining how our intellect, will, memory, senses, and passions relate to our ability to grow in self-governance, increased freedom, and flourishing our personality in the context of the practice of the virtue and vow of obedience. Our vocations, however, are also embedded in the context of spiritual warfare among the principalities and powers; each of us personally must struggle with the inheritance of original sin and of the effects of repeated actual sins. Blessed John Paul suggested that original sin has a different effect in one particular way for women and another way for men.

While traditionally it was often thought that God *punished* Eve for her seducing of Adam into contravening God's law, by placing her under the rule of her husband, "Your desire will be for your husband and he will rule over you," John Paul II interprets this statement as

72. John Paul II, *Mulieris Dignitatem*, no. 24.

not a punishment but rather as an *effect* of the original sin. The woman must work to overcome her tendency to possess those she loves, her inheritance from original sin captured in the phrase "your desire shall be for your husband." As St. Edith Stein observed in her *Essays on Women*, this tendency in a woman, to want to possess those she loves, can extend to her children as well.[73] We women must ask ourselves how our response to men in priestly, religious, or lay vocations is motivated by this effect of original sin, namely, by our desire to possess or cling to a man or what a man does, or, when this is not possible, to try to destroy the man.

In interpreting the words "he will rule over you," John Paul II argues that the man also must work to overcome his specific inheritance of original sin, which is a tendency to want to dominate others. In *Mulieris Dignitatem* he says, "The matrimonial union requires respect for and a perfecting of the true personal subjectivity of both of them. *The woman cannot become the 'object' of 'domination' and male possession.'* But the words of the biblical text directly concern original sin and its lasting consequences in man and woman."[74] This means that just as women must ask themselves when they are acting more from a desire to possess than from their mission welcome new life and to foster its growth in others, men must ask themselves whether they are acting more from their tendency to dominate than from their mission to have dominion.

In *Mulieris Dignitatem*, John Paul II focused more on the roots in Genesis for the systematic characteristics of the sin condition in the modern world, especially as they affect men and women.

> Therefore when we read in the biblical description the words addressed to the woman: *"Your desire shall be for your husband, and he shall rule over you"* (Gn 3:16), we discover a break and a constant threat precisely in regard to this "unity of the two" which corresponds to the dignity of the image and likeness of God in both of them. But this threat is more serious for the wom-

73. Edith Stein, *Essays on Women* (Washington, DC: ICS Publications, 1987), 86–89 and 254–55.

74. John Paul II, *Mulieris Dignitatem*, 10.

an, since domination takes the place of "being a sincere gift" and therefore living "for" the other: "he shall rule over you." This "domination" indicates the disturbance and *loss of the stability* of that *fundamental equality* which the man and the woman possess in the "unity of the two": and this is especially to the disadvantage of the woman, whereas only the equality resulting from their dignity as persons can give to their mutual relationship the character of an authentic "*communio personarum*."[75]

John Paul II points out another challenge for women when attempting to work through the consequences of men's tendencies to dominate and women's tendency to possess, namely, a secondary tendency in a woman to want to be what she cannot possess: "Consequently, even the rightful opposition of women to what is expressed in the biblical words, 'He shall rule over you' (Gn 3:16) must not under any condition lead to the 'masculinization' of women. In the name of liberation from male 'domination,' women must not appropriate to themselves male characteristics contrary to their own feminine 'originality.'"[76]

John Paul II specified that both men and women should recognize specified engendered inheritances of original sin and act to purify them. This is part of our universal call to holiness: "*The inheritance of sin* suggested by the words of the Bible—'Your desire shall be for your husband, and he shall rule over you'—*can be conquered* only by following this path. The overcoming of this evil inheritance is, generation after generation, the task of every human being, whether woman or man."[77]

John Paul concludes with stating the main principle through which both men and woman can overcome this engendered inheritance of original sin: "In Christ the mutual opposition between man and woman—which is the inheritance of original sin—is essentially overcome." He leads us back to the Trinitarian principle: "These words concern that original 'unity of the two' which is linked with the creation of the human being as male and female, made in the image and likeness of God, and based on the model of that most per-

75. John Paul II, *Mulieris Dignitatem*, 10.

76. John Paul II, *Mulieris Dignitatem*, 10.

77. John Paul II, *Mulieris Dignitatem*, 10.

fect communion of Persons which is God himself."[78] Thus we have returned to our consideration of how men and women in complementary vocations in the Church can learn to mutually give of self in service to one another out of likeness of the Holy Trinity.

Conclusion

Drawing together these many reflections on the tradition of obedience in the Church, I would like to point out that Blessed Pope John Paul II (who asked to enter the Carmelites twice in his life) and St. Edith Stein are in a long line of inherited Carmelite spirituality. Beginning with St. Teresa of Avila (1518–82), these great leaders have emphasized both a spirituality of marriage and a spirituality of discerning the will of God through darkness of senses, intellect, and will. In the elaboration by Pope John Paul II, the ordained priest is called to be a living sign of Christ, the bridegroom especially in the celebration of the Eucharist; the consecrated religious alone and in community is called to be a living sign of the bride's response of love for the love of the bridegroom; and the married couple is called together to be living signs of the love of Jesus Christ, the Bridegroom for his Bride, the Church.[79]

St. John of the Cross (1561–1626) opened up the entire mystery of the passive and active dark nights of the senses, understanding and the will. Here, the more common way of living is replaced by the lack of feeling, knowing, and willing so that one's faith can be purified. Obedience becomes a crucial operation during these periods of darkness, in which the only light that guides one is a purified faith as "the one that burned in my heart."[80]

The Carmelite spirituality emphasizes the courage that is needed

78. John Paul II, *Mulieris Dignitatem*, 11.

79. See Sr. Mary Prudence Allen, "Catholic Marriage and Feminism," in *The Church, Marriage, and the Family*, ed. Kenneth D. Whitehead (South Bend, IN: St. Augustine's Press, 2007), chap. 7, 95–144.

80. St. John of the Cross, *The Dark Night*, in *The Collected Works of St. John of the Cross* (Washington, DC: ICS Publications, 1979), Stanzas of the Soul, no. 4, 296.

to obey within the dark nights, and the great gift that obedience is along the increasingly challenging pathway to holiness in contemplative life. The twentieth-century Carmelite nun and martyr St. Edith Stein (St. Teresa Benedicta of the Cross) and Karol Wojtyła both wrote significant books on St. John of the Cross.[81] The practice of obedience in daily life prepared them both for the ultimate gift of their life in service to the Church and humanity.

St. Ignatius of Loyola's (1491–1556) approach to obedience charts the complex ways that spiritual consolation and spiritual desolation work in a person's soul.[82] Depending upon how integrally a person is living a Christian life, these spirits should be interpreted differently. A person needs to learn how, with the help of a spiritual guide, to discern the movements of the spirits so that he or she can overcome deception and be firmly rooted in the Spirit of Truth. Ignatius of Loyola's approach helps in the increasingly intense life of spiritual warfare to obey the right voice at the right time.

He introduced a military model of obedience to God and the Church at the same time that he introduced innovations of method for those following his spirituality. *The Spiritual Exercises* provided a rigorous way to enter into an encounter with Jesus Christ. They awaken in the person an ability to reflect on the movement of the passions within and through a daily and even hourly examination of consciousness.[83] In addition, the exercises can lead a person to make a full offering of "all my liberty, my memory, my understanding, and my entire will, all that I have and possess" back to God, who gave it to him in the beginning.[84]

81. See Edith Stein, *The Science of the Cross* (Washington, DC: ICS Publications, 2002), and Karol Wojtyła, *Faith According to Saint John of the Cross* (San Francisco: Ignatius Press, 1981).

82. See Timothy M. Gallagher, OMV, *The Discernment of Spirits: An Ignatian Guide for Everyday Living* (New York: Crossroad, 2005); and *Spiritual Consolation: An Ignatian Guide for the Greater Discernment of Spirits* (New York: Crossroad, 2007).

83. See Timothy M. Gallagher, OMV, *The Examen Prayer: Ignatian Wisdom for Our Lives Today* (New York: Crossroad, 2006).

84. Louis J. Puhl, DJ, trans., *The Spiritual Exercises of St. Ignatius: Based on Studies in the*

Finally, I offer an example of how men and women in three different vocations can model, through each of their self-gift to others, building the Church in likeness to the Holy Trinity. The late Cardinal O'Connor shared the following reflection in 1997 with the Sisters of Life, a community he had founded:

> What is the essence of the consecrated vow of obedience? . . . the day I became a bishop in Rome some 18 years ago or more, Our Holy Father had just put his hands on my head, and I came down from the high altar of the Basilica of Saints Peter and Paul in Rome. And out of the corner of my eye, I caught this woman pressed practically into the wall, almost trying to conceal herself, and I recognized her as Mother Teresa. I had never met her; she wouldn't know me at all. But I broke from the line from this very solemn, formal ceremony and went over to see her. And all she did was look at me and say, "Give God permission." That, my dear ladies, is the essence of obedience: Give God permission.

I guess that struck me in a special way because I spent 27 years of my life with the Navy and the Marine Corps, and it always intrigued me that whenever you go aboard a Navy vessel, regardless of who the so-called Officer of the Deck is—he could be a very high-ranking officer or he could be a simple sailor. And no matter what your rank is—you could be the Secretary of the Navy—and before you set foot aboard the ship, you ask, "Request permission to come aboard, sir" And it is not until this very senior officer or this very simple sailor says, "Permission granted," that even the Secretary of the Navy sets foot aboard a Navy ship.

> It's as though Our Lord says to us, I need your permission to come into you, to function through you, to use your hands to reach out to others, to use your lips to speak to others, to let others look into your eyes and see me. I need your permission for this. This to me is the real meaning of obedience.[85]

Language of the Autograph (Chicago: Loyola Press, 1951), "Take, Lord, Receive," no. 230, p. 102. In Ignatius's words, "We must put aside all judgment of our own, and keep the mind ever ready and prompt to obey in all things the true Spouse of Christ our Lord, our holy Mother, the hierarchical Church," no. 353, p. 157. See also no. 365, p. 159.

85. Given on July 5, 1997, by Cardinal John O'Connor.

In this wonderful series of events, we see a consecrated religious, Mother Teresa, giving to a young bishop, who later gives in founding a new community, of the Sisters of Life, who give to multiple pregnant laywomen hope for bringing their child to birth and to find it a good home. The Church is built up through the mutual submission and service of men and women in the three primordial vocation in likeness to the love of our Holy Trinity.

Women's Obedience in Marriage

Year	Source	Page in Legg, *On the Retention of the Word Obey*
1582	Manuel Parochorum pro Salisburgensi *obedire* OR	49–50
1587	Bamberg	
1590	Strassburg *gehorsam sein* OE	63
1597	Diocese of Constanz, Switzerland *ihme Gehorsam Ehr* OR	54
1608	Diocese of Passau OE	53
1614	Paul V did not adopt words of SS Peter or Paul "obey" in Rituale	95
1626	Roman Catholics in England matrimony books still used "bonair" and "buxom" with note = "meeke" and "obedient" OE	67
1639	Diocese of Wladislav and Pomerania, Poland *Gehorsamb* OR	55
1644	Directory issued by the Lords and Commons of Scotland OR "Promise to be a . . . obedient wife"	43–44
1654	Ritual Parisiense ad Romani formam *la femme obeissant* OE	61
1662	Unaltered in revision of through 1914 OR Queen Victoria promised to "obey and serve"	33
	her husband OR	34
	Scottish Episcopal Church to "obey and serve" OR	34
1673	Freising *gehorsamb*	
1678	Diocese of Limoges *l'obeissance à son mary* OE	65

Year	Source	Page in Legg, *On the Retention of the Word Obey*
1682	Diocese of Coûtances *de lui obeir comme l'Eglise* OE	64
1687	Diocese of Amiens *la même soûmission que l'Eglise* OE	62
1701	Diocese of Auch *en luy obeissant, come l'Eglise* OE	66
1709	Scottish Presbyterian Church "to be an obedient wife" OR	43
1712	Church of Geneva *promettez. obéir, servir, de lui être soumise* OR	41–42
1714	Diocese of Olmutz OE	53
1720	Archdiocese of Cologne same vows but different duties OR	63
1728	Diocese of Bordeaux *la soumission* OE	61
1730	Diocese of Blois *la soumission*	
1742	Diocese of Strassburg (now French) MC	63
1757	Diocese of Arras *soyez soumise à votre Epoux* OE	62
1763	Diocese of Périgueux *la même soûmission que l'Eglise*	
1784	Diocese of Tournay *Obéissez-lui selon Dieu* OE	64
1786–1892	Protestant Episcopal Church of America "to obey" OR	34–35
1786	Pastorale Parisiense *soyez soumise a votre Epoux* OE	59
1789	Diocese of Seckau OE	52
1838	Diocese of Linz, Austria OE	52
1838	Diocese of Colocz, Hungary *gehorsam* OE	65
1847	Diocese of Breslau, Silesia OR	55
1848	Weslyans in England "to obey" OR	36
1848	Diocese of Prague *Gehorsam* OR, with alternate form of equal vows	54
19th c.	Armenian Rituale *Submitto me* OR	57
1853	Ritual Romano-Salisburgense *ihm gehorsam seyn* OR	49
1876	French Reformed Churches *de lui être soumise* OR	43
1877	Old Catholic Wessemberg Rituale *ihm Gehorsam* OR	58
1886	Diocese of Brixen OR	53

Year	Source	Page in Legg, *On the Retention of the Word Obey*
1892	Kingdom of Poland Uniform "matrimonial obedience" OR	56
	also *obedientiam conjugalem*, *geburlichen Gehorsam* and *l'obéissance* from the Polish	
1894	Church of Ireland "to obey" OR	35

OR, obedience demanded by the rite of marriage; OE, obedience in response to priestly exhortation.

CONTRIBUTORS

SISTER MARY PRUDENCE ALLEN, RSM (Christine Hope Allen), has been a member of the Religious Sisters of Mercy of Alma, Michigan, since 1983. She graduated with a BA in philosophy from the University of Rochester in 1962 and with a PhD in philosophy from Claremont Graduate University in 1967. She was a professor of philosophy at Concordia University, Montreal, from 1969 to 1996 and at St. John Vianney Theological Seminary in Denver from 2000 to 2015. Her major publication is a three-volume work, *The Concept of Woman* (1997, 2002, and 2016).

CHRISTIAN BRUGGER is a moral theologian who writes from his home in Jacksonville Beach, Florida. He is the author of *The Indissolubility of Marriage and the Council of Trent* (2017).

JOHN FINNIS read law in Adelaide and philosophy of law in Oxford, where he has taught law and legal philosophy since 1966. Since 1995, he has also held a chair at the University of Notre Dame. He is a fellow of the British Academy in both the law and the philosophy sections. His main books are *Natural Law and Natural Rights* (1980; 2011), *Fundamentals of Ethics* (1983), *Moral Absolutes* (1991), and *Aquinas: Moral, Political and Legal Theory* (1998). Five volumes of his *Collected Essays* were published in 2011; the fifth volume is *Religion and Public Reason*.

MOST REVEREND ANTHONY FISHER, a Dominican friar and archbishop of Sydney, is currently chancellor of the Catholic Institute of Sydney; adjunct lecturer in bioethics at the University of Notre Dame, Australia; and member of the Company and Board of Identity of the Australian Catholic University. He has published over one hundred academic articles on ethical, bioethical, legal, historical, and theological subjects.

GERALD GLEESON studied philosophy and theology at the Catholic Institute of Sydney, the University of Cambridge, and the Catholic University of Leuven. He is a priest of the Archdiocese of Sydney who taught philosophy and Christian Ethics at the Catholic Institute of Sydney for many years and is now vicar general of the archdiocese.

MARK KINGWELL is a professor of philosophy at the University of Toronto. His most recent book is a study of technology and boredom, *Wish I Were Here* (2019); a forthcoming work examines the politics of risk and vulnerability.

RENÉE KÖHLER-RYAN is the dean of the School of Philosophy and Theology at the University of Notre Dame Australia. She has acted as a consultant on artistic and architectural projects in the dioceses of Sydney and Parramatta. Her publications bring together the thought of Augustine and medieval thinkers with contemporary philosophical issues and the arts. Forthcoming books consider how contemporary philosopher William Desmond is inspired by major ideas in Augustine (2019), and how an Augustinian understanding of reality sheds light on the Catholic tradition of sacred spaces (2020).

MATTHEW LEVERING holds the James N. and Mary D. Perry Jr. Chair of Theology at Mundelein Seminary. He is the author of over twenty-five books, including most recently *Dying and the Virtues* and *Did Jesus Rise from the Dead?* He serves as coeditor of two quarterly journals, *Nova et Vetera* and *International Journal of Systematic Theology*.

INDEX

INDEX

Living the Catholic Tradition: Philosophical & Theological Considerations was designed in Mrs Eaves XL with Mr Eaves display type and composed by Kachergis Book Design of Pittsboro, North Carolina. It was printed on 60-pound House Natural Smooth and bound by Sheridan Books of Chelsea, Michigan.